As Though We Were Dreaming

As Though We Were Dreaming

A Commentary on the Songs of Ascents for Lent

Keith Ruckhaus

RESOURCE *Publications* · Eugene, Oregon

AS THOUGH WE WERE DREAMING
A Commentary on the Songs of Ascents for Lent

Copyright © 2013 Keith Ruckhaus. All rights reserved. Except for brief quotations in critical publications or reviews, no part of this book may be reproduced in any manner without prior written permission from the publisher. Write: Permissions, Wipf and Stock Publishers, 199 W. 8th Ave., Suite 3, Eugene, OR 97401.

Wipf & Stock
An Imprint of Wipf and Stock Publishers
199 W. 8th Ave., Suite 3
Eugene, OR 97401

www.wipfandstock.com

ISBN 13: 978-1-62564-422-0

Manufactured in the U.S.A.

The Scriptural quotes of the Songs of Ascents are from the Revised Standard Version of the Bible, copyright 1952 [2nd edition, 1971] by the Division of Christian Education of the National Council of the Churches of Christ in the United States of America. Used by permission. All rights reserved.

Scripture texts in this work are taken from the *New American Bible, with revised New Testament* © 1986, 1970 Confraternity of Christian Doctrine, Washington, D.C. and are used by permission of the copyright owner. All Rights Reserved. No part of the New American Bible may be reproduced in any form without permission in writing from the copyright owner.

Frontispiece icon sketch "Abraham's journey to Zion" by Laurence Pierson Martin. Used with permission. All rights reserved. www.laureole.canalblog.com

This book is dedicated to the SS Cyril and Methodius Russian Byzantine community at St Elizabeth of Hungary Roman Catholic parish in Denver, Colorado. We have sung the *Songs of Ascents* every year in the Liturgy of the Presanctified Gifts in our journey of repentance.

Open to me, the doors of repentance, O Lifegiver,
For my soul rises early, to pray toward your holy temple . . .
But trusting in Thy loving kindness, like David I cry to Thee,
Have mercy on me, O God, according to Thy great mercy.

—THE OPENING AND CLOSING LINES
OF THE EASTERN TROPARIA OF LENT.

Contents

Foreword | ix
Acknowledgments | xiii
Introduction | xv

1 Introduction to the Songs of Ascents | 1

First Antiphon—Psalms 120–124 | 23

2 Psalm 120 | 25
3 Psalm 121 | 37
4 Psalm 122 | 44
5 Psalm 123 | 59
6 Psalm 124 | 69

Second Antiphon—Psalms 125–129 | 81

7 Psalm 125 | 83
8 Psalm 126 | 101
9 Psalm 127 | 118
10 Psalm 128 | 136
11 Psalm 129 | 150

Third Antiphon—Psalms 130–134 | 165

12 Psalm 130 | 169
13 Psalm 131 | 183
14 Psalm 132 | 193
15 Psalm 133 | 211
16 Psalm 134 | 224

17 Conclusion | 229

Bibliography | 233

Foreword

When Keith Ruckhaus asked me to review his book on Songs of Ascents (120-134), I imagined just one more book on the Psalter. As I read, however, I became delighted by its content, and I am honored to write the forward.

Ruckhaus vividly paints pictures in readable prose of the post-exilic settings from which these "Songs" emerge. He transports the readers into the devastating and harsh conditions of exile where a people never lose sight of their home, Jerusalem. Ruckhaus not only teaches us how these returned-exiles, beleaguered by all sorts of devastation, could sing these Songs of Ascents from hearts filled with joy, but how we the Church might also claim them as our own.

Profound repentance precipitates the return home and anticipates how hopes and dreams arising from the darkness of exile might inspire contemplation and self-examination. Ruckhaus beautifully paints a picture of Ezra's and Nehemiah's rebuke whereby Israel's tears and radical repentance grant their *going up* to Jerusalem from far off Babylon (Ezra 1:11, 7:9). Their disregard for Torah and the prophets as well as forgetting the bitterness of exile nullifies restoration and covenant renewal, especially against the backdrop of the Songs of Ascents. It was in this situation that David prophetically models repentance for the people of God for all generations to come.

Drawing on Eastern Orthodox traditions, Ruckhaus links this scenario undergirding the Songs of Ascents to the Lenten season. While Christians in the Western hemisphere often ignore the richness of Eastern Orthodox spirituality, they lose sight of each Song of Ascents' full beauty and rich heritage that the Eastern Church fathers and mothers have preserved by embedding these premier Hebrew texts into the liturgy of penitence leading to the Paschal feast. This Easter drama and the repeated Orthodox litany of intercession affirms God's loving-kindness in each Song of Ascents: "for You are the Lover of [hu]mankind." Vivid similarities unite the Songs of Ascents and the Sermon on the Mount, as the reader ascends to the house of the Lord, to the holy mountain (Zion), and even mystical staircases ascending to the realm of God.

By candidly relating his own experiences with these psalms, Ruckhaus connects the believer to the rich tradition of lamentation and repentance. Living in the "Front Range" of the Rocky Mountains, Ruckhaus compares mountain climbing with these "ascents" beginning at the base and hoping to summit the mountain: "only one mountain, Mount Zion, looms over and pervades every verse." The trail upward anticipates false summits but through a succession of victories, the sojourner methodically approaches the top.

Most likely, worshipers originally sung these psalms as they ascended up the road to Jerusalem to attend the three pilgrim festivals (Deuteronomy 16:16) or as the priests *ascended* the fifteen steps to minister at the Temple in Jerusalem. Hence, scholars have called them Pilgrim Songs, Gradual Psalms, Songs of Degrees, or Songs of Steps. Later Christians sang these songs on their way to worship before they entered the door of the Church.

In this collection three idioms of revelation—Torah, Prophecy, and Wisdom—work together in successive ascents eventually becoming grounded in messianic hope vividly expressed in Psalm 132. Ruckhaus brilliantly suggests that "the Songs of Ascents have been climbing to this song, only to realize that this last pitch to the summit must be put on hold."

Although the Songs of Ascents were originally anchored in the postexilic setting, how then can we as Christians apply them to Lent and our own deepest and most difficult hours? Bonhoeffer, who asks "how do the words of ordinary men and women become God's word to me?", illustrates this by how Jesus prays the Psalms with us. The Psalter does not preserve these prayers as isolated moments of antiquity, but transforms them to be read within the greater context of scripture. Therefore, within Christian scripture, the Psalter becomes the prayer book *of* Jesus Christ because these psalms are spoken *by* Jesus Christ, and the claim of the New Testament is that they are *about* Jesus Christ. Psalm 2:7, "You are my son; today I have begotten you," is reiterated at Jesus' Baptism. Within Christian Scripture, the Psalter, then, is the prayer book of Jesus Christ because Jesus prays through the Psalter. Bonhoeffer's insight, identifies a new claim of Christianity that Jesus, the Messiah, prays these prayers *with* us, even the Songs of Ascents.

So when we as Christians pray the Psalter, we are not alone because Jesus Christ prays the Psalms with us. When Christ Jesus was on the cross, he prayed Psalm 22: "My God, my God, why have you forsaken me?" but he was not alone because within the inter-testimony of the Psalter, Moses, David, and Solomon are praying with him. Through the cross of Christ, these Psalms have been bestowed to the Church as our old self dies at the cross. The Psalter is then the vicarious prayer of Christ for his Church and with his Church. As members of the body of Christ, we can pray these psalms through Jesus Christ, from the heart of Jesus Christ.

Each Song of Ascents enhances the cultic drama, especially during Lent while participating within the greater Psalter and providing a vehicle for us to express our lamentations, either protesting our innocence as in Psalm 26 or confessing our sins as in Psalms 41 and 51. The living, breathing shape of the Psalter proclaims that Jews and Christians are not alone when praying because Moses, David, Solomon, Christ, and all the Saints pray with them. The Jewish Psalter testifies to Torah, prophecy, and wisdom, and for Christians, it bears witness to a revelation that is more fully revealed in the New Testament as fulfilled in the Gospel. Therefore, we read the Psalms both to cherish our rich heritage of the word of God in Judaism and to understand their new life in Jesus Christ. This is why the Songs of Ascents direct the Church's journey of repentance revisiting both the exile and the cross.

When you read this book, *As Though Dreaming*, allow it to lead you on a journey *upward* that has the power to touch the heart and mind of scholar, clergy, lay person, mystic and even skeptic. You are not alone!

Randall Heskett, Boulder Colorado

Acknowledgments

I AM INDEBTED TO and grateful for the many who have offered their time, energy, and resources to see this project to completion. My family endures the many times when my distraction disables me from being fully attentive to their needs. Thanks to my longtime friend John Narvaiz who faithfully supports me in all my endeavors and who provided financial help for publication costs. Also thanks to Kathy Emme for her energetic and positive editing. I am very grateful to Laurence Pierson Martin for her willingness to provide an original icon sketch of Abraham's "ascent" to Salem (Gen 12–14).

I am also deeply indebted to Father Chrysostom Frank whose faithful service to our parish has provided countless challenging exhortations that have helped to shape and stimulate my own thinking.

Finally, I greatly appreciated the work of René Girard and Raymond Schwager whose game-changing insight into human civilization permeates much of my own thinking.

Introduction

IN THE LITURGICAL TRADITION of the Eastern churches, there is a considerable amount of praying from the Psalms. One may not encounter this, however, if he or she only attended a Divine Liturgy because it is a resurrection liturgy. Little of the Old Testament is read then. But if one participated in any of the hours of the Church—matins, the third, sixth, and ninth hour, vespers and nocturns—one would be immersed in the chanting of not only the psalms, but much of the Hebrew Bible.

Listening to chanted scripture reading tends to, indeed almost inevitably leads to, a kind of sing-songy lullness like singing "swing low sweet chariot" or "Jesus loves you this I know" to a child being held by a loving parent before bed. The words dance off the listener like rain on a roof, all the while the child is descending into a trance-like state of comfort and security just before dozing off. For some who attend Orthodox prayer services, the experience cannot be described in such poetic terms since one is required to stand through the whole thing. Tedious or even torturous may be a more apt description. Admittedly, a bit of austerity is intended. The supplicant ought to struggle a bit to draw near to the Almighty. All this to say that it is quite easy to miss a whole lot of the meaning and force of the text when it is sung as a prayer along with a whole lot of other prayers and combined with candlelight and smoky incense.

We find a similar problem expressed in Ezekiel who apparently sang his prophecies, a kind of Bob Dylan of Babylon as it were (Ez 33:30–33). God complains of Ezekiel's popularity due to his skill as a musician: *My people . . . sit down before you and hear your words, but they will not obey them, for lies are on their lips and their desires are fixed on dishonest gain. For them you are only a ballad singer, with a pleasant voice and a clever touch. They listen to your words, but they will not obey them.* Indeed, some of the monastic Fathers objected to the chanting of prayers as more a distraction than a centering enterprise.

If one is called upon to chant the text, however, all of a sudden he must perk up and pay attention. I can best avoid stammering over my words and the supplicants can best participate in the prayer if I actually read the text within the context of the whole. Even so, a good lot of things can get missed. The advantage of attending the Hours on a regular basis is that one can pick up nuances with each reading. As with most sermons, most of us only catch one or two thoughts that stick or strike a chord with our current experience. For me, this is true of the Divine Liturgy which even though I ritually go through this every Sunday, I still catch a glimpse of the mystery I am participating in.

Being a student of the Scriptures, especially the Hebrew Scriptures, my appreciation of the Psalms has deepened. A heightened awareness of this came during the Great Fast last year.[1] Then, I was able to chant the Third and Sixth Hours at our church. These services are packed with psalms, prayers, and readings from Isaiah. As I continued daily to read these for five weeks, I became more aware of the great struggle of the ancient Israelites to comprehend their relationship with the Lord and their own survival against massive odds. Equally apparent in those psalms was the guttural connection with the gospel.

After the terrible and amazing events of Jesus' passion, his followers struggled to understand the meaning of it especially in light of their growing separation from the Jews. The praying of the Psalms had always been a part of Jewish worship, but the early Christians found great comfort in them as they realized the extraordinary way in which the Psalms connected with the Passion of their Lord. This is so because the gospel story was already genetically encoded in the story of Israel. Everything that Jesus said and did, everything that happened to Jesus relates to that story. It relates not by way of comparison but by way of a continuum.

It is my desire in this book to explore and express some of that struggle of both Israel and Jesus into our experience of repentance. The hope is not just that a worshipper can connect one's own experiences with those of the ancient Israelites and Jews more readily. It is also to help us as the Church to ground our participation in the Great Story. We don't borrow the ancient psalms of the Jew's struggle to reconstitute a kingdom of God; we share in that struggle. That history is our history and

---

1. What is called *Lent* in the western tradition is called the *Great Fast* in the eastern.

that liturgy of penance, anguish and struggle incorporates us into God's ongoing encounter with His people and humanity.

The commentary on the Songs of Ascents (Pss 120—134) here is primarily designed to enhance our understanding of penance during the Great Fast, better known as Lent, and our experience of the Presanctified Liturgy.[2] The basic structure of this book simply follows the sequence of songs as they were written in the Psalms and sung in the Presanctified Liturgy. The liturgical setting in ancient Israel centered on the regional gathering of Jews in the land of Judah at a great festival, perhaps *yom kippur*, the day of atonement. The songs accompanied the pilgrims not just from the outskirts of Jerusalem to the *yulam*, the main courtyard of the Temple, but were also meant to walk us through the great "expedition" from Babylon to Zion. The commentary also connects the life events of the ancient Jews in liturgical celebration with the life events of Jesus and worship of the early church and finally to our corporate and personal journey in the Presanctified Liturgy and through the Great Fast.

Like the Psalms themselves or like being "on the road again," this book at times makes awkward or abrupt shifts in perspective without qualification. I may be talking about the ancient Jews and then shift to comments about personal repentance. I may switch from talking about "they" to "we" to "I" and back to "they" again. But most of all, it is meant to transport us through the great expedition from far off foreign lands to "the city of the Great King."

Even though the book was written primarily for those familiar with the Eastern Christian tradition of the Great Fast and the Lenten liturgy of the Presanctified Gifts, it is my hope that the book is of value to many of other faith traditions including the Jewish tradition. With this in mind, I will at times explain certain aspects of the Eastern Christian worship.

---

2. The Liturgy of the Presanctified Gifts is a special penitent service in the Eastern tradition. Most of the music and prayers, such as the Songs of Ascents, are unique to that liturgy. Worshippers participate in the Presanctified Liturgy twice a week during the six weeks of Lent along with fasting, acts of charity, and confession. My family and I have grown to cherish it as a contemplative and centering guide for the Lenten season.

Abreviations

NJPS   The New Jewish Publication Society, *Tanakh; the Holy Scriptures*

1

Introduction to the Songs of Ascents
The Historical Setting of the Songs of Ascents (Pss 120–34)

The Psalms often directly relate to people of all times in history and in all kinds of different situations because they lack specific historical references. Because of this, it is challenging for biblical scholars to locate the historical situation that might have inspired the text. Even with the forensic tools available to modern research, one can only approximate the various "real life" situations alluded to in the text. Be that as it may, I agree with the consensus at this point that this particular collection of "songs" was composed, edited, and collected in order to encourage and inspire the people of Judah who were laying everything on the line to reconstitute the people of Israel after the great destruction of the city of Jerusalem by the Babylonians (587 B.C.E) and the rebuilding of the temple under Persian rule (515 B.C.E).

The Songs of Ascents fit well into the historical context of the early second temple period, some five hundred years before Jesus. At that time, many Jews had returned to the land, rebuilt the temple, and began the hard work of reconstituting a "land of Judea" under a common rule, without their own king, yet under the imperial oversight of Persia. This set of songs fits especially well into the time frame of Nehemiah and Ezra, over sixty years since the rededication of the temple in Jerusalem. One would do well, in fact, to read the books of Nehemiah and Ezra in conjunction with the Songs of Ascents.

A brief description of the social, economic and political situation in and around the time of Nehemiah goes far to illuminate many of the general statements found in the songs.

A Brief History from the Exile

The biblical history of the kings of Israel and Judah end when the Babylonians leveled Jerusalem and annihilated any remnants of the Davidic royalty in the land of Judah (2 Kings 25:7). For the writers of the books of Kings and Chronicles, there was nothing more to talk about. History as a story of a God and His people ceased at that point.

Ten years before the destruction of Jerusalem, the armies of Babylon seized Jerusalem, deported most of the aristocracy, temple personnel, and royal house, and set up a king from David's house who would supposedly cooperative with Babylonian rule. There was then, a large contingent of Judeans who lost their property, their place in society, and their primary point of reference, the temple in Jerusalem.

Conditions for the first exiles were no doubt devastating and harsh, but the biblical books such as Daniel, Esther, 2 Kings, Nehemiah and Ezra indicate that a good lot of them found places of importance and influence in Babylon. They weren't without resources, and they poured a good deal of them in two different directions: they collected, edited, and wrote scrolls of prophets, prayers, histories, and commandments and combined them into an epic remembrance of Israel that would serve as a foundational document for its reconstitution. What we know of today as "the Scriptures" took on its foundational shape at this time.

Second, they never lost sight of their home, Jerusalem, and devoted time and resources into networks of communication and involvement in the goings on there. This fact alone speaks of a profound sense of resurrection ingrained in the corporate psyche of this people. When Cyrus, the king of Persia, conquered Babylon and issued a decree that deported peoples could return to their lands and rebuild their cities and temples, the Jews in Babylon were ready to act. A primary concern of those with resources among the exiles was to reclaim property seized by others in their absence.

Among the deported, there were still plenty in Babylon who continued to experience a life of extreme poverty and struggle. They were essentially a slave class in Babylonian society subject to all kinds of abuse and maltreatment. Like many who left Europe's harsh conditions in the 19th century for the promise of America or the slaves in the United States after the emancipation, so many Jews in Babylon saw in Cyrus' decree a chance at a new beginning and a flight from poverty and suffering.

Back in the land of Judea, what the Persians called *Yehud*, the region experienced an immense decline in population and resources during the exile. Most Israelites of resources were gone. Clusters of small farmers and merchants struggled to survive and to make sense of the devastation. Opportunistic neighbors from all sides plundered or seized control of small territories within the land. Of the Jews left in the land and outside the general vicinity of Jerusalem, they clustered in small communities reminiscent of the tribal days before Israel had monarchies. There were attempts at establishing local worship centers, resuscitating the idea of local priests or Levites, and a council of Elders. This emphasis on local worship had both good and bad consequences. It compelled many still believing in Yahweh, the God of Israel, to take personal responsibility for maintenance of that relationship. A greater emphasis on personal piety and responsibility for one's neighbor emerged. On the downside, however, many blended their faith with local or foreign customs, many of which were eliminated by the official religion of Jerusalem under Hezekiah and Josiah. The problem of "high places," idols, and sacrificial abuses crept back in.

Similar to the opening up of the West in America, many saw the open unbridled territory as an opportunity for unabated exploitation and newfound wealth. The land had always been a major corridor for trade to which one could expand personal estates through tax, tariff, and loan, given the right collaboration with Persia. Some people, both Judeans and foreigners simply took up residence in abandoned spacious condos or farm estates and with a little entrepreneurial drive became well off and influential. Jerusalem grew as a regional trade center unencumbered by any centralized religious influence, especially of the socially demanding kind found in the Torah and preached by the prophets.

At the time of the building of the temple (523–15 B.C.E), hopes of a resuscitated kingdom of Judah with a temple, a local Davidic king, and a penitent people living under Torah elevated. After Darius firmly establish Persian rule (518 B.C.E), however, nationalistic ideals of a Davidic king were snuffed out. Persia would be the undisputed imperial rule of the land and with that, the Jews in the land and dispersed throughout the empire would have to seriously reevaluate and reinterpret their traditions in order to reconstitute a "people of Israel" in the land of Judah. Many of the high hopes and idealism generated in the dark years of exile were cause for serious soul-searching.

Persia was not interested in regional kings in their provinces, but they were very keen to having loyal and thriving regions able to support imperial coffers. Unlike their predecessors, Assyria and Babylon, whose main tactic for loyal participation was merciless intimidation and cruel demonstrations of force, the Persians wanted provinces to enjoy a limited amount of autonomy and to return to local customs and control. They encouraged the rebuilding of temples and cities and the establishment of a regional "law of the land," as long as it was fashioned in cooperation with the empire and not in defiance of it. This policy was a driving force for the various Jewish groups to come together and establish a "law of the land" that would unite the area and create prosperity. The push to create a binding document for Judah, what we know as "the Scriptures" came partly from the demands of the Persian court.

The challenge of creating a government without local royal sponsorship fell to groups that had already gained respect during the exilic years for their ability to reinterpret Israel's traditions in light of the tragedy. A group of priests inspired by Ezekiel had been formulating a temple and religious reform that would correct the abuses of the past. They placed a larger emphasis on the people being a "holy people" a nation of priests and envisioned how the temple could become the hub of unity and leadership in the land, taking over many functions once under royal administration.

Another group, which was more like a coalition of many groups, pressed harder than ever for the people to unite under the covenant that God had made with the people at Sinai. They believed Israel could reconstitute itself in a confederation of "tribes" similar to the time before Israel had kings and understood the binding force for Israel to be the Torah. As a counter-part to the Priestly slogan of: "You shall be holy as I am holy," the covenant coalition's motto was: "I am your God, and you are my people." They organized a "council of Elders" who could help lead the newly forming province.[1]

After the temple dedication (515 B.C.E) and up until the time of Nehemiah (444 B.C.E), control of the land was divided into three groups:

---

1. The covenant coalition was responsible for the writing of the book of Deuteronomy starting in the days of Hezekiah and Josiah. The book serves as a kind of manifesto or charter of the covenant coalition. Scholars refer to this coalition as the Deuteronomists.

the two mentioned above and the Persian administrators—Jews, Persians, and non-Jewish regional leaders who assured that the interests of the empire were not undermined. The two Jewish groups had differing visions of how best to reconstitute Israel to which there was contention, but they did agree on some critical points. First, they both agreed that a Torah of Moses would be the binding law of the land and to which all Israelites must be subordinate to as a mark of citizenship. They strongly pushed for all Israelites, not just the leadership, to be responsible for covenant obedience.

Out of this partnership of leading Jewish groups a daring innovation was launched. No longer would Israel define itself by a king and his royal apparatus, but by faith. This innovation was not contrary to what Israel had been before, but rather it reflected the deepest longings and primary urges that had always worked its way into the psyche of those who remembered through song, story and liturgy Abraham's daring departure from Haran and his descendents miraculous escape from Egypt. It could perhaps be summed up in such lyrics as: *Some are strong in chariots; some, in horses,/ but we are strong in the name of the LORD, our God* (Ps 20:8); *My father was a wandering Aramean* (Deut 26:5); or *My strength and my courage is the LORD,/ and he has been my savior* (Ex 15:2). Fundamentally, the newly constituted Israel would proclaim that "The LORD is King, He is robed in majesty." This declaration of faith, with its dangerously subversive undertones, dared to set the royal administration of Israel's God as the primary rule of not just the land but of all empires, monarchies, peoples, and tribes.

The primary agenda for Israel to define itself in terms of devotion to the Lord inspired critical religious, political and economic changes. There was a strong sense of solidarity based on the remembrance of the "tribes of Israel" and perhaps by the Greek influence of voting citizens in a democracy. The temple was no longer the king's, but the people's temple. All the people were responsible for the maintenance and propagation of its functions. A "brotherhood ethic" where each Israelite was responsible for the well-being of his neighbor took deep root. Its primary expression was the gathering of Israel at the temple for festivals. There the assembly, heads of households, the Council of Elders, and the priests and Levites gathered as one to deliberate just and righteous laws under the watchful eye of the Lord.

Finally, and this is vitally important to the Songs of Ascents, they felt that repentance was the foundational posture for a reconstituted Israel.

Not all remnants of the old Israel, however, were interested in such a posture. One such group refused even to the bitter end to give up on the dream of a Davidic kingdom which could rise to regional dominance and perhaps even replace Persia. They raised God's promise to David as the absolute standard to which all else was measured. Contrition was a sign of weak faith and even apostasy.

Others, both in the land or dispersed all the way to Babylon, sensed that God justly punished the wicked people—the royal house of David, the royal priesthood, and the aristocracy aligned with the royal house—and left the land to more worthy adherents. Parts of this group were inhabitants of the northern part of Israel who saw their local customs and religious centers destroyed under the reigns of Davidic kings influenced by covenant theology.

But those in control of the government in the early post-exilic period insisted that affinity with the cruel reality of the exile was the only way forward. The bottom line of course was this—all of Israel had failed in their relationship with their God. Contrition over each party's responsibility in that failure was the new foundation to build on and not finger pointing or arrogant stances of superiority or privilege. God had done everything, especially giving the people true prophets to warn them and call them back. Israel did not listen, was recalcitrant and even belligerent. Humility was the new foundation for reformation, not hubris.

Diminishing Hope against Internal Strife

By the time Nehemiah arrives in Jerusalem (444 B.C.E) the city and the region are experiencing a social crisis that threatened the very future of the Jewish people, especially in the land of Judea. Certainly, there were many within or close to Judah's borders who were not connected to Israel's past and saw the reoccupation of Jews in the land as just one more group vying for space in the land. They saw themselves as having just as much right to the land as the Jews and lobbied hard for Persian authority to protect their claims. They especially balked at any notion that land and properties forfeited over one hundred years ago were to be relinquished to some ethnic under-class in Mesopotamia claiming ancient rights to the land.

Although there were external forces at play, the crisis was mainly contested within the Jewish community. High hopes were turning into an abysmal situation. Bitter disappointment heightened the fracturing of rival groups vying for economic and political control and survival. Serious debates raged about the cause and meaning of the exile and its remedy and prevention.

Two deep fissures emerged mainly along economic lines. It can simply be described by the well known phrase: "The rich get richer, and the poor get poorer." This situation, as usual, was grossly disproportionate. The poor class was increasing and the rich consolidated into tighter and tighter circles of prosperity and influence.

The semi-autonomous status of *Yehud* allowed the Jews the chance to experiment with an innovative approach to reconstitute Israel. But of course, empires want subjugated people for one main reason—to fill the coffers of the Empire. Those in places of responsibility were obligated to insure that the rather steep imperial tax was paid no matter what. The demand that it be paid in silver, to which the land of *Yehud* had none of, meant that regional resources be exchanged for it. A lucrative exchange system developed to which most inhabitants were subject to "market fluctuations" that often under priced the value of goods produced.

But the newly formed ideal of a "people's temple" also required every Israelite, even those of little means, to contribute to the ongoing maintenance of the temple. The upper tier priests were secure, but many of the secondary clergy, known as the Levites, were prone to underpayment and sometimes deplorable disparity due to competing notions of provision for them.

The primary driving force behind this disparity, however, was the common, yet ruthless system of usury. The small farmers' livelihood was extremely vulnerable. All it took was one bad crop to cascade one's whole family into the pit of slavery. A farmer or merchant could borrow money from a rich neighbor in hopes of turning one's luck around. Of course, the terms were steep, and the consequences for default were extreme. First, one would hand over his children to slavery. The proprietor of the loan did not necessarily keep slaves on his own estate. The slave market in the Persian Empire was extensive and highly networked. To hand over a child to slavery often meant never seeing them again.

The irony of handing over children was that one's own labor force was greatly diminished, only compounding the inability to repay. The next step was to conscript the owner and the rest of his family and seize ownership of the property. From this situation it is easy to see two things and go far to explain the polarity of "wicked" and "righteous" so evident in the Songs of Ascents.

First, this system of usury was a quick money proposition for those with wealth. It became the primary way one obtained wealth, expanded it, and bought influence with the Persian Empire. The primary vehicle for this system was the court. It was with the elders in the gate where a lender would call his bill due and the debtor called to account. Only a few half contrived accusations jettisoned the process that could destroy a family and pad the pockets of the wealthy. The system was so profitable for some that a good deal of their business week was spent planning for the next default case. This explains the often repeated complaint in the Psalms and the prophets about the conniving, deceitful ways of the rich.

The biblical term for "wicked" is nearly synonymous with "rich," and it was easy to see how explosive the situation could be between those struggling and the well-to-do. This picture is described in Nehemiah 5. Many regional and local families aiding Nehemiah in the building of Jerusalem's walls complain bitterly of the manipulation of the usury system even by their fellow countrymen. Since Jerusalem was a mixed city, Nehemiah's angry reaction to this abuse was targeted to rich Jews and others alike. But Nehemiah's anger especially targeted his fellow countrymen because they ought to have known better. They had the Torah, the prophets, and the bitterness of the exile to inform them otherwise. The great vision of a reconstituted Israel was being greatly compromised by a "business as usual" mentality that superseded the demands of God's covenant. Tensions within the Jewish community between those struggling to survive and those who were thriving under a heartless system of economic disparity were deep, often breaking into near riots during festivals.

It is no wonder how the covenant stipulations for social and economic equity took on an immense appeal for struggling farmers and merchants and even more so from those already marginalized by the system. For many of these, the hope of Israel focused on Jerusalem's ability to unite under one temple, one God, and one Torah. Within the temple precinct, the faithful could renew their hope on a regular basis and the wavering and wealthy could possibly be exhorted by preaching from the Torah from gifted expositors like Ezra.

For many of the wealthy in Judea, both Jewish and foreign, the "Israel project" with its demand for equity was not welcomed. And for many of these, simply ignoring it was a workable strategy. Among the rich who were Jewish, one would simply give lip service to covenant talk merely as a vehicle to keep the current system operable. They still relied on the court system to exact payments and the temple to regulate monetary funds and generate revenue from pilgrims and festivals. Many argued that religion had nothing to do with economics and more aggressively resisted its intrusion in the market place. They could, if necessary, play the trump card against too much push toward the temple and Torah. They could warn Persia of rebellious "king" talk that always brooded among the faithful.

Not all the wealthy, however, were of such a mind. There were those, especially those who had returned from exile and still had regular contact with the exilic community, who sought solidarity with their poorer brother's in the land. They believed in the reconstitution of Israel and put much of their own resources at risk for the project. They faced serious challenges on two fronts.

For one, they had to convince their poorer neighbors that they too were willing to come under Torah stipulations and advocate for economic justice. They had to persuade them away from rebellion and toward working with the system for change. At times, they even had to defend those being taken to court.

On the other front, those of the wealthy class who were in solidarity with the Torah and with their fellow covenant members faced bitter opposition and aggressive tactics to undermine their own wealth and influence in the region. Many saw solidarity with the poor as a recipe for economic ruin. It was folly and madness. The trouble was, this accusation proved to be a real possibility. The rich, both in Judea and Babylon, exposed their wealth to great loss in following through with aiding the poor and advocating for equity. Isaiah puts it succinctly: *The man who turns from evil is despoiled* (Isa 59:15).

At the time of the writing, editing, and compiling of the Songs of Ascents, those desiring to invest in the reconstitution of Israel lived in precarious and tense times. Both poor and rich willing to "trust in the Lord" would be easily tempted to give up on the project, simply concede to the way things are and denounce it as a silly pipe-dream. Visions of a "kingdom come" where justice, righteousness, and fidelity thrive under a loving, rescuing God too readily turned into heartbreaking nightmares.

Psalms, Songs, and Antiphons

He who sings well, prays twice. —St. Augustine

The book of Psalms has spoken to, comforted, and taught people of all faiths. It is the foundational book of prayer for Judaism and Christianity. It has an incredible ability to connect with people in all kinds of conditions and human predicaments. It is especially tuned in to our troubles of all flavors. The book of Psalms is a masterful anthology of the prayers of ancient Israel. No book is more relied on to lead us into prayer and to teach us what prayer is than this book.

The word *psalm* sounds like *song* because it is simply a Greek word for song. In Hebrew, the collection is called *tehelim*, which is taken for the word for praise. The well-known word *hallelujah* derives from the same root word and simply means "praise the Lord." Along with or even perhaps before understanding the Psalms as prayers we should understand them as songs. It has been that way from the time when Miriam sang her song of victory on the shores of the Reed Sea (Ex 15) to our singing the psalms to folk tunes today.

However much we employ the prayers of ancient Israel into our liturgies and worship, we should understand that they were originally meant to be sung. They are lyrics. Those of us in the Eastern liturgical tradition perhaps get a better feel for this since all our liturgies and prayer services are sung or chanted from start to finish. Every prayer is a song and every song is a prayer.

From the Gut—the Origins of Prayer

The origins of song/hymn/prayer come from two different directions. There is the top-down direction. These are public songs inspired by a great military victory and are sung at the victory parade (the origins of our procession). They employ boastful exaggerated language of conquest. This probably doesn't set well with us today, but we must remember that when a city's army leaves town for war, there will certainly be a returning army. The life and death question is always which army will return to the city. Theirs or ours? The relief of seeing the hometown boys coming back was cause for more than a casual "yippie." The hymns of victory were common throughout the ancient Near Eastern world, and Israel certainly experienced some of that.

What stands out about the prayers collected in the book of Psalms and scattered throughout the stories and writings of the prophets in the Hebrew Scriptures is the extent that the "bottom-up" prayers dominate. The Bible places the origins of prayer not in the boastful shouts of victory over an enemy but more in the deep guttural crying out in the darkness of night, whether that darkness refers to the time when there is no sunlight or to the dark experiences of human existence. The first mention of prayer in Genesis 4:26 gushes up from a deep anguish over two men bragging over how many people they have killed in revenge. It was "at that time" that people began to "cry out" to the Lord. As Walter Brueggemann explains, a prayer is first and foremost "sung up."[2]

King David is Israel's rock star of the prayer-song. The Bible witnesses to the basis of his fame. Yes, there were songs sung *of* David as he returned from battles having been one-hundred times more successful than Saul. But few of these songs make the "greatest hits" list. No, the songs remembered are the ones sung *by* David from his wilderness and wanderings collection, where he was a vulnerable and lonesome shepherd or a desperado on the run.

God loved David, and it is perhaps in that curious blend of human vulnerability encased in the mysterious combination of word, voice, tonal sound and rhythm that God so deeply connected with David. The song is open, bare, fragile, from the heart, bonding and transcendent. It is intensely private and public at the same time. The song time travels. It takes us back to sweet memories and calls us to future hopes. Probably like no other, the song infuses eternity in our hearts (Eccl 3:11).

The song can lull us to sleep, but it can also mobilize us. Dr. Roger Payne first recorded the "songs" of the humpback whales in the 1960s. These songs generated the modern conservancy movement, first with the "Save the Whales" campaign and then later the "Save the Earth" campaign. The songs raised the awareness of people around the globe as to the dangers experienced by species everywhere. Dr. Payne explains why this happened. "The humpback whales were the whales that could sing."

The Songs of Ascents comingle top-down and bottom-up prayers without us even noticing the switch. As we proceed through this book, we will encounter the abrupt shifts in perspective common to Israel's songs. They change from first, to second, to third person with ease. They shift from praise to sermon to wisdom to complaint. They run the complete

---

2. Brueggemann, *Israel's Praise*, 78.

spectrum of human emotions from exuberant shouts of praise to guttural groans of despair eked through a curtain of tears.

The song, or *shir* in Hebrew, is mostly in the victory song genre. They are meant to be joyous and celebratory. They are party songs. With this in mind then, we might ask what songs of victory have to do with repentance. Or for that matter, the Israelites might have asked what they have to do with the intense internal conflict surrounding the gathering of Israelites at the Temple. Singing a song with a heavy heart is compared in Proverbs to taking away someone's coat on a cold day (Prov 25:20). The *shir* is generally not associated with mourning, sadness, or melancholy.

Why are these joyous songs of victory and ascent incorporated into the time of repentance during the Great Fast? The response is best experienced as we proceed, on the trail upward rather than explained in the classroom, but it certainly is related to anticipating the victory of God. For the Christian, one always has a kind of cheater repentance. We already know the outcome. Even in Lent, the resurrection is still present. Even as we usher in the Fast at the Vespers of Forgiveness with its shift of somber colors, minor tones, and sober prayers, the Easter songs are sung in anticipation.

Through the Fast and in the Antiphons of the Presactified Liturgy, however, we are jettisoned into the anguish of the Jewish people whose hope of God's kingdom come languished under four great empires over six hundred years. This speaks of one of the more profound mysteries of drawing near to the "Ineffable One." Part of ascending to God is a descent into our failure. The Jews who reentered the land and began rebuilding "a people" insisted on one bottom line foundation—identification with the exile. They insisted that those who had experienced exile best understood the failure of every group and individual involved. Lamentation was the cornerstone for Israel's reconstitution and not smug, finger-pointing exuberance. Israel didn't just fail; it failed completely. Something of this descent before ascent is found in the saying of the Eastern monk St. Silouan: "Keep your mind in hell, but despair not."[3]

Repentance is not really putting on a sad face. It is a re-minding. It is asking us to re-shift our thinking and re-orientate our bearings. It is meant to remind us of our plight without God's mighty intervention, of God's own descent in the destruction of the temple and exile of his

---

3. Zacharias. *The Enlargement of the Heart*, 64.

people and in Jesus' own descent into the plight of humanity and in his death on a cross.

Repentance is about recovering, returning, and reminding our most essential hope, our most essential desire. It is about directing all desire toward the One true desire, to that one true authentic, real and lasting desire.

This is why we mix our songs of hope and joy with our songs of longing and sadness.

The Songs of Ascents as a Literary Set

Palms 120–34 are among the relatively few sets of psalms found in the greater book of the Psalms. We know this especially because of the introductory title given to each of them: "A Song of the Ascents."[4] This particular group of psalms is designed to be sung together. The imagery and themes are artfully woven together into a rich tapestry conjuring up the sensual experiences, emotional gamut and deepest longings of a great "going up." Even the literary structure and features give an ascending feel to its progression.

Themes and Depictions

The more one reads, sings, and meditates on these songs, the more recognizable certain themes and images become. The intent of this book is to encounter these "on the way"; even so, we would do well to familiarize ourselves with the prominent ones here by way of introduction. After all, it behooves anyone embarking on an "expedition" to know something of what one is getting into.

The dominant theme and image is of course an *ascent*, and with that, we can include it with a familiar list of words analogous to the Christian life, all of which refer to movement in a certain direction: journey, pilgrimage, sojourn or passage upward.

The basic Hebrew word is *alah*, to move upward. From that word, however, comes a large variety of meanings and associations, all of which have to do with an upward motion or sense. Since the songs are an entry

---

4. Curiously, the Hebrew word for ascent is plural and it has the definite article in front of it—*the ascents*. This might indicate a well-known "ascent" that includes a variety of little ascents. In other words, my ascent is a part of "the great ascent."

into the temple worship, the idea of climbing the steps to the temple area is certainly part of the reference for these psalms. It is likely that choirs of Levitical singers lined the steps and sang back and forth to one another to spur on the ascending procession of congregants (Neh 12:27–43).

The upward sense can refer to what is immediately higher, like another floor of a building, a set of stairs or a ceiling; however, it is also used to express the extreme heights, like the tops of mountain peaks or the upper limits of the sky. It also refers to the most exalted of rulers, kings. God is referred to as *eliyon*, Most High.

One noun form, *maalah*, refers to steps or a stair case, but also takes on the meaning of a long arduous journey of no return, like a passage. We can picture climbing a mountain pass in order to pass to the other side. One scholar believes an "expedition" best depicts the notion especially in relationship to Ezra and Nehemiah's *going up* to Jerusalem from far off Babylon (Ezra 1:11, 7:9).[5] In this sense, a climbing expedition provides an apt comparison.

A climbing expedition starts with one base, but domineering desire—to reach the top. This desire supersedes and overtakes all other concerns, fears, barriers, or objections. It requires extensive planning, logistics, and along with these, the shedding of all luxury, excess, amenities, or comforts. One must reduce to bare essentials. An expedition demands participation and cooperation with a network of skilled people willing to support the effort, for it is never done alone. One speaks of a climbing expedition in aggressive combative terms. In this sense, the "ascent" is near synonymous with an "assault," for it is fully aware of the enemy, both from within and without, who seeks to thwart the mission.

In one way, however, the climbing expedition analogy breaks down. One climbs a peak because one has not been there before, and once at the top, one descends and returns to his home. But the ascent of the exiles in Babylon or of regional pilgrims struggling in the land of *Yehud*, or of the Church in its season of repentance is a *return* to one's home, to its roots. The return is not to get back to the way things used to be. Those striving to rebuild Israel from the rubble understood all too well the misguided failures of their ancestors. Going back was the only way forward. This is the way of repentance, what the Bible calls "lamentation." Only by reliving, remembering and reminded of the failure of God's people

---

5. Goulder, *The Psalms of the Return*, 23.

to live up to its calling, can they, and we, open ourselves up to a genuine in-breaking of God's kingdom.

There is also a rich spiritual history of comparing our relationship with God to a mountain or a great ladder to be climbed. One of the Lenten Sundays focuses on our struggle against demonic forces in which a famous icon of St. John Climacos is displayed. It depicts the arduous and perilous journey of the monk as he struggles against demons toward God. In the *Hymns of Paradise,* St. Ephrem playfully creates a composite image of paradise as both a garden and a great mountain. He sees every human soul in some proximity to it and moving upward.

Having grown up in Denver, Colorado, the gateway to the Rockies, I too am quite familiar with ascending mountains and mountains being the dominant geographical reference. I could easily orientate my compass by first finding the mountains to the west. The state holds the highest concentration of high altitude mountains found anywhere in the lower 48. My father was an avid mountaineer, and so it is way too tempting not to let some of those memories bleed into the commentary here.

In the Songs of Ascents, only one mountain looms over and pervades every verse—Mount Zion. Zion is a composite icon evoking God's covenantal Presence, especially for those given over to the "Israel project" after the exile. Zion has several geographic points of contact that bleed into each other. It refers to the mound on which the temple is built, but it also refers to whole hill country of Jerusalem, the city buildings, the inhabitants of the city, the worshipping community ascending in liturgical procession, and the hope of a new David.[6] Ultimately, Zion evokes that point of contact between an Almighty loving God and his creatures. Before the advent of Jesus, Zion was the most dominant icon for God's relentless drive, indeed His dogged insistence—called *chesed* in the Hebrew scriptures, "steadfast love"—to meet up with and encounter us humans.

Glimpses of the Top

As we embark on our own expedition through this book, we will encounter other prominent images that give a window into the songwriter's particular hope and perspective, all of which are related to Zion.

One theme is mentioned only once in the Songs of Ascents, but it permeates nearly every verse. None of the inconvenience, exertion, and

---

6. Ollenburger, *Zion the City of the Great King,* 13—22.

stress of an expedition need be experienced if it were not for one giant annoyance—*the dream* (Ps 126:1). We could have been eating sweet cool melons in Egypt or rich, fancy foods in Babylon if it were not for the dream. I could have pursued a "happy life" without reference to the needs of others had I not become a Christian.

It is, then, like my brothers and I going on our weekly climbing and skiing ventures as children. Whether you think it is fun or not, whether you have a strong internal drive toward the top or not, you are getting up at five o'clock in the morning on the weekend, slamming down some oatmeal, putting on your itchy wool clothes, packing into a station wagon while it is still dark and heading for the mountains. You are going simply because you are a part of this family and not some other family.

The dream, as we shall encounter, is both the imaginings of the top of the mountain as well as partial realizations of it. "The dream" has to do with reaching the top, of one's final goal and destination. Jesus expressed the dream this way: "Thy kingdom come, Thy will be done on earth as it is in heaven."

Other reoccurring images relate to the "Israel project." They refer to the great faith effort to reconstitute or resurrect Israel. Ideally, they offer glimpses into the kingdom of God—what it would look like if'n God ran the place—but they are blended into the actual life and hardships of struggling Jews in the land of *Yehud* in the fifth century B.C.E.

The songwriter is especially tuned into the struggling farmer; thus depictions of plowing, sowing, tilling, waiting, and reaping are employed. Images of building a life together similar to what a young married couple might envision also seep in. The lyricist evokes images of building a house, a home, a family, a livelihood and an inheritance. He dreams of enjoying "the good life" where one is settled in. He or she partakes of the fruits of his or her labors, neighborly cooperation, a sense of community and a good night's sleep.

There is one other "image" that dominates the Songs of Ascents. Perhaps the better word is not image or theme, but presence. Throughout these songs, our singers are ever aware of and tormented by a threatening enemy, sometimes just referred to as "they." "They" are variously called wicked, liars, haters of peace and of Zion, war-mongers, taunters, proud, haughty, contemptuous, a devouring predator, and a ruthless plowman. They are ever present as if accompanying the processing expedition from far off Babylon to the very temple itself, impeding and opposing the entourage every step of the way. Indeed, their threatening presence appears to be one of the generating forces for the composition as reflected in the first line: "Lord, in my distress I cry to you!"

The Generators of the Text

Due to the cumbersome and expensive process of producing a "scroll" in the ancient world, the lines between an author, a compiler or researcher, an editor, a transcriber, and a publisher were quite blurred. It is better to understand the faith community or tradition that influenced and generated a text than to isolate a single author.

With this in mind, it is likely that the Songs of Ascents collection was the product of the Levites serving in the temple during the attempted reforms of Ezra and Nehemiah. Some scholars have suggested that Nehemiah was the driving inspiration for its composition, recounting not only a pilgrimage from the surrounding region, but the long "expedition" from exile even.[7] The Songs of Ascents seem particularly aimed at encouraging those who have given themselves over to the "Israel project," believing that the God of Israel still desired to gather His people and to establish an ongoing relationship with them. Similar to its use in the Pre-sanctified Liturgy, they were songs of entrance for the faithful ascending from the region and the city to the temple precinct. The Levites were both the songwriters and performers as they lined the steps on and spurred the congregants upward in song.

Since the Songs of Ascents became fixed in written form, it is quite possible that these songs made their way back to the exiles still in Babylon in the hope of encouraging those who had "settled down" in a foreign land to come home. Even more so, the Songs of Ascents intend to strengthen the resolve of those who had abandoned their home away from home in Babylon, packed up their belongings and set out at great risk to "come home."

In a very real sense, this is what the season of repentance known to us as Lent or the Great Fast is calling us to. We all have settled down into cozy situations of existence. The problem is that that existence is in a foreign land. To varying degrees, we all have acquiesced to a human condition chronically diseased by sin. For some, the home away from home is plenty sufficient and the vision of a true home becomes too implausible, so it fades from memory. For others, the memory of home still

---

7. Goulder, *The Psalms of the Return*, 20–33. Loren D. Crow, *The Songs of Ascents*, 9–13.

lives, but the risk of the expedition is overwhelming fraught with danger and uncertainty. Truly, one could lose it all in such a venture. There are no guarantees of success. There are others who have made the decisive step. They packed the family and are on the way with the bumper sticker "The kingdom of God or bust." But as the hardships of the expedition become real, the temptation is to turn around and go back before it is too late. Finally, there are those who left, made the journey, settled into the land and are overtaken by bitter regret and resentment caused by internal bickering, favoritism, corruption, and incompetence.

Understanding a little about the Levites helps explain the particular themes and emphasis highlighted above. In a lot of ways, they found themselves stuck in the middle as it were.

The exile caused every part of Israelite society to radically reevaluate its role and responsibility for the disaster, and this was true for the class of priests known as Levites. The Bible paints a bipolar picture of them. In pre-exilic times, they were local priests who possibly resisted the agenda of Josiah to centralize worship in Jerusalem. This led to the accusation that they were leading the people into idolatry or abusing sacrificial worship. On the one hand, they were very connected to local communities and needs and often experienced discrimination themselves from the over-reaching royal temple.

The second temple reform attempted to correct the Levitical problem. For one, the distinction between the priesthood descendant from Aaron and the Levitical priesthood was clarified. Only the top tier of priests (Aaron descendants) could offer atonement sacrifices and were allowed into the inner part of the temple. The Levites, however, were responsible for the "people's sacrifices" made in the main courtyard of the temple. The people's sacrifices were those that required the participation of the congregant. It was a fellowship offering which meant that most of the sacrifice was used for a shared meal with family and the Levites.

This two-tiered system may have felt demeaning at times, but the intention was the opposite. It was designed to include or integrate the ministry of the Levites into a one-temple, one-sacrifice system meant to heighten the sense of unity for the beleaguered Israelite community. No doubt, however, the intention was only partially successful. The Levites felt as much as anyone the tension of partially fulfilled hopes against harsh realities and vigorous opposition. They could identify with both the priestly orientated concerns as well as those of the covenant coalition.

The Levites held affinities with the coalition who put a strong emphasis on a brotherhood ideal. As mentioned earlier, this perspective relied heavily on the notion that God had entered into a covenant with Israel. The emphasis was on just and equitable ways of relating to one another. The bottom line was that each covenant member was responsible for not only his own well-being, but the well-being of all covenant members, their families, and even those on the margins.

The Levites were in a similar situation to the struggling farmer or merchant. Their livelihood was equally precarious because the community was at odds over how the Levites should be compensated. Some advocated for the old tribal ideal. They should be without land and completely dependent on generosity. This easily turned into a situation of near homelessness similar to the most marginalized people in the land. Their lives teetered on homeless or emigrant status.

This kind of uncertainly was often compounded by those of the first tier priests who collaborated more readily with the wealthy as a way to keep their own economic situation secure and comfortable. Like those of the coalition, they saw God as one who brings acts of salvation in the real political world to which they lived. They looked to God to act on their behalf.

Because the Levites were responsible for the people's sacrifices, they had more of a pastoral sense than the more separated priests at the top tier. They empathized not only with the farmer or rural merchant, but also with the aristocracy who attempted rigorous and risky identification with the poor.

The Levites, however, were still priests, and that perspective also comes out in the Songs of Ascents. They understood that politics alone cannot move people toward love and responsibility toward others. It also depended on a deep sense of being esteemed as a beloved creature by the Creator. God's love is equally experienced through the joy of a newborn child, a much anticipated rainy season, or a successful harvest. God's "favor" is not just grounded in the exodus, but also in nature itself.

The lyrical beauty and masterful weaving of images and themes found in the Songs of Ascents are best explained as having been generated by those of the Levitical priestly class during the time of Ezra and Nehemiah. They were after all, the skilled singers, songwriters, archivists, and scribes employed at the temple. They were best suited to expresses the balance and tension between rich and poor, urban and rural, covenant and priestly, prophet and scribe, ritual and expository. They experienced on a regular basis in the festivals and Sabbaths generative times of exuberant hope of "thy kingdom come." They knew how true and real the proclamation was: "Taste and see that the Lord is good. His mercy endures forever."

Other Literary Features

Perhaps by design or perhaps by coincidence, the three Antiphons in the Presanctified Liturgy follow a natural division in the text of the Songs of Ascent.

Before I describe the literary divisions in the Songs of Ascents, I want to describe a certain aspect of climbing mountains that provides an apt analogy for proceeding through the songs.

The conventional approach to scaling a peak is to first find a route to a main ridge that leads to the top. Generally, ridgelines allow for the easiest and most direct way to the summit. One problem with this approach is that once on the ridge, one cannot always discern whether the immediate top one sees in front of him is the summit or a "false summit." In other words, once the climber reaches the top in front of him, he may, and often does, encounter another top to scale. He does not know whether the next one in front of him is just another false summit. It is common for a climber to encounter numerous false summits.

A similar kind of picture is given in the structure of this series of Psalms. One can detect in the literary structure an ascent, an arrival at the top with a new realization that it was a false summit, and a descent from the top in pursuit of the final summit.

In a similar sense, we experience several summits as we progress through the Songs of Ascents. In each case, a high point has been reached, but with it a new realization that a greater height is yet to be scaled. We will see how this plays out as the book develops. By way of introduction though, we could divide the three antiphons as follows:

First Antiphon (Pss 120–24)—The going up to Jerusalem.

Second Antiphon (Pss 125–29)—Arrival at the city and passing through "the gates."

Third Antiphon (Pss 130–34)—Arrival at the main court of the temple for sacrifice, a fellowship meal, and a benediction.

A final literary feature deserves attention. The prominent themes and images discussed above are recognizable because of their repetition. Repetition is of course a learning devise, but here, it also promotes the sense of ascending. With each repeat of a word, phrase, or theme, the pilgrim makes one more step up. He realizes that he is not in the same place as he was before. Though it is a familiar theme, something has changed since the last time it was visited.

Even in a subtle literary feature such as this, something of repentance can be gleaned. We revisit repentance every year at the Great Fast and go through the same words, gestures, and liturgies, yet it is not the same as before. Repentance is not a repeat. Perhaps we discover that we have ascended just a little bit more without being very conscious of it. Something has changed since the last time we were here.

The First Antiphon—Psalms 120–124

THE PRESANCTIFIED LITURGY BEGINS with the proclamation of God's kingdom in Christ followed by the reading of Psalm 104. A litany[1] is then chanted by the priest and congregation. The priest then chants the prayer of the first Antiphon.

> O LORD, compassionate and merciful, long-suffering and of great mercy, give heed to our prayer, and attend to the voice of our supplication. Work upon us a sign for good. Guide us in your way, that we may walk in your truth. Gladden our hearts that we may fear your holy name. For You art great and work wonders. You alone are God, and among the gods there is none like you, O LORD, powerful in mercy, and good in might, to help and to comfort and to save all those who hope in thy Holy name.

The First Antiphon Psalms (Pss 120–124) proceeds from the priest's prayer. While the choir leads the congregation into worship, the priest prays and incenses.

The First Antiphon (Pss 120–24) places the liturgical community "on the road" from far off Babylon with the gates of Jerusalem its destiny. In fact, the first song of the antiphon starts on a downhill note. The

---

[1]. A litany is a series of prayers that are spoken by the priests and to which the congregation responds with "Lord have mercy."

expedition is off to a bad start and encounters seemingly insurmountable obstacles. Cries of desperation start the Songs of Ascent (Ps 120). The climber catches a brief glimpse of his goal as he realizes that the Lord is watching over the expedition (Ps 121). In fact, He is on expedition with the pilgrim.

While on the road, the pilgrim reminisces of the good ole' days when Israel gathered at Jerusalem with its king and celebrated the covenant with the Lord. He allows the nostalgia to keep him moving (Pss 122–23:4). Abruptly, and once again, "they" stand by in scornful objection to the expedition. From their lounge chairs they laugh and mock at the folly of such a mission (Ps 123:4). There is a recollection of wits and inner strength and then the climb continues, for they have not reached the Temple (Ps 124).

2

Psalm 120

Unto the LORD[1]

IN THE HEBREW TEXT, the phrase "to the Lord" begins the verse. This is more accurately portrayed in the lamp-lighting Psalms of vespers where first the Lord's name is invoked, "LORD," followed by a call for help, "I call upon you, hear me." It is here where the journey, regardless of its lowly beginnings firmly places its goal. None other than a meeting with "The Lord" will due. As complex, varied, and nuanced as religious faith and practice can be, we need be reminded that the height of our efforts and anguish is none other than a communion with God.

To call on the name of a god or goddess was of course commonplace in the ancient world. There were lots of gods, usually dependent on location. One could readily pick from a smorgasbord of divine aids each with a particular talent or knack.

The name *Yahweh* or some variation of *Yah* was particularly located in the southern Levant and was not restricted to the Israelites. *Yah* was a popular mountain god who was especially called upon to aid in reproduction of crops or herds. He was a rural, not a city god.

The ancient Hebrews understood their god in such a way, but they insisted even more so that God had revealed himself in a dramatic and unique way, a way contrary to any other notion of gods in the ancient

---

1. The version here follows the Revised Standard Version as adapted by the Orthodox Church of America for liturgical reasons.

world. The name revealed to Moses in the desert, "I am" (a word play on the word *yah*) came at a time of deep crisis for the Hebrews. Thus "I am" is especially the one who rescues, who saves, who brings out of the land of slavery.

Yahweh is the most common reference in the Hebrew Bible for the god of the Israelites. But in order to avoid using the Lord's name in vain, the ancient Jewish practice avoided saying the name altogether. When reading the Scriptures out loud then, the written word, *Yahweh*, was spoken as *adonai*, Lord. Thus, "the LORD" in our English bibles is the substitute name for *Yahweh*.

For the ancient Israelites and for us today, the Name mostly invokes the sense of a God driven to interaction and communion with humans. His desire is to draw near and even live among us. Even more so, He works unceasingly to "draw all men to Him." To call on the Lord (*Yahweh*) means to call on a one of kind god who wants communion over conscription, covenant over contract, liberation over slavery.

In my distress, I cried

The Hebrew word for distress, *tzarar,* has a general sense of being bound, restricted, cramped, squeezed, tightened, swallowed, overwhelmed, or closed in on. It does not carry a mild sense of anxiety or stress, but of being in dire straits. One can easily get the sense of being smothered or suffocated, like a boa constrictor who raps its coils around a victim and patiently waits for each exhale to gently tighten its hold, making the next breath shorter than the one before.

As a child, I was claustrophobic. I vividly remember the sweeping sense of panic when confined to a small dark place. Particularly, I felt like I could not breathe, that I would suffocate.

The prayer of Jonah amply portrays the sense. He was not only engulfed by the sea, but even more so, he was swallowed by a great fish. Even ancient peoples understood that a person does not survive in a fish that is underwater. This is double-death, an imminent and certain extinguishing of life with no possible way of escape.

> *In my distress I called to the LORD,*
>   *and he answered me.*
> *From the midst of the nether world I cried for help,*
>   *and you heard my voice.*

> *For you cast me into the deep, into the heart of the sea,*
>   *and the flood enveloped me;*
>   *all your breakers and your billows passed over me.*
> *Then I said, "I am banished from your sight!*
>   *Yet would I again look upon your holy temple.*
> *The waters swirled about me,*
>   *threatening my life.*
> *The abyss enveloped me;*
>   *seaweed clung about my head.*
> *Down I went to the roots of the mountains;*
>   *the bars of the nether world were closing behind me forever*
> (Jonah 2:3–7)

This kind of distress is used to describe Joseph's "anguish" as he was lowered into the well by his conniving brothers (Gen. 42:21). It is not a quiet annoyance or nuisance—it is compared to the kind of tormented anguish of a woman in the pangs of child birth (Gen. 3:16, Jer. 49:24).

Tzarar can speak of all kinds of "difficulties" or hard times as it were, but in the case of David, it is mainly speaking of men who seek his life. Certainly, this is a major theme in the Psalms, especially the ones attributed to David. Thus, it is not difficulties brought on by natural or incidental causes, but ones brought on by other human beings. It is the hostility, harassment, abuse and violence experienced by other humans, especially those who are closest to us. The ones who should be our friend, colleague, neighbor, or loved one is the worst and most intensive kind of distress. This is indeed the complaint of the song here.

It is the sweeping sense of shame that overtakes the one whom the crowd or gang has converged upon. It is that choked feeling of shame as the many single out the one who is unsuspectingly smothered by the newly formed league as they hurl and heap fatal accusations upon their target like stones on a pile.

The psalms attributed to David vivify this best. It is ultimately the suffocating humiliation of being completely overtaken, defeated, and overpowered by one's enemies to the extent that even God has abandoned the "loser."

> *Be not far from me, for I am in distress; (tzarar)*
>   *be near, for I have no one to help me.*
> *Many bullocks surround me;*
>   *the strong bulls of Bashan encircle me.*
> *They open their mouths against me*
>   *like ravening and roaring lions.*

> *I am like water poured out;*
>   *all my bones are racked.*
> *May heart has become like wax*
>   *melting away within my bosom.*
> *My throat is dried up like baked clay,*
>   *my tongue cleaves to my jaws;*
>   *to the dust of death you have brought me down.*
> *Indeed, many dogs surround me,*
>   *a pack of evildoers closes in upon me*
> (Ps 22:12–17)

The distress most often brought up in desperate prayer in the Psalms is inevitably from other humans and mostly humans acting in a kind of conspiring collective sense. The enemy is addressed as simply "they," and by a variety of other terms that we will encounter. Most importantly, of all the people who will accompany those on expedition, the enemy is ever present and ever pressing. They vigilantly lurk, seeking the prime opportunity to devour.

Climbers know of such an enemy. He is called "weather." It is ever present, often benevolent. Good weather can make for an ascent of shear beauty, majesty and exhilaration. When the weather is clear and mild, one can have a "hills are alive with the sound of music" experience of harmony with nature. But always lurking, brooding, congealing is weather's bipolar unpredictability. Especially in high mountains, weather goes from beauty to devouring beast within a matter of minutes.

Need we be reminded that Jesus also knew of such enemies.

That he may answer me

In the second part of this opening verse we are reminded of the double-play or ambiguity of prayer, for the petitioner declares in the midst of such impending doom that *He answered me*. Some have attempted to avoid the difficulty with this statement by making it a subordinate clause—"that he may answer me," but most versions read it straightforward from the Hebrew—"and he answered me."[2]

The term invariably appeals to someone who has some power or authority to reverse a bad situation. First and fundamental, an answer is given simply because the superior one grants a hearing. He responds

---

2. The Septuagint, however, may lend itself to such an interpretation; *pothen*—from hence, where.

by listening. The word carries strong overtones of a court case where someone is on trial. Job, for instance speaks frequently of "answering" his accusers. If one is surrounded by an avalanche of accusation, the presence of an impartial judge generates a tremendous hope. The accused is vindicated simply in being given a fair hearing.

Sometimes, as is the case of Elijah (1 Kings 17:3–4), the answer comes as a favorable gesture or sign. It is a positive indication that acquittal is forthcoming.

Nehemiah's (Neh 1:1–11) situation aptly depicts the tension of answered prayer. Upon hearing of the dreadful conditions in Jerusalem, Nehemiah is inconsolably vexed. He mournfully prays to God, and the answer comes in the form of the King of Persia granting him leave to return to Jerusalem. The "answer" for Nehemiah was to begin the arduous exodus or expedition back to Jerusalem. Before he can *go up* to the holy mountain, he will first have to *go down* to Jerusalem. Just as Abraham had to leave his father and engage in the dangerous migration (descent) in order to engage the promise, so too Nehemiah. Thus, God answered Nehemiah, but as the opening verse of the Songs of Ascents immediately indicate, this "answer" would lead Nehemiah into even greater perils and trials. Indeed, others perceive Nehemiah's hope mission as an act of war (Ps 120:7).

We must never forget that Israel's (and our) cry for deliverance in the Roman occupation of first century Palestine meant the deadly descent of the Son of God.

Nehemiah relies on God's past "answers" to prayer as the foundation for future help. The prayer of Jonah is a prime model of the dynamics of prayer, and it helps us grasp the tension between a request heard and a request acted upon. In the case of Gideon (Ju 8:8), there is just a negative response to a request or petition. The answer can simply be no, access denied. In the case of Jonah, we are asked to imagine Jonah saying this prayer in the belly of a fish. This prayer gurgles to the surface from the deep as Jonah's last breath. Jonah goes so far as to admit that God had brought the disaster upon him. But ironically, it is where *the bars of the nether world were closing behind me forever* that Jonah proclaims that God heard his voice.

And here is the mystery beyond words about this kind of desperate, lastditch cry for help. Somehow and in some way, Jonah sees a vision, a foretaste, of being in the Presence of the Lord again. He sees himself back in the Temple. He sees himself, as we see ourselves in the singing of the antiphons in Pre-sanctified Liturgy, approaching the Temple, ascending to the Holy Mountain.

My father was an avid mountain climber who took his children on many a climb. The anxious anticipation over the plans and preparation for a big climb come to a swell as one first lays eyes on the mountain. Its towering presence looms as both challenge and threat. One is irresistibly beckoned into its magnetic sphere. It must be approached. It must be ascended, for if one makes its summit, great rewards are received. It is not the feeling of having beat the mountain as much as being received as a cohabitant and correspondent to its majestic presence. Certainly, something of this feeling is envisioned in Jonah's impossible assurance of resurrection in the very heart of death.

The spiritual tradition of the Christian East has long held the insight that to be drawn close to God in Christ, one must imitate Christ in that he descended before he ascended. In the death, resurrection, ascension of Jesus all prayers have already been answered. In the second coming of Christ all of our current and future prayers are answered.

As is quite possible in the case here, the initial answer has jettisoned the petitioner into a new and even more threatening crisis. From the salt-misted shores of the Reed Sea to the riverbanks of the Jordan is a vast and life-threatening desert.

Deliver me, O LORD, from lying lips,
And a deceitful tongue

There are several words in Hebrew that denote a rescue of some kind; *natzal* conveys a sense of reclaiming or recovering something or someone to its rightful place, even by radical and forceful intervention. Thus Amos 3:12 speaks of a shepherd who violently snatches away parts of a sheep that is already in the clutches of a lion's mouth.

Most certainly here the petitioner is facing a life-threatening situation brought on by humans, for they are conspiring, plotting, scheming against his life. And they are unified against him. They speak with one mouth and one tongue. The focal point of their unity is the victim whom they have selected to annihilate. Their weapon of choice is that of accusation.

My son loves to watch a show called "The Deadliest Warrior." Each episode analyzes the weapons and battle tactics of two different warriors and then pits the one against the other in a computer simulation.

Most of the weapons are gruesomely effective and ancient peoples such as the Israelites would have a frightful familiarity with some of these. Oddly though, the psalms speak incessantly about one kind of weapon with horrifying terror—the false accusation. Like an avalanche, it only takes a tiny vibration to set off a monstrous and deadly cascade, a force so overpowering that it is only exhausted by the expulsion of a target.

The force of this deadliest of weapons is its unifying character, for all the voices have coalesced into one set of "treacherous lips" and one "deceitful tongue." It must be remembered that there was no judicial system as we know it today. There was no investigation or forensics to verify the truthfulness of crimes. There was no legal council, no police force, and no jury of peers. One could appeal only to the judges in the gate, which were tribal elders and this only a few times a year. A person would be acquitted or condemned mainly on the basis of witnesses, simply on the basis of "filing a charge."

The Israelites were especially sensitive to the precarious nature of accusation as is reflected in the Ten Commandments—*You shall not bear false witness*. The wisdom writer observes that of the seven things God hates, all of them are related to the bearing of false witness (Prov 6:16–19). How toxic an accusation was just coming from one voice. But accusation is a powerful magnet able to suck in a host of vitriol into its sphere.

Realistically though, the accusation is extremely destructive even today with all kinds of safeguards in place. It only takes an accusation to get a teacher fired. An angry teenager can merely report abuse, and a family is torn apart. A congregation can disintegrate with the accusation of a minister's sexual misconduct.

In the Psalms as well as in most of the Old Testament, however, the deceitful tongue is mostly related to conspiring to overtake a leader (Neh 1:1–11). There were no elections, no peaceful transference of power. There were only kings and only two avenues for change—succession or assassination. Usually it was a combination of both. Either way, it usually entailed gruesome upheaval, the annihilation of rivals. Again, we must remind ourselves of the double-way of prayer. Before this prayer becomes my prayer, it was the king's prayer. Even today and in a very real way, a leader is just the next victim being dressed for sacrifice.

It was, then, serious business for a king/leader and the community to pray for protection. It is the petitioner's very life that is at stake even at the first whispers of gossip.

I suggest, however, that there is a two-fold concern here, and this other concern may draw us closer to the relationship with repentance. The song is sufficiently general about the source of the deceitful tongue to possibly include the petitioner himself. Perhaps he has or is sorely tempted to engage in the same tactics to save himself. There is one surefire way to deflect the accusation from locking in on him—promote a counter-accusation. Engage in the whole nasty business of conspiracy and political intrigue. Create an even more appealing target. The petitioner struggles deeply to reciprocate deadly tongue with his own brand. This will save him, but will it save the situation? Let someone else take the fall. After all, to reciprocate violence with violence is the way things are.

This temptation is powerful indeed. One needs only to reflect on the temptations of Jesus in the wilderness to grasp the destructive power of accusation. We must remind ourselves that Jesus resisted the temptation to engage in his own brand of political intrigue that made him vulnerable to political annihilation.

What shall be given you?
 And what more shall be done to you,
 you deceitful tongue.
A warrior's sharp arrows,
 with glowing coals of the broom tree!

Who can avoid being sucked into the vortex of accusation and counter-accusation? Our petitioner laments living in a place where this monster engorges off of every juicy, finger-pointing morsel. He is sorely tempted to reciprocate his own brand of vitriol against his accuser. To match lie with lie, deceit with masks.

To pause here, there is real wisdom that the prayer of St. Ephrem is daily repeated during our time of penance—*Grant me to look upon my own transgressions and not to judge my brother.*

In our psalm, the lyricist catches himself. His prayer turns completely away from the Lord, and confronts the enemy head on, in himself as well as in his real human adversaries. Just like our Lord in the wilderness, he directly engages the devil. He interrogates the "lying tongue." He speaks to the tongue as if he were a fraudulent investor, a ponzi schemer. What dividends or returns do you think you will gain by investing in my destruction? If you scheme deceptively, what kind of profit do you hope to make? Before the tongue can answer, he cowers over the tongue with the irrefutable truth—your own destruction!

To make the point, the metaphor changes from bankruptcy to a city under siege, which may in fact be the real life situation of the psalm. Nehemiah's work force faced physical assaults as they worked to build Jerusalem's walls (Neh 6). He envisions deadly archers, mighty men, on the walls cascading sharp armor piecing death upon the city's attackers. And if they attempt to scale the walls, showers of infrared coals will sear away their flesh.

Woe is me, that I sojourn in Meshech, that I dwell among the tents of Kedar.

Once more, the prayer switches directions. Now the petitioner descends even deeper in despair, crying out a woe! Most often a woe is a curse upon the enemy. Appealing to the gods to bring down destruction on one's enemies was what most ancient peoples thought of as personal prayer. Indeed, one can find woes being uttered in both the Old and New Testaments—"woe *to you* who . . ." Here, however, it is the last ditch cry of one who has come to wits end. It is the final hope against hope, a gasp of exasperation.

The expression "woe *to me*" is limited to the anguish of the prophet, mainly Isaiah and Jeremiah. Their anguish echoes the complaint found here. The treacherous words of a brother now turned adversary threaten to devour all.

> *But I said, "I am wasted, wasted away.*
>   *Woe is me! The traitors betray:*
>   *with treachery have the traitors betrayed.*
> *Terror, pit, and trap*
>   *are upon you, inhabitant of the earth;*
> *He who flees at the sound of terror*
>   *will fall into the pit . . .*
> *The earth will burst asunder,*
>   *the earth will be shaken apart,*
>   *the earth will be convulsed.*
> *The earth will reel like a drunkard,*
>   *and it will sway like a hut;*
> *Its rebellion will weigh it down,*
>   *until it falls, never to rise again.*
> (Isa 24:16–20)

A critical characteristic is noticed when the prophet speaks a woe to himself. In particular, it is an enemy *from within* whose venomous words cut so deep. The prophets consistently conjure up the same images to depict the feeling. The one desiring to be faithful to his God should find himself among likeminded brethren, colleagues and countrymen who together strive toward goodness, righteousness, and faithfulness. Instead, it is like being an immigrant in a foreign land, living in a culture with no rights and vulnerable to unceasing injustice and scornful taunts.

Meshech and *Kedar* are obscure places outside of Israel's boundaries. *Kedar* was more a transmigrating shepherd tribe in Arabia than it was a settlement. Both could possibly have been stopping stations for exiles on their "trail of tears" to Babylon (Isa 21:13–16) and for those returning from the exile. Like the petitioner in the psalm, Isaiah feels like a stranger even in his own country when he is confronted with a vision of God in the Temple:

> *Woe is me. I am doomed. For I am a man of unclean lips, living among people of unclean lips.* (Isa 6:5)

Jeremiah expresses that same dilemma as the petitioner of Psalm 120. The accusing tongue is a contagion that infects all alike. Who can avoid its indiscriminate drive? It is a wild fire consuming everything in its path:

> *Woe to me, mother, that you gave me birth!*
> *a man of strife and contention to all the land!* (Jer 15:10)

Both Isaiah and Jeremiah express terror where accusation and counter-accusation swirl to an explosive pitch. The prophet understands that he is as culpable as his enemy/brother and needs a radical cleansing from the Lord. He does not presume to be more righteous than his enemy and therefore the Lord should be on his side. He understands more clearly than his rival that the destruction of all is at stake, not just him or his enemy. Thus he prays despairingly that if God does not intervene, all is lost.

Too long have I had my dwelling
  among those who hate peace
I am for peace; but they are for war.

Nehemiah's return to Jerusalem conjures up the haunting cry of prophets past. He has returned to the charred rumble of the once glorious abode of his God. He is here on a peace mission, but he lives among a people who only conspire war. They mock with scornful threat, and they devise plans of destruction.

> *On hearing this, Sanballat the Horonite, Tobiah the Ammonite slave, and Geshem the Arab mocked us and ridiculed us. "What is this you are about to do?" they asked. "Are you rebelling against the king?" My answer to them was: "It is the God of heaven who will grant us success. We, his servants, shall set about the rebuilding; but for you there is to be neither share not claim nor memorial in Jerusalem." (Neh 2:19–20)*

> *When Sanballat, Tobiah, the Arabs, the Ammonites, and the Ashdodites heard that the restoration of the walls of Jerusalem was progressing . . . they became exceedingly angry. Thereupon they all plotted together to come and fight against Jerusalem and thus to throw us into confusion . . . Our enemies thought, "Before they are aware of it or see us, we shall come into their midst, kill them and put an end to the work." (Neh 4:1–2, 5)*

Nehemiah also had to deal with a defeatism from within, for even the resident Jews were saying:

> *Slackened is the bearer's strength,*
>   *there is no end to the rubbish;*
> *Never shall we be able,*
>   *the wall to rebuild.*
> (Neh 4:4)

To thrive on constant contention is to hate peace, and the petitioner of the psalm continues his lament that he lives in such a place. Yet there is no cursing of enemy here, just the self-talk of one on the brink. *I am for peace, but they are for war.*

To call a woe upon oneself is to bewail the ruinous nature of our humanity. In a discussion about faith, religion and atheism, Terry Eagleton explains how genuine faith must "go all the way down."[3] By this, he means that faith must include reason, but it must go beyond reason to a gut level notion of love. "Faith is a kind of love, a commitment," he says:

> "A tenacious commitment when one is at the end of his tether, in darkness and in pain and fear, not knowing what the hell was going on, but refusing to give up on what he saw as the source of his life and love."

---

3. Eagleton, "Conversation with Terry Eagleton" Templeton Foundation.

For Eagleton, atheists commit a fundamental "category mistake" when they start with a positive view of human history. This inevitably leads to starting at the top and descending into human despair. Faith on the other hand starts at the bottom, with a tragic view of history. It starts in the tragedy of the exile and a prophet cruelly hung on a cross. It starts with lamentation not congratulations. Genuine faith must at some point cry out: "Woe is me!" "Woe to us!" As Eagleton says, faith is the ability to "start at the very worst and still have some vestige of hope."

A season of repentance is much more than just a personal inventory of sins, vices, and bad thoughts. It bewails the violence that to this very day we humans rely on to get along. It may be disingenuous for us to pick and choose our penance. This is why we as the Church take the journey of repentance and why we revisit the exile and the cross. This is why Mary of Egypt is one of the key icons of the Fast.[4]

This is why Jesus taught us:

> *Blessed are they who mourn,*
>   *for they will be comforted.*
> *Blessed are the peacemakers,*
>   *for they will be called children of God.*
> (Mt 5:4, 9)

---

4. In her youth, Mary was a prostitute who "worked" the pilgrimage circuit. She was miraculously converted as she watched the Christians worship in Jerusalem. She spent the rest of her life in repentance, wandering in the desert.

3

Psalm 121

**I lift up mine eyes unto the hills,
  from whence does my help come.**

When last we left our explorer, he was looking at the prospect of violent conflict. He makes the bold declaration, a promise to himself that he is for peace and not war, but this is easier said than done.

As he walks the road toward Jerusalem, he drops his head in grudging resolve, but then there is a sudden reversal. He musters new determination. "I will lift my eyes to the hills from whence my help comes." If we imagine that the expedition is still in route, we presume that his vision sight is more imaginary than physical. Still, the phrase implies a kind of internal exertion or mental effort.

Lifting the eyes is a frequent phrase in Biblical prose. It can refer to arrogant demeanor. We all know the look. Mostly it connotes an intensity of focus, to examine more closely, to pay attention. Even more so, it refers to a recalibration of one's desires, an inventory of deepest longings, and a redirecting of devotion.

During the exile the phrase took on a new intensity as the prophets call those cowering before the dread appearing, mighty gods of Babylon to lift up your eyes "to the heavens." They called on the "stripped ones," the literal meaning of an exile in Hebrew, to envision the grandeur of God that cannot be depicted by the paltry chiseling of stone idols and gold plating of carved wooden gods. Thus the prophet proclaims:

> *To whom can you liken me as an equal?*
>   *says the Holy One.*
> *Lift up your eyes on high*
>   *and see who has created these*
> (Isa 40:25–26).

Time and again in the foggy shame of exile, the prophets conjure their eyes upward to the highest of heavens and there fix on eternity.

As to the expedition still in route, the eyeball effort is focused on "the hills." Lifting the eyes has little effect if it does not find an object of gaze, a fixed point, a destination. These are not any hills or mountains, but those of only one unique place—Zion. It is for certain that this is a clear visual reference. The hills that enfold, protect, and fortify Zion is a towering symbol of Yahweh's presence.

If one aspect of repentance is the realization of our desperate state, another is to focus on a visible sign or symbol of God's Presence. My wife and I have made many trips to Nebraska to visit her folks. The golden plains of the prairie have their own kind of statement, and I have learned to enjoy my visits there. On our way back, we could always be comforted when the blue Rocky Mountains appear on the distant horizon. It is a real visual sign that we are approaching home. At times when the encroaching weather threatened, we would squint with anxious anticipation for the first sign that our trip home was making real progress.

Just as a climber envisions making it to the top, so the pilgrim ponders in great anticipation his arrival in Jerusalem. Certainly, if this was primarily an image in his mind, it would have been of great comfort and increased anticipation to repeatedly conjure up the picture.

In the introduction, I mentioned the phenomenon of false summits. If one encounters several of these on the ridge, they can sap strength and resolve. It was amazing, however, what extra bursts of energy and fortitude one found with only a small glimpse of the summit in sight.

The hills of Zion are not just any old mound, for in the eyes of the songwriter, Zion is the very source of his "help."

Although the Hebrew word for help, *ezer*, can have mild references to being an aid or assistant, it mostly refers to someone who comes to the aid of someone in a life-threatening situation. Often it refers to one who intervenes in a crisis. Here we must remember the profound distress of our petitioner. Most people in the ancient world lived under the constant threat of annihilation. The book of Judges depicts the unpredictable and horrific violence common folk had to be aware of. This included local marauders as well as large organized armies seeking to stretch their territories. Most ancient people could point to a "ghost town" somewhere nearby. This line, then, reminds us that our singer is not longing for Jerusalem primarily to participate in a grand party. He needs a rescuer, someone to come to his aid and pry back death's powerful grip.

My help comes from the LORD,
who made heaven and earth

The strength and towering majesty of "mountains" remind the singer of the reliability of God. Just as one can count on hills never to move, so one can count on a true rescue from this God of Zion.

It is perhaps difficult for us to understand the profound sense in which God's real presence and involvement in the Israelite's daily life was bound to Zion. What is always implied in the Psalms is that Zion is the place where he chose to dwell. It is the sole prerogative of Israel's God to choose Zion as his place of abode. God's occupation of Zion is the clearest possible evidence that He has established a "beachhead" or headquarters in which to orchestrate his global campaign. Here the King of Zion will wage His own kind of war against all his foes, against the nations. The Lord's conquest will not be by means of armies, weapons, political intrigue, siege-works, massacre and pillaging. It will not be military might and political influence, but by the Spirit as the prophet Zechariah proclaimed (Zech 4:6). A law of justice and mercy will go out from this beachhead that will relentlessly march its way throughout the earth. *From Zion shall go forth instruction,* the prophet Isaiah proclaims (Isa 2:3). Because of this, Zion will be the place of pilgrimage for all nations. The whole world can draw close to the Presence.

For extra force, our singer assures himself of God's ability to rescue him from death's grip. It is not just that God established his beachhead on the mountains of Zion. He made those very hills. The phrase, "who made heaven and earth," is repeated several times in the Songs of Ascents, and it carries a certain connotation to it. It is one of several repetitive phrases in the Songs of Ascents that serve to bind the set of psalms together and to provide a stair-stepping effect to it.[1] Although the Israelites harbored notions of a creator god throughout its history, it was mostly overshadowed by the mighty saving acts of God in birthing

---

1. Crow, *The Songs of Ascents*, 157.

Israel. Yahweh was primarily a saving God. It was not until the Israelites suffered the devastating conquests and deportations of Assyria and Babylon that they were confronted with gods who appeared for the moment mightier than Yahweh.

After all, in every generation and culture, other gods appear to be more powerful than the "Mighty One of Jacob." This disparity becomes so great at times that the faithful can only envision radical and extreme reversals. This is what gave birth to "apocalyptic" literature. God will have to completely eradicate the present world in order to reestablish his kingdom. In our day, the "gods" of the market place and technology rule the day, and the appeals to the god of Israel are discredited and even denounced.

Oddly, it was these foreign countries and under the shadow of massive, stone-sculpted gods, that Israel's awareness of the greatness of their god swelled. Whatever claims their captors' gods of ruthless conquest could make for the moment, Israel began to retort: our God made the very stones and wood that you make your idols from. You make and fashion your idols, but our God fashioned the heavens and the earth (Isa 40:18–31). The kingdom of our God is not restricted to one small plot of ground. Even more so and even in contrast, the Israelites began understanding their God as one who could establish his empire on earth without military conquest.

In our singing of the Songs of Ascents, the repetition of the phrase "who made heaven and earth" is a near manifesto and mantra with powerfully subversive undertones.

**He will not let your foot be moved;
he who keeps you will not slumber.**

For the Israelites, and really for us as well, we are talking about real, down-to-earth help from serious perils of life on planet earth. As much as we all would like to secure a pleasant afterlife, when we "cry out for help," we are looking for life-saving help. It needs to be here and now. For anyone who has struggled with addiction, a natural or economic disaster, a debilitating illness or political upheaval, the relief needs to be close at hand. The essential operative notion in the ancient world is that if *somebody* doesn't come to my aid, I will certainly die. This is the essence of "bottom up prayers."

We like to think of ourselves today as being able to take care of our own dilemmas, and to some degree, this is true. We have mega-systems in place than can buffer us against terrorist attacks, natural disasters or economic downturns. Not so the ancients. There was little in place to ward off even a small happenstance from becoming a disaster. Salvation came almost exclusively from human aid and intervention of some kind.

It may be, however, that our world is returning to a time like the ancients. Since the "Great Recession," we are reminded of our economic vulnerability. It is apparent that decisions made in corporate meetings can send shockwaves through the whole global system. Decisions made by a few in distant places may mean an economic disaster for a family.

Thus in verse three, the perspective shifts. Up until this point, there has been a person speaking directly to God, someone who is in dire straits, whose earthly existence is threatened. This person is looking for the God from Zion to rescue him. This can be anyone's prayer.

But the voice shifts in verse three. Now it is someone or a group of people, a choir as it were, that responds directly to the original petitioner. The plight of that one is also the plight of the community. As he goes, so goes the community. If he perishes, they perish. If he is victorious, then they are saved. If he makes it to Zion, then they will survive the perilous journey to the abode of God. It is the choir, then, who interjects with their own prayer born out of a mysterious confidence that God is *with us* through his chosen instrument of salvation. The "hopes and fears of all the years" are bound up in the success of this One coming to Zion.

The psalm begins with an image of one approaching Zion, periodically straining the eyes in hope of its mount appearing on the distant horizon. He has passed through remote and unfriendly territory, *Meshech* and *Kadar*. The choir senses the urgency of his journey and assures him (and itself) that God's preserving hand is with him.

Even though the roads to Zion are jagged and uneven, passing through steep ravines and narrow passes, Yahweh will not let his foot slip (Ps 121:3).

Many a time along the way, one's eyes will become weary. One will not always be alert enough to watch for danger of wild animals, thieves, hostile territory, or even logistical problems. The Lord, however, does not weary like humans. He will stay alert even when our pilgrim must stop to rest. God volunteers for the night watch.

The "rescuing God" from Zion is also a *shamar*, a guard, a sentinel. Perhaps the pillar of fire in the wilderness on the night of crisis at the

Reed Sea is alluded to here. *Shamar* mostly refers to keeping guard or overseeing a place, especially at night. In other words, it speaks of being alert, especially to covert or stealth attacks. To make the point and to spur on the faint-hearted traveler, this verb is repeated six times in the course of six verses. The word connotes direct and engaging action, intimate involvement.

Behold, he who keeps Israel
  will neither slumber nor sleep.

Once again, the repetition and embellishment of the phrase, *he will not slumber*, gives the feeling of ascension and progress. The verse adds extra emphasis by starting with a "behold." The word *hinah* is a demonstrative pointing to certainty—"certainly," "assuredly," "without a doubt." Not only will God relentlessly keep his eyelids from drooping, he won't even need to sleep at all. He never needs winding. He neither slumbers nor sleeps. In the last part of this verse, the perspective of the one and many emerges. It is in God preserving this one chosen individual that God is *keeping all of Israel*. He is forging the way for all those who will return from exile. As goes the One, so will go the many. His plight is our plight, his destiny ours.

The LORD is your keeper;
  the LORD is your shade on your right hand.
The sun shall not smite you by day,
  nor the moon by night.

Our choir still envisions the saving one on his arduous expedition to Zion. It is peculiar that the choir is looking far into the distance for its help, yet our sole petitioner is looking only to Yahweh from Zion. Weather conditions are of course a major concern for anyone who travels, yet our choir sings in reassurance that God is sun, wind, and water proof.

The repetition of the divine name again provides the sense of ascent, but it is also for powerful effect—Yahweh alone is the bodyguard, guide, and weather shield. The phrase "the Lord is your shade on your right hand" depicts a curious image of God as a humble servant, but perhaps it pictures more an entire entourage accompanying our traveler. As in the case of Nehemiah, the king of Persia amply provided enough provisions for him to safely complete his mission. The official sponsor of Nehemiah's mission was the overshadowing presence of the king's will and decree.

As if to exhaust every possible situation, the choir gives up the details and resorts to generalizations to cover all the bases. With each emphatic proclamation of the Name the choir emboldens our sole traveler upward to the holy mountain.

The LORD will keep you from all evil;
  he will keep your life.
The LORD will keep your going out and your coming in
  from this time forth and forever more.

4

Psalm 122

THE SUBTITLE OF THIS Psalm differs slightly from the previous two in that it adds "of David."[1] This is a bit problematic if we are considering the whole group of psalms being postexilic. The songwriter has a huge repertoire of lyrics to choose from Israel's "songbook." It is simply the tools of the trade for any composer to attribute the important influences of past "masters" on his own music.

Wynton Marsalis is an excellent example of this. When discussing his compositions, he can speak of a Milesesque (characteristic of Miles Davis) or Ellingtonion (signature sound of Duke Ellington) phrase or even section of a composition. Sure it is Marsalis' work, but the "flavor" of the section is so characteristic of an earlier composer's "sound" that it could just as well have been him. The trained ear would not only be instantly transported to that innovative sound of an earlier era, but also taken back to the times that produced both composer and composition.

Most important is the reconnection between this *one* who is going up to Jerusalem and David who did not rest until the house of Yahweh was built. Both are imagining an already built temple and a well-fortified city where the tribes are gathering from north and south for a great harvest festival where the kingdom of Yahweh and his righteous rule will be recognized and celebrated.

David dreamed of a scene never before witnessed in Israel. The king led the priests, Levites, tribal elders, and pilgrims in a procession leading up to the temple. Singers and musicians lined the staircases lifting each

---

1. The preposition "of" is represented by one Hebrew letter that can also be translated "for" or "to" depending on the context.

step of the faithful with praise to God for his mighty deeds. Likewise, the expedition leader of this psalm now finds himself among a caravan of like-minded friends.

The mission now has the flavor of a pilgrimage. It is an expedition for sure since our supplicant is coming from distances beyond the borders of Israel (Ps 120:5). It is a long awaited return. He must trudge a far and foreboding distance just to see the city protruding over the horizon, yet that will only be the beginning of an exceedingly greater destination, one like David's. The city walls are dismantled; its gates are burned and porous. The Temple stands as a haunting monument to Israel's shameful recalcitrance to the gracious call of their God.

Zion was to be the highest of mountains. The people of Israel were to lead all the nations toward a different kind of kingdom. One not ruled by fickle gods, violence, tyranny, suspicion, pretense, oppression and injustice, but by mutual respect of neighbor, care for the vulnerable, and a powerful bond between God, king and subjects.

The most radical aspect of this kingdom was the proclamation that Israel's God would be the King. But while on the way, our singer will reminisce about a time in the distant past when one "beloved" by God believed with sometimes reckless abandon a dream born in the distant bulrushes of the Nile. David saw the vision conceived from a different kind of god in a different kind of heaven. This was not the usual dream of the gods of great kingdoms whose only concern is that humans feed their gluttonous appetites and attend to their impetuous whims. Rather, it was a dream of a God who desires to draw all people unto Him, into an everlasting bond of love, a realm of blessing where all can survive and thrive.

The Hebrews had always thought that the mighty deeds of God in the past were a blueprint of the future. Hence, the songwriter and his travel companions sing a "golden oldie" from the songbook of David. They nostalgically imagine themselves among the procession following the sign and seal of their King's mighty presence (the ark) and His dancing coregent (David) up to the place where the King will set up permanent residence. From there and from then on, there will be life, goodness, peace and prosperity for all.

As participants in the song ourselves, we are compelled to join the expedition. If David saw this determined band steadfastly marching toward the "beautiful city" he would rejoice. He would drop everything and follow. He would say: "I rejoiced when I heard them say; we are going up to the House of the LORD."

I was glad when I heard them say,
let us go into the House of the LORD.

It is a shame in my day that going to church is viewed as an obligation or drudgery. For certain, there were those in the days of Israel that felt the same about going to Jerusalem.

"What a hassle and expense it is to make such an uncomfortable and risky trip. I have to close the business for weeks, and hope to heaven that when I return my managers haven't ruined the place or even worse embezzled me for all I'm worth. We have local holy places where we can have festivals. We don't need to go all the way to the big city just to be overcharged by every tourist trap on the way. Besides, this is just a scam by that crackpot king in Jerusalem to feed his coffers with my hard earned money."

There were those in Israel's day who like today didn't see the vision and weren't able or willing to dream the dream. They sat in the distance and complained about that dancing fool of a king. With pointed finger, they mocked, accused, and scorned those making the trip, those who somehow and somewhere smell wisps of salty mist from the lapping shores of the Reed Sea and ever so faintly hear Miriam's tambourine rattle as voices begin to sing: *I will sing to the LORD for he is gloriously triumphant;/ horse and chariot he has cast into the sea* (Ex 15:1–3). Unlike the childhood rant that "words shall never hurt me," the taunts of those detractors pierce with deadly force. They cut to the very marrow of one's bones. The songs of Israel are full of such bitter experiences: *Our souls are more than sated/with the mockery of the arrogant,/ with the contempt of the proud.*(Ps 123:4).

For those who believed that the dream was true, the announcement to go up was an occasion for inspiration and joy. Forgive me for the crude comparison, but it might be similar to parents saying to their children: "Kids, we're going to Disneyland!" Such joy, such anticipation, such longing energized by the hope of realization.

Our feet have been standing within your gates,
O Jerusalem.

The verb tense here has created problems for interpreters, and this is largely due to how the translator views the historical/setting of the *Songs of Ascent*s. Our traveling entourage sings as though they have been to the

Temple before. They reminisce as though it was only last year that all the tribes gathered with David or Solomon for a glorious celebration of the Kingship of Yahweh. They recall the heart-pumping exuberance as the memory of their tedious and perilous journey is being erased with each step as they approach the very gates of Jerusalem as they walk through the gates with heads cocked one way and then the other. Their eyes look upward in wide-eyed wonder as a seemingly endless stream of diverse people solemnly yet joyfully ascend in one chorus of thanksgiving.

It is at this juncture in the ascent of these songs that a certain tension is accented, and it is a tension that we, even today, are engaged in. It is the same tension that pulled at wandering Abraham, the Hebrews in the wilderness, of David as he dreamed of building a kingdom of righteousness, and of the Jews of Jesus' day as they were awaiting the complete restoration of "the kingdom of David." Even to this day, the Church as well as the Jewish people hope for "Thy kingdom come." It is a tension that sometimes leads to despair more grievous than if there were no hope at all. It is the tension of hope partially realized.

This is in fact where the issue of faith really comes into play. It is as the writer of Hebrews has said: we have evidence now of things still hoped for (Heb 11:1). But this is less than a comfortable situation. It is the place between promise given and promise fulfilled.

While still at the king of Persia's table, Nehemiah rejoices when he hears the decree. Return to Jerusalem. He makes his preparations for the arduous journey. He travels through inhospitable territory, all the while remembering the bitter "trail of tears" that his people traveled in the opposite direction. With the distance diminishing to Jerusalem, anxiety swells with both joy and trepidation as images of "the glory of Israel" past repeatedly jog the conscience.

Now, the expedition imagines itself actually entering the gates of Jerusalem, and the stories of the city's demise are jolted into bitter reality. It is as if Nehemiah was saying: "I stand now within the gates of the beloved city, just as my ancestors did for centuries past. But I stand where glorious gates are nothing more than charred rubble, inglorious reminders, symbols and signs of Israel's stubborn resistance to God's gracious invitation."

Here, we might pause and remind ourselves of our repentance. Although there is in the Hebrew bible some ranting against other nations and its wicked ignorance of God, it pales in comparison, to the soul-searching grief of Israel's own failure to live up to their calling. Nothing hurts our world more than the refusal of God's people to faithfully respond to God. We too have "arrived" at the very gates of the great city only to stare with wounded heart at a city decimated by half-hearted response and distracted passions.

Jerusalem, built as a city bound firmly together,

This, of course, is not how the story ends for our expedition leader nor for us, for Yahweh's faithful march is irreversable. Our singer sings of glory past, not so he can nostalgically wish for "the good old days," but to recall the past as a guiding map of the future. For this singer, the city itself is a blueprint of what God's people are. The way Jerusalem is situated and was built upon is a powerful "icon," a window into how God views his people.

First, he speaks out the name of the city and beckons all to pause and listen. "*Yerushalaim.*" Listen again as the soft sounding syllables stream effortlessly in a line dance of unity. "*Yerushalaim,*" city of *shalom*, of peace. Throughout the rest of this song, our singer pushes the limits of the imagery—city of peace. Both words, "Jerusalem" and "peace," are strategically conjured up three times in this song.

The very fact that it is a city that God loves is marvel enough. The Israelites have carried with good reason a high degree of suspicion about cities. There, tools of war are forged. Kings arise to take what is not theirs and leave only insurmountable burdens of conscription. The gods of city kings are insatiable, ever driving for more food, bigger boundaries and more glory. Cities always have pharaohs, and pharaohs never have enough bricks. So, one should marvel that a transient god content to live among nomadic shepherds should even care about a city, let alone choose to *take up residence* in one.

But this is no ordinary city. The main reason for her peace is that it is inaccessible and unsustainable. It is a rock mound[2] pushed up by arid hills from the desert floor. It has little natural resources, especially water, to generate its own commerce. It is off the easily travelled highway routes of commerce. Her life totally dependends on travelers and merchants. She is a destination city whose survival depends on attraction beyond economic necessity.

Its geographic makeup combined with its architecture creates a postcard design of God's desire for his people. It is a city *tightly bound together*. The verb to bind *(habar)* has a basic sense of tying, weaving,

---

2. The word *tzion* simply means barren mound.

or binding together, usually with cords or ropes. Oddly, it is also used to refer to some kind of magic that actually uses ropes to, in a sense, bind someone to a curse. The picture is, of course, that the binding element is strong and secure, not easily undone. The city is zip-tied. Our lyricist views the buildings of the city which are mortared to each other as a picture of the common destiny of the faithful. Perhaps a comparable picture is that of quilting, sewing separate pieces of fabric into a whole blanket.

The adverb here is one of the main Hebrew words used to describe unity, oneness, or togetherness (*yachad*). It is often used in reference to a unique, priceless relationship with a beloved person or thing that cannot be replaced. For instance, in the well-known story of Abraham's sacrifice of his son, God describes Isaac as "your son Isaac, your *one* (only—*yachad*), whom you love (Gen 22:2, 12, 16). The description of Isaac—son/one/love—is repeated three times in that story, intensifying the powerful passions at play in the drama.

In this psalm, it is likely that the compact density of the buildings ascending to the temple intensified the sense of a city acting as one personality, as one living thing. Somehow the compact nature of cities, not just in terms of buildings, but more so in terms of its life, takes on a distinctive feel or personality. Even today, we create songs memorializing our city experiences: "New York, New York," "My kind of town, Chicago is," "I left my heart in San Franscico," "I wish I was in New Orleans." We never reminisce this way about suburbs because the individual houses stand apart from each other. There is enough distance and fences between each house to lose any distinctive ambiance for the place as a whole. It does not bustle with its own distinctive rhythm and characteristic vibe like a city can.

For many of us today, we can only imagine being "tightly bound together" in a living situation as a thoroughly miserable proposition. We love our fences, our distance, our social networks. We especially don't like the idea of being bound by someone else's need, necessity, or even worse, his sin or idiosyncrasies. Today's spirituality mostly envisions communion with one's self and with nature. For sure, solitude is a critical component to anyone's spiritual health and growth. All Christian spiritual traditions emphasize this. One cannot, however, lose sight of what is an ever-driving vision of God the Father—to unite all things unto Himself (Eph 1:10). God incorporates. God calls each individually, and each person must personally respond to God's gracious initiative. But it does not stop there. God beckons one to a family, a people, a city, an assembly, a house, a body, a priesthood, and a citizenship (Eph 2:22).

> **to which the tribes go up, the tribes of the LORD,**
> **as was decreed for Israel,**
> **to give thanks to the name of the LORD.**

The lyricist continues recalling the city map of a united Israel. He retrieves ancient dreams hardly realized. But there was a time, nearly five hundred years gone, when all the tribes of Israel went up to Jerusalem, from the Negev and Beersheba in the south and as far as Dan in the north. This was a tiny insignificant patchwork of peoples, tribes as it were. They were bound together by an even more ancient memory born among bulrushes and bricks without straw. Under the shadow of bitter toil, they experienced a miraculous intervention. They saw a new light, a god who favors the oppressed one, the poor one, the victim, and the slave. They experienced a god who will fight Pharaohs and cast out gods from the heavenly court.

They were bound by a vision that people can live together without dominance, fear, rivalry, and violence. Such dreaminess, of course, always butts up against the hardcore realities of survival on the planet. We must have commerce. We must have trade. We must have armies and weapons. We must perpetually feed the insatiable dragon in our basement or we will perish.

The idea of a league of tribes, cities, or "states" was not unique to ancient Israel. All of the ancient empires were able to amass huge armies and immense resources under the auspices of some unifying banner. Kingdoms were built upon the slaughtered corpse of some previous god or goddess who had come under the collective condemnation of the "heavenly court." The victim god was sacrificed to the needs of the greater good.

There was no such sacrifice Jerusalem was founded upon. Instead, its foundation was a saving intervention by God. Just as Moses led the people out of the threat of complete disintegration by the hand of Pharaoh, so David rescued a loose confederation of settlers against the daunting threat of an ever increasing and ruthless flow of newcomers to the region called the "Sea Peoples," some of whom were known as the Philistines. The "united colonies of Israel" was scarcely a fierce fighting type. They were generally more interested in a peaceful life of tending their crops and herds. Their main defense, especially north of Jerusalem, was that they were "hillbillies." The hill country in which they settled provided a natural barrier to marching armies.[3]

---

3. Finkelstein and Silberman. *The Bible Unearthed*, 109—111.

In this unique character of David, the haphazard confederation of settlers was miraculously delivered from being annihilated or run off by a foreboding giant. Jerusalem became a crowning symbol of God's amazing favor towards David and for this motley and unruly group of settlers called "Israel."

These colonies were not generally known for their congeniality. Each little group of towns preferred to stick to themselves. They would only ban together because of some economic or militaristic threat. This way of defense had mixed success as the book of Judges amply testifies, and at times, these tribes could just as easily and ruthlessly turn on each other. It was the overwhelming threat of the Philistines that forced the Israelites to ban together, but it was David and his miraculous fighting feat that united Israel like never before.

David's fierce guerrilla warfare tactics won him a reputation among the tribes, but his love and zeal for his God was equally famous. David wanted his own love of God to be a trademark of every Israelite. He envisioned a unified people who would "give thanks" to the Lord, and hence he was driven to find a place where all the tribes could "go up" in one chorus of thanksgiving to their God.

Of course, Israel's history is marked mostly by a long, bitter, and violent split between the northern tribes, which the historical books of the Old Testament call "Israel," and the southern tribes under the name of "Judah."

It is this tortured history of civil discord that is especially seen in this psalm as being healed. Our English translations don't pick up the nuance found in the Hebrew text. It is the "tribes of Yah" that are mentioned here, a phrase peculiar to the rallying cry of the northern tribes.[4] Truly by the time of the exile "the tribes of Yah" were virtually non-existent. The ruthless destruction of Samaria, the capital city of Israel, and the merciless exile of the inhabitance by Assyria had essentially wiped Israel off the map. At that time, however, many still faithful to *Yah* in the north found refuge in the south. This group of northern refugees profoundly affected the writing and formation of the Hebrew Bible. Thus, the vision of a united Israel was kept alive.

It is convenient for most of us to settle into our own comfortable Christian "tribes" and then think that this is all that matters to God. Even worse, we establish our own religious or Christian identity in opposition

---

4 Goulder. *The Psalms of the Return*, 46.

to some other form or expression of it. From the earliest call of Abraham to the early church, true "orthodoxy" understands the very heart beat of God to unite all things unto himself. Honestly, a true unity with all Christians appears to be impossible. But let us never make excuses for ourselves. The real and visible disunity of Christians is perhaps the paramount sin of the Church(es).

Let us, however, be somber here. The unification of "the tribes" lost to hatred, rivalry, and strife was just as unrealistic for our lyricist here as it is for us today. Here, we must allow ourselves to be confronted by God's desire (We always talk of wanting to do God's will, but do we?). The songwriter here expresses one of God's deepest longings—a unified people.

Unification always seems like a complicated matter, and it was just as much so for our post-exilic writer of this psalm as it is for our hierarchs today. Even so, our writer sets forth in the rest of this psalm the foundational elements for a united, reconstituted Israel. Again, our lyricist looks to the past as a blueprint for the future. Again, the composer is not deterred by the obvious and checkered "real" history of Israel. He knows full well that the united kingdom under David and Solomon was short-lived with the fissures of division festering faster than the temple construction. But when David engineered the bringing of the ark of the Lord into the city and on to the temple mount, there truly was a time "when all the tribes went up," together as one and with one voice giving thanks to the Lord."

In the vision of unity poetically expressed here, three critical elements are needed. First, the tribes "go up" specifically to "give thanks" in grateful response to the "decree for Israel" (v4). The decree has its foundation in the Passover night in Egypt (Ex 12:1–3). Importantly, it was to "the *whole community* of Israel." The Hebrew word in both the Exodus passage and here refers to a specific assembly or group who has been *called* or *decreed* to be together. It is, therefore, very close to the New Testament concept and word for church, *ekklesia*.

Ekklesia basically means the "called out ones." The call or decree in the Hebrew bible was especially for a covenant renewal festival (Deut 12). The decree to assemble in one place is meant to counter the Israelite tendency (and our own) to "do your own thing" (Deut 12:8). The decree has irretrievably bound this loose confederation of tribes into one city gathered around one God. The decree has bound their destiny just like the houses inside Jerusalem have been mortared together (Ps 122:3). "One man's ceiling is another man's floor" as it were.

The tortured history of the "decreed of Israel" painfully reveals the failure to live up to this calling. It was rarely manifested. The assembly around Solomon's dedication of the Temple (1 Kings 8:5) was but a brief respite. Some 250 years after Solomon, a "reformation" movement in Judah, starting with Hezekiah and ending with Josiah, briefly revived and even extended the unity movement. A complete secession of hostilities between warring brothers was a central rallying cry. The unity movement is most clearly laid out in the book of Deuteronomy, but its agenda has its stamp on the most influential portions of the Hebrew bible including Genesis through 2 Kings, most of the prophets, and the Psalms.[5] At the heart of that agenda is a call to a singular devotion to the Lord:

> *Hear, O Israel, the LORD is our God, the LORD alone. Therefore, you shall love the LORD, your God, with all of you heart, and with all your soul, and with all your strength* (Deut 6:4–5).

Of pinnacle importance to the assembling of the tribes at one place was for Israel to *give thanks* with one heart and voice to Yahweh. The basic notion of offering thanks is based on a common imperial arrangement of the ancient Near East. A powerful king seeking to expand his empire would usually first offer an alliance to a small regional king. It is a kind of "I've got an offer you can't refuse" type of proposal. The lesser king would vow allegiance to the greater king and agree to implement the royal policies of the empire. They would contribute to the prosperity of the greater kingdom in terms of goods and services. The local king is a vassal or vice regent for the greater king. Once a year, the regional king would sponsor a "covenant renewal" festival in which the lesser kingdom would make a public proclamation of loyalty to the empire. They would bring gifts, tokens of the kinds of goods and services to be supplied on a regular basis, and they would renew their commitment of loyalty. In return, the imperial king would promise peace—protection from enemies and a share in the wealth of the kingdom. Also at these treaty renewal festivals was a rehearsal of punishments should this vassal king and his subjects seek to renege on this arrangement, either by seeking independence—usually in order to become a great empire itself—or by seeking a counter allegiance with an up and coming rival kingdom.

Israel had a unique twist to this common imperial arrangement. Instead of Egypt, Assyria, or Babylon being their imperial king, it would

---

5. I called this unity movement articulated by the book of Deuteronomy in the historical introduction to this book as "the coalition."

be their god, Yahweh. Instead of the king being a god, God would be king. Yahweh's vice regent or vassal king was of course the king residing in Jerusalem. The picture, then, of all the tribes of "Ya" going up to Jerusalem to "give thanks" was a critical aspect of maintaining a unique relationship. Again the key aspect of a covenant renewal festival was to renew one's exclusive loyalty to the imperial king. The regional king was the key leader in showing subordination and loyalty. Our lyricist here sings a song of nostalgia and lament. The sadness of this ballad is exacerbated not so much by Israel's past failure, but even more so by Israel's imperial King and God who with dogged persistence and passionate love (His *chesed*—steadfast love) refuses to give up on "the dream" regardless of how his subjects respond.

There the thrones for judgment were set, the thrones of the house of David.

Not only were the king's subjects to "go up" in order to give thanks, but it was in the place of unity were right judgments could be made. Anytime one lives with other human beings, disputes arise. There can be little peace and prosperity if it only applies to the few; thus, justice cannot be neglected. One of the most grievous and persistent condemnations of the prophets was that the festivals of the people tended toward excessive wild parties than a gathering place for all. The prophet Amos has the audacity to sarcastically call people to the worship centers to indulge in sin (Amos 4:4). In a dramatic scene fraught with tension, Jeremiah confronts a festive procession in Jerusalem, reminding the assembly of Yah that the unique relationship of the Lord with Israel and the Temple in Jerusalem means nothing if the Lord's righteous decrees are not practiced (Jer 7). Isaiah proclaims a major reason for the fall of the city and destruction of the temple was the corruption of justice:

> *Rather, it is your crimes*
>   *that separate you from your God.*
> *It is your sins that make him hide his face*
>   *so that he will not hear you* (Isa 59:2)
> *Their feet run to evil,*
>   *and they are quick to shed innocent blood.*
> *Their thoughts are destructive thoughts,*
>   *plunder and ruin are on their highways.*
> *The way of peace they know not,*

> *and there is nothing that is right in their paths;*
> *Their ways they have made crooked,*
> > *whoever treads them knows no peace.* (Isa 59:7–8)
> *The LORD saw this, and was grieved*
> > *that right did not exist.*
> *He saw that there was no one,*
> > *and was appalled that there was no one to intervene.*
>
> (Isa 59:15–16)

The Mighty One of Jacob is not obliged to favor a worshipping assembly just because they are the right people in the right place. Indeed, the prophets' message was customarily delivered "at the gate" (Jer 7:2). This was the place where "the thrones of judgment" were set. This was the place where violations, crimes, and grievances could be deliberated with "the wisdom of God for giving judgment" (1 Kings 3:28).

At the gate, a free Israelite brother, many of whom had sacrificed everything just to return to the land, forfeited his inheritance in Israel and once again returned to the bondage of Pharaoh.[6]

The New Testament church was not immune from turning a blind eye to the "little ones" gathered for worship. Paul roundly condemns the Corinthian's habit of the well-off throwing lavish parties as part of the worship while making the low-lifes of the congregation stay outside only to get the leftovers (1 Cor 11:17–34).

In the Hebrew bible the issue of justice at the gates consistently refers to the wealthy and well-to-do and the constant temptation to take advantage of the needy. This is especially grievous when it is all done under the guise of high-minded piety. As in the case of Nehemiah, the common folk were in great distress because the wealthy landowners were taking excessive interest on credit, virtually enslaving their brothers and sisters (Neh 5). These people were not free to participate in the work of rebuilding the city and temple. In other words, God's kingdom was being grossly undermined by the maltreatment of the underprivileged. Nehemiah was so angry about this that he filed charges against all the nobles of the city (Neh 5:6). An audacious move indeed!

That the weak and vulnerable must be included and treated fairly by those espousing allegiance to the Lord was, of course, the persistent message of Jesus. Jesus also "filed charges" against the aristocracy, a move which partially led to his demise. Sober indeed are the words of Jesus that it is entirely possible to claim to follow him and yet be cast

---

6. This will discussed at length in Psalm 127.

out of the kingdom for neglecting to heed his words about including the poor (Mt 7:12–23).

Our status as "rich" should cause some seriously consideration in a time of repentance. The Bible consistently calls us to a concern for the poor that goes considerably further than simply giving donations. It calls on a radical paradigm shift. It challenges the very notion of being rich and poor, of wealth and poverty. The consistent understanding of "the poor" in the Psalms is that all those who worship the God of Israel are the poor.[7] This very understanding of the poor as those who worship God in truth is foundational for all of Jesus' teaching on the poor. Jesus starts the list of beatitudes with "blessed are the poor" indicating that a poverty of spirit is the fundamental character of any who would worship the true God.

The throne of judgment is utterly essential to an authentic re-gathering of Israel. The worshipping community cannot be whitewashed veils for greed, hatred, and self-interest. The God of Israel will have it no other way. The songwriter understands the disastrous history of Israel who presumed their god to be like all the other gods whose only concern was to be fed and admired. As long as a temple is maintained, sacrifices are offered, and boastful exaggerations of the gods' might and splendor are sung, then the gods will let us get on with establishing our economic ventures and consolidating our wealth.[8]

Perhaps our own repentance, our own culpability and complacency in this regard, goes much deeper than what we imagine. If our church does not attract the poor, if there are not the disadvantaged in our midst, then we have cause for somber reflection.

Pray for the peace of Jerusalem!

When my brothers and I would mountain climb with my parents as kids, my dad would strategically carry a bag of lemon drops in his pocket. Anticipating the inevitable complaint of "I'm tired" or "How much farther?" or "I can't take another step," Dad would point to some location in the immediate distance and promise a lemon drop when we arrived there. We kids could not imagine what it would take to accomplish the whole climb, but those lemon drops provided extra incentive to keep going.

---

7. See: Ollenburger, *Zion the City of the Great King*, 68–70, and 115–16.

8. See: Brueggemann, *Israel's Praise*, 55—87

In this psalm, our journeyman has time travelled to distant times past as persistent motivation to keep moving towards his destination. In this verse, however, the expedition must turn toward the reality of the times and to what lies ahead. The task of rebuilding the host city for the temple now ominously stands before our singer like a majestic mountain beckoning to be climbed. There is still a spiraling trail ahead. There is still an ascent that must be attempted. And there is the very live possibility of failure. Without sacrificial effort, heightened stress, and volatile contention, the vision will fade to a fanciful wish. A failure of wills appears eminent.

Our expedition leader draws on inner strength to focus all attention to the task at hand. *Pray for the peace of Jerusalem (v6)*. Once again our songwriter relies on the very name of the city to create a catchy tune the fainthearted can savor in one's mind like lemon drops in the mouth. The songwriter strings together homonyms to hypnotically remind of the prize at hand—*shaalu shalom yerushalaim*; pray (*shaalu*) peace (*shalom*), city of peace (*yerushalaim*). It is a mantra with each new step: "pray peace, city of peace. "Pray peace, city of peace."

The prayer continues. The author is convinced that the repetitive lyric will become the theme song to those who dare to keep singing. The very thing longed for will be realized from within. As one earnestly asks of God to "pray peace, city of peace," one's own love of that place will also become one's own peace. *Yishlavu ohavakah—May all who love you be relieved.*

The dancing lyric on peace continues in verse seven. May there be peace (*shalom*) within your walls and relief (*shalah*) within your towers. That even the watchmen on the towers are at ease speaks of a security extending far beyond the city walls. There is not even a rumor of enemies mustering for attack. All are quieted.

For the sake of my brethren and my companions,
  I will say peace with you.

The singer concludes his dance of peace by reminding his fellow explorers that the task of peace is not just for one's own sake, but even more so, it is for the many who are still homeless, the disenfranchised far off in distant lands or next door. It is for those whose hope flickers to near extinction. It is for those who also must pack up their belongings and make their own expedition to the great gathering. It is for those like Tobit who lament in foreboding and inhospitable land: *Your festivals shall be returned into mourning./ And all your songs into lamentation* (Tobit 2:6).

5

Psalm 123

THE NEXT TWO SONGS round out the first antiphon, and they prepare the way for the expedition's approach to the city. The expedition will arrive to a ruined and humiliated city. Despite the circumstances, the dream is that the city can once again host the residence of the King. It will be the center attraction for a reconstituted Israel that not only includes the remnant of all the exiled tribes of Israel, but also all the nations and families of the world. The expedition has travelled through inhospitable territory yet still faces a tangled logistical nightmare compounded by violent protest. A daunting task.

Our singer once again turns to ardent petition and then to zealous exhortation. He comprehends the magnitude of his own ineptitude and weakness. Even more so, he comprehends the seriousness of the threat.

Over the past decades, we have learned to take threats more seriously in the aftermath of a series of shocking school shootings. Those who are in positions of trust are now trained to take seemingly off-hand or casual comments of threat with much more gravity. Even our increased posture towards threat still pales in comparison with what most people in the ancient world had to deal with. For the first three centuries, Christians struggled with the ominous cloud of the Roman Empire's hostility toward them. It only took but a wisp of accusation born sometimes by a flash of impetuousness or flighty inconvenience to send a cascade of bloody slaughter down upon them. Even in many places of our world today like the Congo, Somalia, or Mexico, slander turns to slaughter and rumor turns to riot in an instant.

Our prayers for protection hardly compare when we have a massive military enterprise and a sophisticated police force in place. I say this not so much as commentary on our socio-political structure, but to help us realize on a deeper level something about prayer and trust. Throughout history, when most common folk in the world have prayed to God for protection, they truly "cry out" in desperate hope against hope. They truly have *no one* to protect them, not a shred of visible evidence of something on the horizon. It is a living reality that only God can help them. The prayer for help is better compared to a woman with children in a Somali refugee camp than us driving through a bad part of town. Those who have experienced chronic illness come closest to the kind of guttural groan of one's deepest self when faced with the specter of a merciless and powerful force that has set out to ravish.

Like the first two psalms, a life-threatening opposition dominates this song.

To Thee, I lift up mine eyes,
O Thou who art enthroned in the heavens.

In the stair-step fashion of the lyrics, the supplicant returns to an earlier theme and then elevates it a few steps higher.

The shift from flirting with the lower limits of despair to turning one's gaze toward some object of hope is repeated incessantly in the book of Psalms. Indeed, one could study most of the prayers recorded in the Hebrew bible and find this fascinating characteristic. The creation account of Genesis 1 expresses it in cosmic terms. Even in and *especially* in the midst of chaos (Gen 1:2), the wind of God rustles.

The supplicant relies on appropriate imagery to muster inner strength. As he was still in route to Jerusalem (Ps 121), he imagined inner strength being renewed in him with the first glimpse of the rising hills around Jerusalem (Ps 121). There he relies on the visible presence of the hills to spur him toward an even more powerful, yet invisible, reality. Here his focus ascends even higher than the hills of Jerusalem, even higher than the city walls and its interconnected city dwellings. He even intently focuses his gaze beyond the temple mount. It is *to You who are enthroned in heaven.*

The question easily arises as to how one can intently direct one's eyes towards something that is not really accessible to the eye. How does our ancient supplicant look to God sitting on a heavenly throne? We should not too readily delegate the petition to figurative speech or to spiritualizing. When the composer had earlier set his eyes toward the hills, he was in route to Jerusalem. He could only see the hills in his dreams; even so, they were real visible mountains that he was orienting himself toward. I say this not to hermeneutically toy with the verse, but to point to a tension in prayer that we share with our ancient counterparts. It is the tension between the visible and the invisible, but even more so, the tension of God's presence and absence.

We Christians have such spiritualizing tendencies that we sometimes fall into a kind of pious heresy. We readily disconnect God from our own reality. We would do well to explore how the Israelites struggled with this tension. To do so would not only help us sympathize with the struggle of God's people in times past, but also clarify for us a critical aspect of prayer—how did they and how do we understand God's *real presence* in our midst? In prayer, how does one focus all physical and mental attention and energy toward that which ultimately reaches beyond all our senses?

At the heart of the Songs of Ascents is a profound longing for the reestablishment of Zion. As even we ascend with our songwriter in the chanting of the songs, we catch a glimpse into the inseparable bond between a God and His people and a unique place where that is profoundly expressed. There is no other ancient people who persistently struggled with the tension between a God *who made heaven and earth* (Ps 121:2), who is enthroned in the highest of heavens and yet one who dwells in a tent, a house (1 Kings 8:13), or in an even smaller box (ark). He is above all other gods, yet there is no place, not even in Sheol, that is beyond His reach. He is hidden (1 Kings 8:12), and yet his glory is for all the earth to see.

This tension heightens in intensity at the temple that Solomon built:

> *Can it indeed be that God dwells among men on earth? If the heavens and the highest of heavens cannot contin you, how much less this temple which I have built! Look kindly on the prayer and petition of your servant, O LORD, my God, and listen to the cry of supplication which I, your servant, utter before you this day. May your eyes watch night and day over this temple, the place where you have decreed you shall be honored; may you heed the prayer which I, your servant, offer in this place. Listen to the petitions of your servant and of your people Israel which they*

offer in this place. Listen from your heavenly dwelling and grant pardon. (1 Kings 8:27–30)

Two things in this prayer of Solomon address the dynamics of God's presence in relationship to prayer. First, God is uniquely and *really* present when His "servant" offers prayers for himself and for God's people. The Temple offered that unique place where all of God's people direct their attention (lift up their eyes) solely and unanimously on God. In one sense, all the Psalms are the prayers and hymns of God's messiah, his anointed one. The "servant of Yahweh" is the primary supplicant to which priests, Levites, singers, tribal leaders, and the faithful follow behind.

Second, God cannot fit into a temple anymore than an elephant can fit in a shoebox, but God's *glory* and *name* can abide there. Under these two designations, the Israelites were able to express the dynamic of God's Presence (I am with you) and His transcendence (Yet does God dwell in a temple?).

In Israel's more ancient past, God's glory was closely tied to the ark that profoundly symbolized God's Presence. It was especially a military symbol of God's immediate presence in crisis. It symbolized God's saving act of victory, of the victorious, conquering God. In other words, it is Israel's primary icon of God's decisive action, of the God who defeats his enemies. The king upon the throne is closely aligned with "the hand of the Lord." The ark was placed in the holiest part of the first Temple.

The ancient Israelites also spoke of "the Name" dwelling at the Temple. In many a sense, the Name is an all-encompassing term for "the glory of the Lord" which finds its particular centerpiece in the ark. The Name closely aligns to the written covenant that was placed inside the ark. Unique to Israel is a strong connection with word, with covenant. Reference to the Name, synthesizes icon with word requiring, demanding even, response, engagement, communion, and reinterpretation.

Visions of enthronement intensified with the prophets (Isaiah 6, Ezekiel 1, 10, Daniel[1]) as the wavering of God's chosen people comes to a high-pitched crisis before the exile. In other words, the worse things got in the real world of religious infighting and political intrigue, with real life consequences like massacre and exile for inhabitants, prophets such as Isaiah (Isa 6) and Ezekiel (Ez 1, 8) see a reality that is both transcendent and counter to the obvious. Yes, the visions border on the hallucinogenic,

---

1. Jeremiah does not have a throne vision, but his visions revert back to the fighting god of the exodus story. God reveals himself to Jeremiah as a king going out to war.

blurring the ordinary with the fantastic, yet they reveal the true situation to those whose fear and anxiety has distorted their ability to see through it. At the very heart of the enthronement visions of Isaiah and Ezekiel is a radical claim that teeters on the blasphemous—"I saw the Lord," says Isaiah (Isa 6:1). In a storm cloud epiphany, Ezekiel sees a man seated on a throne and proclaims that it was the "God of Israel" (Ez 10:20).

The picture of God seated on a throne points to an essential aspect of prayer for the Israelites as it does for us even today. It points to the sole prerogative of God both to will and act. This is inherent in Israel's great confession of faith that the Lord our God is one. For Israel, there is only one God in whom to look to for all one's needs, hopes and desires.

Behold, as the eyes of servants look to the hand of their master,
   as the eyes of a maid to the hand of her mistress,
so our eyes look to the LORD our God,
   until he have mercy on us.

We are on the other side of the historical rift when slavery was a common experience, so the metaphor of slaves looking for a sign of approval from their master is simply not going to have much of an impact on us, or if any, a negative one. The imagery may be somewhat analogous of an employee seeking affirmation from a manager or a child from his parents, but even here, the feeling may not be as intense as what the ancient songwriter is trying to convey.

The other day, I watched one of those television shows where they make a competition out of seeking the most talented singer/entertainer. One can see the obvious twinkle of fame in each contestant. Just to get to the televised competition rocketed the contestant's exuberance. Many of the contestant's relate the thrill of performing before a televised audience ranging in the millions. They testify how encouraging the roaring applause of the studio audience was. But all the affirmation leading up to his/her performance diminishes in comparison to the critical juncture that immediately follows. Each contestant stands alone, exposed to either humiliation or an adrenaline flood of emotions as the judges give their verdict. Each contestant looks with anxious anticipation for the slightest look or gesture that would indicate the approval of the judges. Many contestants relate that the affirmation of a judge made all the physical and emotional stress wash away in an instant. Repeated often is the tearful response of a contestant that the judges' affirmation made all of the years of struggle and doubt worth it. If we can relate to this comparison, we are closer to understanding the emotional impact the ancient songwriter intended.

The image of slavery is perhaps a curious one given the heightened tension around usury and slavery mentioned in the historical introduction. Given that many in Judah were on the verge of losing their share in the "Israel project" to economic disaster and slavery, this may have not been the best choice of analogies. It may, though, have been a subtly subversive one for both poor and rich alike. The claim that the poor are slaves of the Lord means that no one else should dare attempt to seize what does not belong to them. It could serve as a "do not trespass" sign.

As well as serving as a warning to the wealthy, the slave metaphor could have served as a reminder to the rich that they too belonged to the Lord and therefore were bound by the demands of their master. In a picture similar to the parable of the unforgiving servant (Mt 18:23–35), the rich had no right to call a fellow servant to account when he himself was solely indebted to his master.

Most importantly, the petitioner strains for just a glimpse of the enthroned One's *hand*. The hand of a king is a common phrase in the Bible which signifies that decisive moment where a decision or judgment is finalized and the whole apparatus of the kingdom is put in motion toward making the appeal of the supplicant a reality. One's whole life can literally hinge on the motion of that hand.

A major yet almost imperceptible shift occurs here which bears attention. As is frequent in the Psalms, the petition moves from singular to plural, from a private to a public appeal. The supplicant's humble movement toward the throne in heaven serves to also encourage others to do the same. Again, the community of the faithful never prays alone. They pray with the king, the servant of the Lord. We don't just pray to Jesus, we pray with Jesus. Likewise the one leading the prayer and procession turns from asking only for himself. It is now we and our prayer, because ultimately Jerusalem and the holy temple do not belong to the people of God; they belong to the King who is seated on the heavenly throne.

The last phrase of verse two interjects an almost imperceptible yet laser beam focus to this song. The prayer leader has set a stare down with the one upon throne. Our eyes will not relent or will not blink until *he has mercy on us*. The prayer includes a call to persistence, fortitude, and focus, but it also relies on the right perception of the God whom one is appealing to.

From the first pages of Israel's sorted history from Adam and Eve to the disastrous destruction of the northern and southern kingdoms, the people of God proved to be a mostly faithless, thankless, and recalcitrant lot. Torturous is the historical read with occasional flashes of hope amidst a sea of irresponsible infighting and destructive rivalries. Countless are the conflicted prayers of those who profoundly understood the grievous nature of Israel's collective insubordination and guilt. Any human king would have been done with them a long time ago.

We have here a first glimpse at what is a central and critical theme undergirding this whole set of songs. It has been alluded to from the opening call for help, yet awaits explicit identification in the opening verse of Psalm 125—*trust in the Lord*. These are nice words but the supplicant here is up against insurmountable odds. He has come with but a small entourage to rebuild the city and restore the temple from ruins. Those opposed to such a venture surround Jerusalem, control the countryside, and have enough military capacity to crush it. As was discussed in the opening psalm (120), the primary source of anguish and torment is the collective condemnation from the enemy.

But the supplicant has boldly fixed his eyes on the *One enthroned in the heavens*. But for what reason? Yes, God can be fearful. He has shown wrath and judgment toward His wayward people, but bottom line, the *Lord is merciful*. In rapid succession, mercy is called out three times. Thus he unwaveringly appeals to the Lord to show favor, confident that this appeal will not go unanswered.

The word for favor, *hanan*, accents the underserved nature of an action by one someone who has the power to make or break the life of the supplicant. For instance, there is no reasonable cause or explanation as to why Esau who was doubly cheated by his wimpy conniving little brother should run to meet Jacob, throw his arms around his neck, and repeatedly kiss him (Gen 33:4). That action was completely unreasonable and unwarranted. No logical calculating person should respond like that.

The *hinan* of God is frequently appealed to in the Psalms and often with the common cry: "How long, O LORD? . . . How long?" (Ps 13:2). In this case, it refers to an extended time of shame and humiliation from the contemptuous, cynical, and haughty opponents who have amassed into a mob, hell bent on a lynching (Ps 13:3–4). The "how long" question intensifies with Israel and Judah who suffered the devastation of their life and culture for over one hundred years. They had been reduced to nothing. But many who want to see the people of God forever gone viciously attack the faint hope of being resurrected from the dead. They want the history of God's people to stop here. This bold complaint that God is procrastinating is solidly based on the surety of God's mercy. In a sense, it is like children who manipulate their father or mother based on the unabashed confidence that he or she will give in. That parent is a softy, a squish. And again, the supplicants here only need the slightest sign or gesture to indicate that the full rescue or redemption is on the way.

Most people struggle deeply with the wrathful images of God in the Bible as well they ought. Some of them are quite disturbing. I can address little of that here, but to conclude from those depictions that there is a stark difference between the God of the Old Testament and the God of the New is to blithely ignore passages such as this. The bottom line for the petitioner here is the same for all who approach the True God—at the very core, essence, and foundation of our life, the life of earth and of the universe is Love. The belief that Love is the resonating tone of all creation is the only foundation of prayer.

This affirmation undergirds the litanies of intercession in our Orthodox liturgies. We should not miss its power because of its repetition: "for You are the Lover of mankind." The Bible itself struggles with the seemingly maniacal rage of God at times. God can punish to the second and third generations those "who hate me" (Ex 20:5). But God's anger pales in comparison to His love that extends beyond the thousandth generation. The belief that Love is the elemental core of existence was miraculously "revealed" to Israel and the affirmation that "His steadfast love endures forever" is the golden thread woven by the Spirit of God that binds the Holy Scriptures together.

For we have had more than enough of contempt.
Our souls have been sated
  with the scorn of those who are at ease,
  The contempt of the proud.

The collective supplication for mercy daringly pushes the limits of humble petition, for despite the fact that mercy is undeserved, the supplicants still present reasons for God to act. But even here, their case is based not so much on airtight logic, but on a radical presumption about the God to whom they are making their appeal. To paraphrase Paul, the greatest of these things is love. To "trust in the Lord" is to stake one's own hope on this fundamental posture of God towards his people. Again Paul talks crazy when he speaks of the weakness of the All Mighty (1 Cor 1:25) that He loves humans. On this basis the supplicants boldly make their appeal.

The repeated phrase, *we have had more than enough*, comes out perhaps understated in our English translations. In the Hebrew, it is simply two words. The first word translated as "more," *rav*, is used to describe multiplication, becoming great, having an over-abundance. We can get a feel for this in the well-known blessing of God bestowed on humankind at creation (Gen 1:28): "Be fertile and multiply (*rav*)." Negatively in the story of Noah (Gen 6:5), *rav* is used to describe the excessive violence that humans have come to. It is also the word to describe excess in size or quality like large frightening armies (myriads or legions) or a king who has amassed hordes of plunder from invasions.

The second word, *sabah*, is commonly used with the verb to eat. Thus it means to eat to the full, to be satiated or stuffed! Thus, those on expedition are sick unto death, having eaten humble pie much, much more than what one would think is humanly possible. The pain is excessive and deep. The use of the Hebrew word "our souls" instead of simply the pronoun "we" draws attention to the chronic nature of the wound. It has cut within an inch of one's life. It has nearly sucked out one's existence.

The thrice appeal for God's favor in this song serves as an antibiotic against the threefold virus their enemies has unleashed: *contempt* and *scorn* from those who are *at ease*. Over all, it is the contagion of contempt.

This Hebrew word, *buz*, is mostly found in wisdom literature where it is usually associated with pride and wickedness. Wickedness is never directly linked to what we would call crimes: murder, abuse, drunken brawls, foul language, vandalism, etc. Rather, wickedness is connected to *conniving* to do wrong, *planning* to inflict injury, or conspiring to destroy someone; in other words, wickedness is primarily malice. And always, these malicious ones form a crowd or a lynchmob (Jb 31:34). It is a contempt that has collectively singled out a victim to unleash its own internal anger and violence and deflect it away from itself.

This word is often translated "laughingstock" which of course refers to putting someone up for both public punishment and humiliation.[2] For the one targeted for such collective violence, the contempt is experienced as shame. In the Old Testament, shame is the external reality of being publically humiliated to the point of being shattered or dismayed. It is to

---

2. Laughingstock was a latter derivative of "whipping stock."

be taken down by the collective condemnation of a group, of one singled out for communal retribution. The internal emotions associated with being ashamed run the gambit of negative feelings such as confusion, shock, horror, surprise, consternation, remorse, awkwardness, and anger. All of these are but the effects of being publicly humiliated.

The next two lines that finish off this psalm further clarify this kind of humiliation. It is the *scorn of those who are at ease*, and *the contempt of the proud*. The Hebrew word for scorn, *laag*, is derived from the verb to stammer or stutter. Isaiah (33:19) speaks of the humiliation from the Assyrian army taunting them in a foreign language. The soldiers guarding the walls hear only gibberish; nonetheless, they know exactly what kind of frightful threats and cursing is conveyed. Mostly, the picture is of "talking stupid" or "sounding like an idiot." It is taunting pure and simple.

The pain is further compounded by the source of this mocking from *those you are at ease*. The taunting is especially from those who have the wealth and power to secure their own well-being and comfortable life. In Nehemiah's case (Neh 3:36), this mocking comes from those who are settled in the land. Most of these people, simply took over lands and house left vacant by the exiles. These possessions to which they have grown accustom became their wealth and security by simple default. Jeremiah speaks of those who have not been exiled, who didn't have their whole life ripped out from under them. They are *undisturbed* by the horrible plight of others (Jer 12:1).

They are not only at ease, but arrogant. The Hebrew word is derived from the word for dove. In our culture, a dove is mostly associated with peace and calm, but the ancients connected them more with their "uppity" behavior. Doves are known for their beauty as well as a kind of cocky stature and walk. They are not only at ease, but they strut around in proud displays meant to deliberately provoke.

The exiles had grown accustom to the taunts of their captors, but this song reflects the shocking experience by those returning to the land. Expecting a welcome from their brothers, they received scorn. Instead of help, they received haughty resistance. Their hometown had changed dramatically in their absence.

Psalm 123 begins a mini-set within the larger first unit sung in the Presactified Liturgy that moves upward to a great call to trust God. The next psalm continues to express the agony of the congregant's situation but with increasing infusions of confidence and hope.

6

Psalm 124

A Song of Ascents of David

IN THE STAIR-STEP FASHION of this series of songs, David is once more brought to mind. Before, we were to imagine David joining the great expedition to establish Jerusalem (Ps 122). Here, the historical allusions are broader and vague, but the ascending congregation recalls the conquest of the Lord over Israel's enemies of times past. Because of the Lord's favor towards David, David experienced countless miraculous escapes against overwhelming odds.

If it had not been the LORD who was on our side,
  let Israel now say

The last psalm left the entourage on a sour note as they passed by the Rolling Hills Estates where people wagged their heads from poolside recliners in pathetic disbelief at the expedition now disheveled from the dust bit climb.

The abrupt shift in voice at the beginning of this psalm signals yet another bold burst upward coming from previously unknown reserves from within. The voice is of one from among the assembly who turns from head-bowed trudging to a motivation-spewing head coach in the locker room. This renewed hope finds courage in the memory of victories past.

Regardless of the ingeniousness and military talent of the leader, however, the song reminds all who look with hope that the one and only factor for success against vicious and dangerous opposition is whether Yahweh is "for us." Again, the appeal is for the Lord's mercy.

As discussed in the previous song, favor is something undeserved. There is no warrant or case that could be brought to procure it. It is not like a court case were one can present evidence or logical argument to compel the judge and jury that a positive outcome is warranted. No, the appeal can only begin with "I have no right to this." It is as the famous hymn always sung at the end of Billy Graham crusades: "Just as I am without one plea." It is never an issue of fairness, but of favor. It is never an appeal based on merit, but on mercy.

The recollection of David in the title of this song, reminds the assembly that the collective hope of favor before *the One enthroned in heaven,* is firmly establish in the *favored one.* The way the story of David reads reminds over and over again that it was God who chose David, not the ingenuity or political calculations of men. There is one primary reason: God loved David. He found a posture in him that was essential to any supplicant. It was not his military daring or his political savvy. It certainly wasn't his model family life or his questionable, religious piety. Rather, it was his readiness in any situation to respond to God. No matter how much David faltered, David was willing to turn to God, to keep responding to God. He did what Adam and Eve refused to do. David ran to God when questioned; the first couple hid. David sought forgiveness when his irresponsibility was exposed; the first couple hoped for God's forgetfulness.

This is part of what our repentance is about. If we choose to follow the model of this favored one and, of course, of Jesus to whom David was but a forerunner, then we must learn and keep on learning to turn toward God in any situation. Keep responding to God. Make every situation one in which God has access to us. Be a co-respondent with God.

Ironically, the singer continues to push the limits of a non-argument. This song is moving in two directions at once. It continues to directly appeal to the one enthroned in the heavens. It steadfastly fixes its target on the only One who can truly make a difference. It zeroes in on a bottom-line posture of God that above all He is merciful.

The verse also presents a bottom-line about what "chosenness" is about. Chosenness has been, and still is, a posture that can turn quite ugly. The history of Israel and the Church is riddled with all the ugliness of humanity in the name of God being on "our side." Being favored or chosen by God does not equate to privileged status and smugness. It is not an opportunity to boast or an excuse to oppress others. Or as Jesus put it, it does not mean slamming the doors shut to the kingdom (Mt 23:13), not only restricting access to mercy for large swaths of people, but ironically excluding one's self as well. If we can learn anything from the prophets and the ruin of Israel and Judah, it most certainly does not mean that God will sanction our behavior regardless of what it is.

The song also seeks to "preach to the choir." It is for *Israel to declare*. It calls on the petitioning congregation to have the right posture of prayer. This is, in fact, what much of prayer is about—putting the petitioner in the right frame of mind to make *any* appeal to the God of heaven. This song warns the congregation against a flippant approach to the throne all the while strengthening and raising up those who would put full trust in the merciful God.

This song is a kind of spiritual conditioning necessary for all those who put their trust in the Lord. At its core, it trains the soul to combat one of the worst enemies of a supplicant's prayer to God—smugness. In the parable of the publican and the Pharisee (Lk 18:10–14), Jesus warns of this destroyer of effective prayer that easily and often overtakes.

In the Christian East, spiritual pride is the archenemy of the monk. The oft mentioned spiritual struggle of a monk who battles for years in solitude mostly refers to the monk's struggle against "vain glory," an illusion that his own spiritual prowess has enabled him a deeper access to God. This struggle is often thought to be a terrible fight against demons.

This psalm follows a common pattern of prayer found in the Psalms and the Old Testament, that of historical recollection.[1] A main feature of historical rehearsal is not only to remind the worshipping congregation of how they came to be. Even more so, historical rehearsal seeks to *relive* the past saving events and pull the congregants into the ongoing saving acts of God. It pulls the supplicant's prayer for blessing and protection into God's current events. It re-orientates the myopic concerns of daily life toward the great concerns of God's dealing with this world.

If it had not been the LORD who was on our side, when men rose up against us

The allusions as to who the enemy is and what situation is referred to are quite general. This I believe is deliberate, for these few verses evoke

---

1. Exodus 15:1–18, Judges 5, 1 Samuel 2:1–12

a reminder of *all* of Yahweh's mighty saving deeds. Like a forensic artist who creates a composite image of a criminal, so here a composite image of Israel's enemy is drawn.

First, the opposition is simply "man." We've encountered already what is common throughout the Psalter. The enemy is the "wicked," the "proud," "evil-doers," and so on. Even these designations are general, but here it is just simply *humans*. As the primeval history of Genesis 1–11 reminds us, humanity has an almost magnetic compulsion to move away from its Maker and opt for its own violent version of human hope.

The story of Israel going all the way back to Abraham has seen countless opponents: Abimelech, Joseph's brothers, Pharaoh and the Egyptians, the Moabites, the Canaanites, the Philistines, Damascus, Assyria, and Babylon. And of course, let us not forget the biggest opponent of them all—*the rival brother*, for the primary focus of Israel's history as told in the Old Testament is of the disastrous civil strife between northern Israel and southern Judah.

This rivalry between brothers so consumed Israel and Judah that God nearly vanished from the picture. And if we want to uncomfortably bring in the messy issue of God's anger, we may want to at least be reminded that God's anger is almost exclusively aroused and intensified by the inability of His own people, touched by miraculous intervention and possessing a powerful revelation of an alternative reality for mankind, to behave differently than their gentile neighbors.

Humanity here is said to "rise up" in contrast to the congregation who is "going up" in these songs. The words are different in Hebrew. As already mentioned, the *alah* of the singers refers to those on expedition who are not only hoping to reach the Holy Mountain, but rebuild it. They are ascending to a dream that carries into eternity. It has both a present and a future character to it. Humanity also rises up, but ironically only as a cheap imitation of God's mighty deeds. The Hebrew word for this kind of action, *qum*, refers to rising from a prostrate to an upright position. It denotes getting stirred up in opposition to something else, to take a stand often *in opposition* to something.

Thus in just one verse, the lyrist summarizes human history up until this point: humanity opposes God.

This is the starting point for any genuine repentance. It is as Paul says; we were once "enemies" of God (Rom 5:10) and "strangers to the covenants of promise" (Eph 2:12). We come from the stock whose genetic makeup is rebellion against God. There are those in our culture who aggressively oppose God and actively seek to undermine the Church. These people we unfortunately give far more attention than is warranted. By far more degenerate is the posture of most of us who opt for the pretense of indifference. God is neither here nor there. We simply opt for *non-response*. This is but a glossy makeover of the former.

I must dare say that we cannot experience the Lord's favor and know what it means for Him to be "for us" or "on our side" unless we are willing to examine the extent to which we have been and still are fundamentally resistant to Him. Repentance is about turning resistance into response, and the "us" whom *God is with* and to whom God will protect and defend are those who willingly place themselves in the middle of this intense struggle first within one's self, then within the Church, and then in the culture we live in. They understand the real battle being waged between the "we" who have taken a stand to oppose God, and the "we" who have boldly laid down the arms, who have surrendered. They are the humble who truly understand that "if it were not for the Lord, I would have perished."

Then they would have swallowed us alive,
   when their anger was kindled against us.
Then the flood would have swept us away;
   the torrent would have gone over us, the raging waters.

The songwriter conjures up mixed metaphors commonly used in the Ancient Near East to refer to the fearful prospect of being annihilated by an invading army, or as the case in this psalm, being taken to bankruptcy court. It is like being caught in a flood or a trap. Both depictions, however, are compared to being eaten or consumed by a great beast. The metaphors not only serve to evoke God's mighty saving deeds at the Reed Sea (Ex 14–15) and the sparing of Jerusalem under Assyrian siege (Isa 36–38), but also to summarize the whole history of God's many and ongoing "amazing rescues." Moreover, the images recount the recurrent miraculous intervention of the Lord in sparing God's people in the exile and their "escape" from Babylonian captivity.

The depiction of the enemy (humanity opposing God) is clear regardless of the metaphor. They seek to completely devour God's people. The picture of being eaten by an enemy is universal in the ancient world. In verse three, our English translation accurately conveys the notion in

Hebrew of being *swallowed whole*. It is the word used to describe the wholesale consumption of Jonah by the great fish. Perhaps many of us have seen videos of great snakes that can engulf its prey twice its size. The picture is of being completely overtaken and the destruction complete.

In verse six, the consumption is like being devoured by wild beasts. Again, I have seen film of lions or crocodiles that vociferously tear and rip at a carcass until only hide and bone remain. Whether overtaken by a flood or devoured by a beast, the fearful prospect is compounded in that the victim is still "alive." It does not have a peaceful death, and then it is devoured. No, the victim is horribly conscious of its oncoming doom. Prophets such as Habakkuk (Hab 3:16) and Ezekiel (Ez 4) describe the dreadful horror of a protracted siege of a city where the inhabitants can contemplate their own demise in excruciating dullness of time.

The lyricist makes clear what force lay behind these acts of consumption—raging anger. *Charah* is one of the most common Hebrew words to refer to the expression of anger. It is one of many Hebrew words derived from a *CH-R* root that even the pronunciation may have a pirate-like snarl to it (the CH has a back-of-the-throat sound to it like coaxing up flem). The words derived from the CH-R spelling have powerfully negative connotations: dung, dry, desolate, waste, ruin, struck down, sword, tremble in fear, fear, anxiety, strip, expulsion, exterminate.

The prospect of the concentrated and collective anger of men upon a victim is so frightening that the ancients could not directly speak of it. The reference to rage is metaphorically spoken of as a fire that is out of control, like a wild grass or forest fire. It takes on a single personality and is nearly impossible to predict let alone contain or defend. It can suddenly change directions with devastating consequences. One translation powerfully conjures up the more accurate description: "in their burning rage against us."[2]

There are many different directions a commentary can go to discuss men's anger, but here, we must be reminded that this kind of rage is *collective* and is singularly focused on a target. The victim is one who has for whatever reason attracted the collected anger of a group like metal to a magnet. He is a scapegoat for the collective, a sacrifice for the good of the whole. The collective nature of the anger is particularly evident in the metaphors of fire, flood, and devouring beast. The imagery of a bird-trapper best depicts the selective target of the victim. It is one of the most

---

2. NJPS

common metaphors in the ancient world to describe a city under siege.³ Annihilation is the goal.

All this, however, is more a commentary on the Lord than on the horrifying prospect of men's rage. The emphasis of this song is not so much on the victim, but on the *God who defends and rescues those who have become targets of collective hate.* The God of the Israelites and of Jesus is a defender of victims. The allusion to God's rescue at the Reed Sea here is meant to remind that the primary reason why one can trust in God is that one can always count on the Lord to defend the victim of collective violence.

It is easy enough to see how the metaphor of being swallowed alive and whole by a great fish easily relates to being swept away by a flood. Both speak of the inevitable doom of one caught in such a predicament. Verse four draws out the picture of being caught in a flood in remarkably similar fashion as the song of Miriam does in Exodus 15. There, of course, it was the pursuing Egyptian army, also full of consumptive rage (Ex 15:9), who was overtaken by the waters. The victory is in the collective rage itself. Rage turns on those who presume to wield it. This is craftily portrayed in the Reed see incident by the Egyptians' own chariot wheels getting bogged down in mud the harder they pursue their victim.

Once again, Israel is humbly reminded that they could have just as easily been caught in that flood "had the Lord not been on our side." The difference between the raging Egyptians and the fearful Hebrews did not lie in any inherent quality within either of them, but only in the God who acts on behalf of victims. God was on "their side" because *they* were the targets of collective oppression. They were the victims of empire building agendas. These verses are a critical precursor to the next series of psalms that speak of confident trust in the Lord (Ps 125:1). God is on the side of the Israelites to the extent that the Israelites remember that God *executes justice for the oppressed, who gives food to the hungry, who upholds the fatherless and the widow, who watches over the sojourner and who will bring the way of the wicked to ruin (Ps 146:7–10).*⁴

---

3. Crow, *The Songs of Ascents*, 53.

4. These verses are chanted every Sunday in the Divine Liturgy as one of the entrance songs.

> **Blessed be the LORD**
> **who had not given us as prey to their teeth.**

For the third time in this song, acknowledgement of the Lord's life-saving mercy is proclaimed this time as a pronounced blessing. Blessing carries a similar idea as praise or thanks, but with a stronger emphasis on reciprocity. Blessing is one of the most prized commodities in the ancient world. It is what every human has a guttural desire for—*to survive and thrive.*

As the stories of the patriarchs in Genesis accurately depict, blessing is something that can only be granted from a greater to a lesser, so it is a bit baffling how we "bless the Lord" when most of the time it is us who seek blessing. This is where the reciprocal relationship becomes prominent, and again, it speaks something fundamental about prayer. Blessing must be asked for, and its reception depends totally on the recipient's humble and grateful acknowledgment of the source. Even more so, the recipient of blessing binds himself to the continuity of the giver's heritage. It declares complete indebtedness that is impossible to renege.

The story of Jacob who stole the blessing from Esau reveals something of the dynamic of blessing defined above. It is difficult for us to see how Jacob is blessed after such a disgusting display of conniving and deceit. Truly, Esau seems to get a raw deal, but powerfully implied in the story is a major flaw in him. Esau's flippant attitude about the blessing reveals a major breakdown of blessing. He wanted to survive and thrive but without binding himself to his father. He wanted blessing without strings attached.

Might I suggest that this is often behind our own requests to God. Every person in the world wants to survive and thrive. The fact that I as a Christian seek that from God is not all that distinctive. The true distinction is the extent to which I am willing to align my life with the Father's heritage.

> **We have escaped as a bird**
> **from the snare of the fowlers.**
> **The snare is broken and we have escaped.**

The Hebrew brings out the force a little stronger than our English pronoun "we," for it is their very *souls* that are at stake. The soul is often connected with the word for life as in the narrative of humankind's creation (Gen 2:7). God breathed into the *adam,* and he became a "living soul." A primary sense of the soul (*nephesh*) in the Old Testament is that of taking in life. It is the drive, passion, and desire to partake of life. The *living soul* is one who is hungry for Life, and when the Life is taken away or imprisoned as it most often is in human existence, one's very essence is at stake.

As it is in the case of the congregation in this psalm, so it is even today. The primary source of denial of life comes from other humans. This is precisely what is being lamented here. The social arrangements of humanity constantly seek to manipulate, entrap, and devour that God-breathed desire in every human to take in the goodness and wholeness of Life as God intended.

As mentioned already, this reference to being trapped like a bird most likely conjured up numerous powerful historical images from Israel's past. Many times a situation seemed hopeless, and yet the Lord somehow "fought for Israel" and made a way of escape. I believe the metaphor here has a double referent with regards to Israel's most tragic event—the exile. One part refers to the inhabitants of Jerusalem who were in the first stages of the exile. The initial strategy of the Babylonians was to subdue Judah, not destroy it. They took away the rebellious king and the Temple apparatus. They installed their own "governor" who would supposedly be amiable to the policies of the Babylonian Empire. Thus, there were Israelites in Babylon and Israelites still in the land. A fierce debate ensued as to whom were the true faithful, the ones in captivity or the ones occupying the land. Jeremiah's prophecy of the good figs and the bad figs aptly describes this conflict (Jer 24).

Those who stayed in the land continued their rebellious agenda to the dismay of the prophets Jeremiah and Ezekiel who advocated subordination. It was this posture that brought on the complete destruction of Jerusalem by fire and the slaughter of its inhabitants. The first part of this referent then is to the parents and grand parents who did not resist what had come upon them, voluntarily accepted refugee status, and went into exile. They escaped the fowler's trap.

The other part refers to the Babylonian captives who have been granted permission to return to the land of their fathers to rebuild and reoccupy the land. It is the "we" of Psalm 124 who have made the arduous expedition. They risked all, especially a settled and comfortable life, to take up the dream of a reconstituted Israel. Verse seven describes the trap as simply fallen apart, a likely reference to the degenerative state of the Babylonian empire, which as empires go did not last very long.

In both aspects of this metaphor, the rescued ones who confidently declare that the Lord was "on our side" are the ones who willingly accepted exile, did not stubbornly resist the Babylonians, and became refugees.

Embedded here is a powerful reminder of our own repentance. In a world of tremendous upheaval, there are many who tenaciously cling to some form of "the way things were." This is natural, but at some point one must examine to what extent that desperate clinging to a former vision of how to faithfully live actually becomes an impediment and obstacle to what God is currently about. We need be reminded that those who stubbornly resisted the Babylonians and insisted on protecting the Temple in Jerusalem at all costs are the very ones who brought on its complete demise. This psalm powerfully affirms that the ones who experience "the Lord being on our side" are the ones who first accepted their status as refugees as the book of Hebrews reminds (Heb 13). There is nothing in this psalm or in the story of Israel's exile that indicates that this was an easy and painless thing to do. The book of Lamentations aptly describes the true experience.

This same sense of accepting or embracing "refugee" status as a precursor to entering the kingdom of God is most evident in the ministry of John the Baptist. "In the wilderness," one must prepare for the coming kingdom, not in the centers of power, prestige, and wealth. Indeed, it is those "cities" that consistently uproot and devour.

> *Blessed are the meek,*
>   *for they will inherit the land.*
> *Blessed are they who are persecuted for the sake of righteousness,*
>   *for theirs is the kingdom of heaven.*
> *Blessed are you when people insult you and persecute you and utter every kind of evil against you [falsely] because of me. Rejoice and be glad, for your reward will be great in heaven. Thus they persecuted the prophets who were before you.* (Matt 5:5, 10–12)

Closure of the First Antiphon

Psalm 124 closes the First Antiphon. It started with a cry for help and God's answer coming in the call to begin the expedition. Through Psalms 120–24 and in roller-coaster fashion, we descended and ascended through foreboding and inhospitable territory squinting for just a glimpse of our destination. Every obstacle that sapped energy and determination was countered with historical rehearsals of the Lord's mighty but not always readily apparent Presence. Our goal is reunion with God on the Holy Mountain, but by surprise we also encountered Him unexpectedly on the way.

By this point in the Songs of Ascents, all the key themes have been introduced. As we continue, the struggles of getting to Zion will be revisited in even more heightened intensity—personal fear and doubt, internal and external hostility, windows into God's vision of humanity, and hope arising against the backdrop of despair and resistance. Our singer began the expedition in the land of his captors far away from Jerusalem and surrounded by hostile opposition, yet as he continued to appeal to God, he found fellow travelers both past and present willing to join the expedition. The entourage sang of Jerusalem's past glory in the steady march toward that holy place with each squinted eye straining for just a glimpse that their mission might meet realization.

The Second Antiphon—Psalms 125–129

AFTER THE FIRST ANTIPHON is sung, a Little Litany (prayers of intercession) follows. The priest chants the Prayer of the Second Antiphon:

> O LORD, in Your displeasure rebuke us not, neither chasten us in Your wrath, but deal with us according to Your tenderness, O Physician and Healer of our souls. Guide us unto the haven of Your will. Enlighten the eyes of our hearts unto the knowledge of Your truth, and grant unto us that the remainder of the present day and the whole time of our life may be peaceful and sinless, through the intercessions of the Holy Theotokos and of all the saints.

He then proclaims the eternal kingdom of the Holy Trinity and the choir confirms with "Amen." The choir begins the Second Antiphon as the priest incenses the Presanctified Gifts.

In the second Antiphon (Ps 125–29), the expedition sees the hills of Jerusalem peaking up on the horizon. With renewed vigor the upward pace quickens. This antiphon quickly marches us first to the hills of Jerusalem (Ps 125), then through the hostile city (Ps 125:4–5), and on to the Temple precinct where a great sigh of exuberant relief bursts forth (Ps 126:1–3). Yet even in the midst of congratulatory hugs, whispers of doubt weave their way into the jubilation. This is not the final summit (Ps 126:4–6). Even so, the expedition now pauses and takes inventory. They listen to speeches by master climbers assuring the faint hearted to keep going. There is promise of great rewards, visions of sun-baked blessing, and images of the good life (Ps 128). They have beaten the odds so far. They have overcome their foes. They have conquered each new challenge and tamed every obstacle. Onward the must go (Ps 129).

7

Psalm 125

Upon arrival to the city, a whole new set of challenges arose, for the expedition found the city in shambles and occupied by hostile company. A sinking feeling overtook as inner strength evaporated. Even as all self-confidence faded, the assembly reminded each other not of the ever present and energized opposition to the "Israel project" but of a powerful and extraordinary truth about the God of Israel. To put it in the words often repeated in Orthodox prayer: "The Lord is merciful and the lover of mankind." The singers somehow mustered the faith of Abraham who believed that a peculiar God had reached out to him with unmerited favor and asked only one amazing thing of him in response: *trust God*.

All of the songs so far have led up to this point. The rest of the songs of ascents reflect on this critical juncture. Thus, the first verse of Psalm 125 is the centerpiece and pivotal point of the whole series. The key word is *trust*.

The expedition grew in trust as they drew nearer to their destination. Joy must have swelled up in them as the first sign of hills poked through the horizon and increased in intensity with each step closer. As each one plodded with invigorated step, the doubts, fears, and anxieties must have melted away. But as the songs continue, the trials of getting to the city will be revisited in even greater degree as the traveling entourage must convert to a construction crew.

I am reminded here of major, climbing expeditions like those to Mt. Everest. After years of preparation and months of logistical planning, packing, and traveling, an expedition finally reaches the foot of the mountain. From base camp, however, a new set of logistics is now implemented. Base camp must be established, and a series of camps must be set up all the way up the mountain.

There are numerous tensions at play in Psalm 125. Certainly, our singer's ascension to the mount is fraught with an undergirding unease. At the center and cause of the tension are the one's trusting in the Lord. In other words, the ascension itself is both an act of trust and a cause of unease.

The metaphorical interplay of reversals in this psalm revolves around mobility and the immobile. The hills of Zion are immovable yet ascending and encircling like an army preparing to siege a city. Similarly, the seemingly established rule of wickedness will be unsettled. The homeless who trust in the Lord will find an abiding inheritance while those who build estates off of unjust gain will find themselves wanderers. In other words, it is those who are actively ascending, trusting the Lord with every step, doing good, and advocating for justice who will find a home, settle down, and find rest.

Great caution must be exercised here. We can too readily associate ourselves with the trusting ones who are righteous do-gooders and presume that we have nothing to do with evil, wickedness and corruption. In other words, the tension in the song is not meant to be easily resolved. This is not trust. Trust in the Lord is not a way to end tension or avoid conflict. One cannot even begin to trust the Lord if one is not willing to live in the tension. Trust in the Lord is its own home all the while accepting our unsettling settlement. It is what Walter Brueggemann aptly coins as "a precarious trust of landedness."[1]

Those who trust in the LORD are like Mount Zion,

Trust is surrender, and surrender is something the prophets repeatedly called the people of Israel and Judah to do. The antithesis of surrender is resistance, and repeatedly the people of God refused God's call to *not* resist the Assyrians and the Babylonians.

We can easily get a feel for the basic element of the Hebrew word here for trust, *batach*, for it suggests lying face down on the ground as we do in prostrations several times during the Presanctified Liturgy. Rather than raising a white flag as a sign of surrender, it is possible that ancient armies threw their weapons down and laid face down hoping for the best.

---

1 Brueggemann, *The Land*, 59.

In a sense then, trust carries the notion of being passive, still, or quiet. It is the perfect gesture of non-hostility. This probably doesn't set well with many of us whose compulsion is to "do something" about a crisis, to secure our own security.

This verse can easily lend itself to the kind of intransigence that leads to religious intolerance. In other words, we can very easily turn our bull-headed stubbornness and arrogance into a virtue not only sponsored by God, but conveniently guarded by Him against all criticism. To remind, everyone puts their trust in something: guns, money, power, or luck. It is here, however, where the singer reminds that the *act* of trust is totally dependent on the *object* of trust. Appropriate trust is firmly grounded, as Mt Zion is, not in one's self but in a God whose response to even a minimal amount of trust on our part is full on, complete, and enduring commitment.

Trust, *batach*, is related to belief, but is not the same thing. Belief has to do with putting confidence in someone, especially in response to a promise, as when Abraham responded to God's word (Gen 15:6). Belief is prompted by the extended hand of another.

On the contrary, trust in the Psalms and in the prophets is the antidote for fear as when Isaiah proclaims in the face of the approaching Assyrian army: *I am confident and unafraid.* (Isa 12:2). Trust in the Lord is the alternative response to a life-threatening situation.

Isaiah perhaps best characterizes the meaning of trust. One might even say that this is Isaiah's message. The word is particularly connected to Zion where a radical, even miraculous, reversal will occur. At Zion, God will defeat all the nations whose kingdoms are built on haughtiness, pride, violence, treachery, greed, and ruthless power. The poor, on the other hand, who are grossly dependent and in distress (*tzarar*), who have been coerced into surrendering to systems of human exploitation, will find refuge (Isa 24–26).

This great reversal will culminate in a feast on Zion "for all peoples." The feast will have the effect of destroying the "veil that veils all peoples,/ The web that is woven over all nations" (Isa 25:7). In terms reflecting the resurrection, God will "destroy death forever." The LORD God will wipe away the tears from all faces" (Isa 25:8).

Trust for Isaiah has everything to do with what one is going to hold on to in a crisis (Isa 25:9). It is not Zion itself that is important, but rather the act of deliverance performed there that becomes a symbol of the God who delivers. Isaiah as well as much of the Psalms connects praise (as a victory song), rejoicing, deliverance, and trust around the symbol of Zion.

There are a couple of critical qualifiers to this proclamation of the nature or foundation of *trust in the LORD*, for it is extremely tempting for trust in something else to take precedence to a detrimental effect. First and in every case, the basis and focus of the trust is *the LORD*. This may seem like an obvious point, but the Israelites clearly lost sight of that.

In one of the most profound confrontations in the Bible, Jeremiah must confront the worshippers in Jerusalem who were placing their trust in the *place* rather than the *person* (Jer 7). Even more so, they had lost sight of the kind of God who was said to defend Zion. They presumed Him to be like an imperial deity whose main concern was protecting his investment and keeping his source of self-aggrandizement intact. As Jeremiah forcefully argues, the Lord of Zion is also the Lord of the covenant. He expects behavior in keeping with a covenant people.

Their costly mistake can just as easily be ours. The Jerusalemites got the phrase turned around. They heard more: *those who trust in Zion are like the Lord*. They were placing their trust in Zion, a powerful icon of God's mighty presence for sure, but not in the Lord. We should not be slight in our criticism of those silly ancients when this gross error is constantly repeated in every generation. Religious institutions are not holy and inviolable in and of themselves. It is only the God who is present there that makes it holy. Nor should we concern ourselves with distorted fears of outside invaders. The consistent message of the prophets is that the greatest threat to religious freedom is *internal*, not external. The monastic tradition bears witness to us—one can be completely free even inside a "cell."

The other error is an extension of the "trusting in Zion" mistake. It confuses the metaphor saying: "Those who trust in the Lord *are* Mount Zion." This kind of distortion may even be more grievous than the one above, for it again distorts what is centrally important. It directs the focus away from the Lord and onto to the one supposedly trusting God. It makes the action of trust more important than the object of trust.

This error also played itself out in Israel's history. When Nebuchadnezzar first besieged Jerusalem, it was meant to be a corrective measure, not a destructive one. He emptied the Temple and took the nobles of the city into exile. At that time, Jeremiah insisted that the Israelites *not resist* this because the nation's troubles were due to a covenant breach with their King, Yahweh. The king of Babylon was merely God's instrument.

The regent ruler that king Nebuchadnezzar established to replace the rebel king was supposed to implement Babylonian subjugation. The opposite occurred to a disastrous effect, and here is the reason why. Those still left in Jerusalem presumed that God had punished the former occupants of Jerusalem and replaced them with the "good people." They called those in exile the "rotten figs" and themselves the "ripe figs." Their main proof was, of course, that they actually occupied Jerusalem. They were the true Zion based on a seemingly good argument—they physically occupied the space. Their control over the institution and the city was for them proof positive that their own trust in God was strong while those in exile was weak, non-existent, or distorted.

In yet another of Jeremiah's bold confrontations, he shockingly reverses the rotten/ripe fig slogan, saying that those in exile were the ripe figs (Jer 24). And why? The ones who were radically uprooted were the ones who began to relearn (another word for repentance) what it meant to put their trust in God *alone*. They lost everything. They truly became poor and had to learn to *trust in the Lord*. They had to critically decide whether to opt for the dream over against a stark reality. In the end, those who proclaimed most loudly about Zion ended up being the most stubborn and recalcitrant. They confused their own physical occupation of space and smug self-confidence with the Lord's promise of Presence based on *favor*, unwarranted goodwill. In 587 BCE, Jerusalem was burned to the ground. Its inhabitants massacred or exiled. Zion returned to its origins. Once again, it was just a barren heap.

Jesus had to confront this same kind of distorted trust in his own time. He scathingly rebukes the kind of mentality that would place more stock in religious symbols and institutional icons than in the One and True God who is the source of such things. There were some religious teachers who were making fine points about when an oath should be considered binding. They said it is not enough to simply swear by the altar or temple, but by the gold of the Temple. Jesus reminds them that it is God alone who makes any religious artifact, however venerated it is, worth anything at all (Mt 23:16–22). The fact that this same temptation, which is peculiarly a religious one, still plagued the Jewish community nearly 500 years after the destruction of the temple reminds of the precarious lure of false piety.

It is not simply a matter of trust, especially measured in quantities. As Jesus instructs, a puny amount of faith is enough, *if* it is directed toward the right god (Mt 17:20). Thus, my prayers sometimes seem impotent because I simply did not address them to the True God. I confused the mighty One of Jacob as the god of vengeance, the Holy One of Israel as a petty ledger-keeping god.

The promise here is precarious as it is hopeful. Everyone places his or her trust in something. The issue is what or who? If it is anything except the Lord *alone*, it will lead to boastful self-confidence, but also inevitable ruin. As has already been discussed (Ps 120, 123), the "enemy" of the Psalms is consistently portrayed as "haughty," "proud," and "complacent." It is the Lord who makes one's trust "immovable."

This kind of radical trust "in God alone" fundamentally understands that there is no other viable alternative. This is what places our sense of trust into serious question and is again, a cause for repentance. If we are honest with ourselves—a major component of repentance—we must admit that our trust is more in money, guns, and power than in the Lord. This is always the case with those who have money, guns, and power. This is not the case with "the poor."

The connection between radical trust, the poor, and Zion are so integrated, that it is impossible to grasp the meaning of Zion without it. The word "Zion" mainly denotes a dry heap, a worthless mound. Its geographic value was next to nothing. It had no natural resources or beauty, was hard to get to, and was not near major trade routes.

Zion, however, is almost exclusively used in poetic verse. It is a favored term of the prophets, such as Amos, Micah, and Isaiah and quickly took on a symbolic or iconic flavor to it. Zion is an idyllic reference to the inhabitance of Jerusalem whose geographic "height" above the rest of Israel ought to equally correspond to them being model citizens of the covenant with Yahweh. They were to be the model city of covenant living. As Isaiah proclaims:

> *I will restore your judges as at first,*
> *and your counselors as in the beginning;*
> *After that you shall be called*
> *city of justice, the faithful city.*
> *Zion shall be redeemed by judgment*
> *and her repentant ones by justice* (Isa 1:26–27)

Zion was to be a "city on a hill" that would so exemplify a radical alternative to the violent, exploitative, and often merciless kingdoms of Israel's neighbors by upholding the weak and disenfranchised that the nations would abandon their murderous ways and flock to that holy hill to see for themselves. Furthermore, they would return to their own lands and city embracing the covenant living of the Lord for them.

> *In the days to come,*
> *The mountain of the LORD's house*
>   *shall be established as the highest mountain*
>   *and raised above the hills.*
> *All nations shall stream toward it,*
>   *many peoples shall come and say:*
> *"Come, let us climb the LORD's mountain,*
>   *to the house of the God of Jacob,*
> *That he may instruct us in his ways,*
>   *and we may walk in his paths."*
> *For from Zion shall go forth instruction,*
>   *and the word of the LORD from Jerusalem.*
> *He shall jusge between the nations,*
>   *and impose terms on many peoples.*
> *They shall beat their swords into plowshares*
>   *and their spears into pruning hooks;*
> *One nation shall not raise the sword against another,*
>   *nor shall they train for war again.*
> *O house of Jacob, come,*
>   *let us walk in the light of the LORD!* (Isa 2:2–5)

Most of the prophetic proclamation in addressing Zion, however, is scathing because Jerusalem not only neglected the covenant requirements but also wantonly pursued the opposite. It became a city just like the others, established more by murder, conspiracy, and gross pursuit of wealth at the expense of the poor. Instead of a place where all from the king and priests on down humbly present themselves before a righteous God, it persistently became a covenant community that walled itself off from the poor, not even allowing them access to the Lord (an accusation Jesus also brings against the city (Mt 23:13–15). Zion became a community of pious pride, distorting chosenness into privilege, merciful favor into a commodity, and trust in false piety as collateral.

> **Which cannot be moved, but abides forever.**
> **As the mountains are round about Jerusalem,**
> **so the LORD is round about His people**
> **from this time and forever.**

It is also important to remind that Zion is not the equivalent for the temple. Rather, Zion is the "hill" that the temple is placed on. In other words, Zion is the foundational plot where God can place his Presence. Again, the prophets remind that it is not the land per se that is the critical component, but a people who trustingly commit to a covenant relationship with this God who proclaims exclusive kingship over them. Again, the metaphor must remain clear. It is not the real estate that is foundational but the continuing act of a trusting people in a just God that "abides forever."

It is this very truth that the early church affirms of Mary the mother of Jesus who clearly and foundationally lived out. Admittedly, sometimes the poetic metaphors found in liturgical expression about Mary seem to runaway with themselves—holy heifer, queen of heaven. But Mary's unqualified trust in God is the foundation to which God was able to abide in. With Mary, the act of trust and the object of trust are perfectly situated, creating the perfect "space" for God to be "with us." Thus Mary is called Zion, the new Jerusalem:

> *Shine, shine new Jerusalem,*
> *The glory of the LORD has shown on you*[2].

In the psalm verse there is a curious interplay with what is supposedly immovable and inactive with what is movable and active. Even the words themselves act out the interplay. First, there are those who are in an active state, a transient state of trusting. We know this because they are on their upward way from Babylon to Jerusalem. Trust is exercised with each unsettling movement upward. Ironically then, it is this kind of "trust on the go" that the singer assures is *immovable* and *settled in*.

The trusting refugee finds a permanent home. It abides forever. And it is a secure home.

The Hebrew word for move used with the negative here, *mot*, carries strong connotations of security, like securing a city from attack by

---

[2]. A prayer spoken by the priest in Divine Liturgy after the congregation has participated in the Eucharist. The lyric is also found in a hymn to Mary during the Easter season.

building strong walls that can withstand a siege and battering rams. To remind, such was the mission of Nehemiah. And here again, it is sorely tempting for us to blur the distinction between a security that comes in trust, and the security that we want in economic and militaristic ways. In this regard, the security that comes from trust in the Lord is reciprocal. The more one trusts in the Lord, the more trust one has in the Lord, the more one becomes immovable or secure in that trust, the more one trusts that trust. Like churning butter, the more one keeps swirling it, the more it solidifies.

Trust in the Lord has a built in security to it. The lyricist beckons his listeners to look upon that majestic hill and be reminded that it is not going anywhere. It stays put, like a rock on the ground, and so it is with trust that is firmly fixed on the Lord.

The quality of trust *in the Lord* cannot be shaken, moved, or distorted for one reason—the Lord. And for this reason the singer extends the metaphor. Zion does not stand alone. It is not a mountain popping up out of nowhere. No, mountains surround it. It is situated in hill country.

Here, I am reminded of a climbing trip I took with my father and brother to the volcanoes in Mexico. One of the most striking features of the climb was that these towering volcanoes jettisoned up from the valley floor solely in isolation. It was an anomaly when we reached the top because there was no spectacular scenery. These mountains simply popped up through the clouds in lonely solitude. They were not situated in a mountain range. There were only the mountain, the clouds, the sky, and us. I vividly remember how odd that felt.

With the visible hills of Jerusalem firmly in sight, the singer beckons the expedition to also see how the object of their trust, the Lord, is responding to their trust. Here again is the word play with the moveable and the fixed. Zion does not tower in lonely solitude, nor does one's faith. It is a misnomer to insist too strongly that one's faith alone saves. Hills don't go anywhere, nor do words on a page, but in both cases here, there is a critical movement the trusting ones must see. Just as God was brooding over the primordial waters of chaos, so the Lord encircles the trusting ones.

The word *saviv* in Hebrew strongly connotes a kind of circular movement, a churning, that insures solidity and invincibility, like an army surrounding a city. The verb is variously translated as enfold, encase, surround, and even churn. In this song, it is the ones "trusting the Lord" who are "his people." The enduring quality of the Lord's "churning" presence twice repeated in the first two verses perpetually responds to the trusting ones. Trusting moves the Lord to enfold or surround His people, and that movement spurs further trust.

We find this curious back-folding word play come out clearly in a scene for the Assyrian siege of Jerusalem. Then Sennacherib's army was on a seemingly unstoppable invasion of the territory. When he prepared to attack Jerusalem, he made an appeal for Hezekiah to surrender the city to which Hezekiah refused. The odds of a positive outcome for Hezekiah were so minimal that Sennacherib scornfully asks: "What is this trust that you trust?" In other words, what is the basis or foundation that you repeatedly wrap your confidence around? (Isa 36:4). Hezekiah demonstrates the answer as he retreats to the temple and makes his appeal to the Lord alone (Isa 37:16).

Confidence is a useful word here, for it combines faith (*fide*) and active partnership (*con*—together with). Those who trust in the Lord alone swirl around Him as He in turn enfolds them in a hurricane-style generative force.

This enfolding, churning, protecting presence of the Lord toward His trusting ones does not have a term limit on it. It is *le'olam*, eternal. In that stair-stepping lyric, the phrase is repeated and embellished in verse two not only to reinforce the point but also to remind of the ascending quality of trust in the Lord. It gets stronger with use.

The eternal quality of trust in the phrase "now and forever" echoes the promise of Yahweh to king David. David's kingdom was to be forever, yet the Babylonians put a complete end to the Davidic dynasty. The promise of David was buried under ruins and lifeless exile. Here the singer beckons himself and his listeners to let hope ascend in the act of trust. He calls the faithful to take on David's abiding trust in God. He steps up the commitment level of Israel. One cannot just depend on someone else to trust God above all else. Each covenant member must exercise the trust in the Lord that David did. This, the singer reminds, is where the Lord's eternal promise lies.

Even though the mission was to secure the city by rebuilding its walls, this critical lyric reminds that it is the interplay between a trusting people and even more so the Lord's response that truly secures the city, that truly makes our lives "safe."

The scepter of wickedness shall not rest
  upon the land allotted to the righteous,
lest the righteous put forth their hands to do wrong.
Do good, O LORD, to those who are good,
  and to those who are upright in their hearts.
But to those who turn aside to their own crooked ways,
  The LORD wil lead away with evildoers.

An abrupt shift occurs here as if our heady lyricist has been jolted back to reality. Even to this day, there are those who oppose God's people and his alternative vision for humanity. For our lyricist, the opposition is exerting a considerable coercive influence on Jerusalem. Even though the expedition has arrived at base camp, they still must get past the guards. Even though the temple is situated in the center of the city, it is surrounded by hostility. The expedition faces a major obstacle in its final push to the summit. They must pass through the *scepter of wickedness*.

With ingenious literary play, the next three verses situate those "trusting in the Lord" encircled in the center surrounded by hostile foes, like a wagon train surrounded by Indians. The very words on the page imitate the real situation they are facing, and it demonstrates how the "trusting trust" in the Lord secures them. It also boldly proclaims the flip-flop kingdom of God that moves the intransigent and stabilizes the transient.

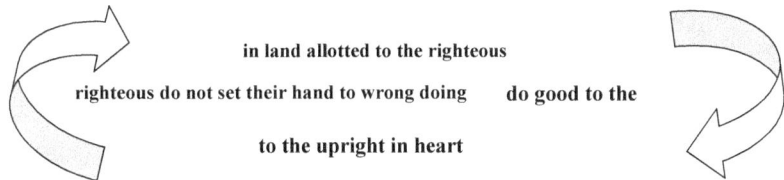

The scepter of the wicked shall never rest

in land allotted to the righteous

righteous do not set their hand to wrong doing   do good to the

to the upright in heart

in their crooked ways act corruptly   go the way of evil-doers.

The use of a rod or scepter as a symbol of authority and power to punish was well known in the time of monarchies up until a few hundred years ago, but the symbolic impact today is negligible. Perhaps a policemen's "badge" is the closest symbol we relate to. The symbol "to serve and protect" is backed by the ability and authority to punish if necessary. The rod was referred to in shepherding terms (Mic 7:14)—to lead, to count, to protect—but as Israel faced powerful imperial gods and armies, the references became negative and associated with excessive and violent displays of force, abuse, oppression, and tyranny. Yahweh is spoken of rarely in such vicious terms, but when He is, it mainly refers to the inherent, imperial violence of the Assyrians and Babylon. In that case, the Lord is pictured as "breaking the rod of wickedness" used as a truncheon to beat down rather than an instrument of guidance and protection.

The lyrical form of much of the Psalms often puts in stark contrast "the righteous" and the "wicked" for rhetorical effect. As readers of the Psalms, we must be cautious lest we fall into a smug posture roundly condemned by the prophets and Jesus. The lines are often blurred and this was certainly the situation Nehemiah faced upon returning to Jerusalem.

After several years of intense labor and struggle to rebuild the walls of Jerusalem, Nehemiah discovers that many of the wealthy Israelites are seriously undermining the effort (Neh 5:1–9). In behind the scenes negotiations with non-Israelite residents of Jerusalem, they have been lending money to the poorer Israelites, many of them are returning exiles who are seriously struggling to get established. They charge such excessive interest that they are literally enslaving their fellow Israelites, taking advantage of their vulnerability.

Nehemiah is outraged and takes his fellow well-to-do citizens to task. They are playing the "dreamy" intentions of Nehemiah and those who share his vision against those who vehemently oppose the project fearing a loss of political control and income. As is often the case with those with wealth, their top priority is to make sure that regardless of how the political winds blow, their wealth and station remain intact. These Jerusalemites are not vehemently opposed to "the dream." It is just that the political and economic winds are shifting, and they are jittery about where it will settle.

Settle is the key word here, for the songwriter emphatically declares that this way of operating, so common in the world, will not *rest*. The Hebrew word, *nuach*, literally refers to pastured sheep. Thus it does not just connote stopping somewhere, but rather securing a field in such a way that the sheep can feed and lie down free from predators. The desire to have a "home" where one can settle in without threat is nearly universal. The lyricist reassures, however, that procuring it by "wickedness" will always be counterproductive. To hold on too tightly to what one has, especially that elusive sense of security, ironically leads to a perpetual uneasy sense. Thus in our day, when there is any kind of social, political, economic, and even environmental uncertainty, it is said that the markets are "nervous." There is hesitation and "hedging."

Unfortunately, those with wealth, power, estates, and influence all too readily appear to be secure while those who struggle to make ends meet must genuinely struggle with a huge amount of uncertainty. Sorely tempting it is to abandon high ideals in the face of day-to-day realities.

What rules Jerusalem as the expedition arrives is labeled "wicked." The term *rasah*, occurs throughout the poetic portions of the Hebrew bible and is mostly associated with violent behavior toward the weak and defenseless. They are enemies of God because they prey on the vulnerable, and in this respect the wicked are viewed as opposing God (Ps 10:2–3, Ps 9:17–18). The word is often associated with criminal activity especially violent.

It is easy for us to associate wickedness with gangsters or drug lords, but the lines between legitimate and illegal enterprises were nonexistent in the time of Nehemiah. Even today, however, these lines between markets and "black markets" are blurred.

The idea that "there is no peace for the wicked" (Isa 48:22) is undergirded by a reciprocal notion of violence. Violence only begets violence, or as sometimes popularly expressed: "What goes around comes around." It is a belief that regardless of appearance, violence towards others is "unsettling."

The wicked complete their entrapment around "the trusting ones" by being described in verse five as *crooked* and *evildoers*. The first word here invokes a sense of twisting or bending and is opposite the general idea of righteousness as being straight. The idea of twisting is further described by the verb "turn aside" which connotes wandering off. Anyone who has sat down with a car salesman to discuss price senses a winding, meandering discussion meant more to cloak than to clarify. It is definitely not straightforward.

Evil-doing (*ewen*) connotes bringing on trouble, sorrow, or misery. It is often found in parallel with "toil" so it carries a strong connection with hard labor. As with many Hebrew words, *ewen*, has both positive and negative denotations. Positively, it means wealth or strength. Interestingly, Hosea uses both (Hos 12:8), fusing unfaithfulness, idolatry, and adultery with economic and military strength. In a sense, one man's strength or wealth is another man's brokenness and poverty. *Ewen* is usually seen as the consequence of "crooked" ways. In other words, the corruption of some usually means the hard labor of others, and it is this very thing that works against righteousness, leads to veneration of false gods, and is denounced repeatedly by the prophets. Evil doing is often associated with lying speech and conniving.

There is one more characteristic of evil doing and it does not escape our lyricist. This kind of violence is contagious, and thus the prayer and warning is added: "lest the righteous set forth their hands." It works its way so subtly into the daily goings on of commerce that even those who wish to "do good" are tempted to ignore or turn away. We need not ponder long of how tempting this kind of evil is. One, especially one who has wealth and is part of the aristocracy, either cheats or manipulates the system to one's advantage or he may not be in that class for very long. Historically, the wealthy tend not to advocate for economic fairness. The singer here is fully aware that the lure of wealth easily overtakes "righteous" intensions.

It is especially unsettling "in the midst of the land allotted to the righteous." In an ironic flip-flop, the singer boldly asserts that the most unsettling thing for the wicked is the righteous, already defined as those trusting in the Lord.

The word "allotted" is a good one here because we can easily make the connection with "lot" and "lottery." Real estate in the ancient world was awarded by divine "lottery." Literally, it was determined by casting lots—throwing stones out and determining an outcome from it. The best comparison is throwing dice, and dice may in fact be a vestigial remain of such a practice. In basic terms, the gods gave it. This perspective was especially the case of small villages or farmers who had no other way to make claim on a piece of land. This notion of divine allotment was very powerful in the ancient world. This notion was intensified for Israel by the exodus event. The land was not "for sale" really. Thus the sin of kings so roundly condemned by the prophets is that they seized the inheritance of others.[3]

Carefully, the lyricist chooses the next phrase qualifying the fundamental right of deed. In Israel, one inherits property primarily by righteousness more than by genealogy. Again, it is easily tempting for one to consider himself righteous by virtue of belief in God, or as in the case of the Israelites, by birthright. The stark polarities combined with the rather general category of righteous and wicked set forth here readily lends itself to a misread. We can start by the context of the Psalm itself.

---

3. The strongest example is the seizure of Naboth's vineyard by Jezebel that sets the prophetic protest in motion (1 Kings 21). See also Deut 8.

First, the righteous are already identified with "those who trust in the Lord." Carefully, the lyricist chooses the next phrase qualifying the fundamental right of deed. In Israel, one holds property title primarily by inheriting *righteousness*. Ownership of the land is not determined by a property deed, by simple occupation of the land, or by inheritance, that is by divine right. It is by trusting in Yahweh.

I am reminded of the beatitudes in which Jesus says the meek shall inherit the land. To this day, biblical statements like "the meek shall inherit the earth" or that the land is assigned to those who trust in the Lord is absurd by all appearances, as some outspoken atheists of our day like to point out.

The righteous are contrasted with the scepter of wickedness discussed above. The righteous are those who structure their lives and livelihood in ways that are just. Righteousness, *tzadek*, is synonymous with justice and it has everything to do with treating others justly, especially economically. The lawgiver puts it succinctly:

> *You shall not keep two differing weights in your bag, one large and the other small; nor shall you keep two different measures in your house, one large and the other small. But use a true and just [tzadek] weight, and a true and just [tzadek] measure, that you may have a long life on the land which the LORD, your God, is giving you.* (Deut 25:13–15)

Second, the righteous are further characterized as those who "do good". The word for good, *tov*, mainly refers to visible expression, something clearly seen. A prime example is the creation story where God pronounces the goodness of creation only upon it becoming visible. In this respect, it was necessary for light to come forth before all other acts of creation. Only upon seeing something does God pronounce it as good.

I suggest that this is not necessarily how we tend to look on the value of goodness. We tend to look at it as something internal, hidden, and conceptual. Goodness does have this aspect to it as will be discussed below, but we should be leery if it rarely finds visible expression. The Hebrew simply converts "good" into a verb, something like: "I am *gooding* about today." Good creates value. Again, the singer understands clearly that the wickedness is being played out in reality; mainly in the way humans with resources are behaving toward those with little resources.

Third, they are "upright in their hearts". The word for "upright" (*yesher*) is a synonym of *tzadek*. Whereas *tzadek* connotes straight as opposed to crooked or winding, *yesher* pictures more of level and even as opposed to rocky or uneven. It counters evildoing. It eases the hard labor of over-bearing task masters.

Either way, the singer adds an important qualifier. Whereas with the words such as righteous, good, and evil refer to actions with ill or beneficiary consequences, here the singer addresses the inward aspect. Goodness, righteousness, and equity must be "in the heart." If we take our cue from the earlier Songs of Ascents, we can say that it is not just talk of equity, but something that proceeds from true desire and carries its way to real works of goodness.

Uprightness of heart is a quality that cannot stand on its own, but must be connected with trust in the Lord.

Peace be in Israel.

This statement seemingly comes out of nowhere. Outbursts of joy and confidence in the midst of despair are common in the Psalms. Jonah's prayer, to remind, is a prime example.

The singer laments a heightened tension here that seems irresolvable. Wickedness, evildoing, and corruption have the ascending ones surrounded, pinned down on all sides. The singer, however, strongly implies a return to his opening assertion. *Trust in the LORD.*

In this last curt line, the lyricist steps up his confidence, opting for the dream over the compulsion of reality. Both words, *shalom* and *Israel*, are conceptual more than factual. The Scriptures amply testify that the hope of a people united by the worship of one God and living together in a just society in such a profound way that the nations of the world would abandon their ways and follow the example of Israel was more rumor than reality.

A united people called Israel was only briefly glimpsed at over a six hundred year period under such legendary figures as Abraham, Moses, Joshua, David, Solomon, Hezekiah, and Josiah. That glimpse, butted up against the antithetical response of Israel and Judah, tormented the prophets. Apart from that, the accusers during the construction of the second temple were entirely correct:

> Let it be known to the king that the Jews who came up from you to us have arrived at Jerusalem and are now rebuilding this rebellious and evil city. They are raising up its walls, and the foundations

> *have already been laid. Now let it be known to the king that if this city is rebuilt and its walls are raised up again, they will no longer pay taxes, tributes, or tolls; thus it can only result in harm to the throne. Now since we partake of the salt of the palace, we ought not simply to look on while the king is being dishonored. Therefore we have sent this message to inform you, O king, so that inquiry may be made in the historic records of your fathers. In the historical records you can discover and verify that this city is a rebellious city which has proved fatal to kings and provinces, and that sedition has been fostered there since ancient times. For that reason this city was destroyed.* (Ezra 4:12–15)

Yet, despite the torturous history of a divided, bickering, warring, and obstinate people, there was an abiding current, a profound sense, a precious dream that all the resistance in the world could not squelch despite the dream being mostly imprisoned underground or at the bottom of wells. It is a dream born from the bulrushes of the Nile. It is an unnatural hope to humans, yet it relentlessly bullies its way into our existence doggedly pushing us forward the more the waters of the Reed Sea recede.

Truth be told, the unity of God's people today is more a fanciful afterthought than anything to be taken seriously. We keep breaking up into smaller and smaller entities, unable to reconcile differences. "Church" is equally relegated to a conceptual reality, as is "Israel" of old. We are all too familiar with the litany of sin, vice, lust for power, corruption, rivalry, and indifference that plague even a local gathering of believers, let alone the long history of the institution(s). Christians today are hard pressed to articulate a meaningful description of "the one holy apostolic Church." For the most part, we hardly understand what it is, nor can we muster a high value to it among the list of priorities for daily living.

Yet the Songs of Ascents beckon with each line and each step to keep on singing, keep on plodding, to keep looking upward. It invites us to join the expedition, continue the perilous ascent, and to welcome God's dream into our lives despite being surrounded by opposition. Even though for us Christians the life and resurrection of Jesus jettisoned us upward like nothing before in the story of God's people, we are reminded at Lent in the singing of these psalms that we are still ascending and our expedition is still in progress.

> *Blessed are the poor in spirit,*
>   *for theirs is the kingdom of heaven . . .*
> *Blessed are the meek,*

for they shall inherit the land.
Blessed are they who hunger and thirst for righteousness,
  for they will be satisfied...
Blessed are the clean of heart,
  for they will see God...
Blessed are they who are persecuted for the sake of righteousness,
  for theirs is the kingdom of heaven. (Mt 5:3, 5, 6, 8, 10)

8

Psalm 126

THERE IS A SENSE in this song that the expedition is cresting its long sought after objective. The climbers have breached through a daunting obstacle and have made a final push to the summit. They have arrived at the threshold of the temple itself. Shouts of joy burst out where once desperation cried. Giddy laughter congeals with tears of relief. The pilgrims sifted the soil in the hands and kissed its walls. They kissed each other! It had mainly been a fanciful hope wrapped in sleepy images butted up against stark realities to the contrary. The dream had become real and the reality a dream. Now, each step springs the expedition upward with quicken pace. Laughter ascends to shouts of joy and joy to affirmations of God's greatness. God's greatness bears repeating as the expedition now turned procession bounds upward in spirals of joy.

    Climbing high altitude peaks as a child did not seem to get easier with experience for me. There was always the labored breathing, the weighty lead feeling in the legs, the compulsion to sit down and not get up, the whines of "how much farther," the worry of amassing dark clouds and accelerating winds. It was funny then, when my brothers and I would catch a bulls-eye view of the summit. Instantly, all drudgery vanished as rival brothers race to the top. Yes, running at fourteen thousand feet shocks the lungs in an anaerobic frenzy, but who cares. The goal is within grasp!

    When we reach the top, we first bend over in heaving gasps for air. Imagine then, our bewilderment as we realize that the tip of ground we are standing on is not the top. It was a false summit. As we come to the sober realization, we must once more gather our wits and recalibrate our objective. All is not in vain, however. We have come too far to turn back, and now we see what the false summit had blocked from our view. We see more clearly even in disappointment the goal set before us.

The arrival at a "false summit" is quite evident in this psalm. Barely had the expedition caught their breath and the groggy pilgrims wiped the dreamy sleep from their eyes before the realization hits them. This is not the summit.

There is a spiraling kind of interplay in here that speaks to us as much as to the original recipients of the song. It is the false summit that intensifies the polarity between the fulfilled and the unfulfilled, between dreams and reality, between what is and what needs to be.

In this song, joy partners with sorrow; "they" pair up with "us," laughter with tears, abundance with barrenness, hard endless toil with rewards, turning back with doubling down on the future, returning with reconstitution, repentance with resurrection.

When the LORD brought back those who returned to Zion,

The exhilaration of the moment immediately focuses on the primary orchestrator of the Jews' joyous return. Yes, they *went out* from Babylon, but the Lord *brought them back*. This bi-directional action is reminiscent of the Hebrews' great escape from Egypt. Even though Pharaoh *spit them out* and the Israelites *went out*, it was the Lord who *brought them* out like a fisherman reeling in his line. No one has ever come to God on his or her own without the Lord baiting, luring, and reeling him in first.

The tension of the fulfilled and the unfulfilled in this opening line spills over into the very translation of the verse. Scholars struggle with the verb tense, some using past, some present, some future.[1] In liturgical time, the time of the Lord's action dance with each other. They play off of each other.

The translation puzzle centers over a word play with what the Lord has or is doing—returning or restoring (*shuv*)—and the object of that action—"those who returned to Zion" or the "fortunes of Zion" (*shivat*). The trouble centers around the word used to describe the object of the Lord's action to return or restore. Some understand *shivat* as derived from the same word as return, *shuv*. Thus, the Lord has "returned" (*shuv*) the "returning ones" (*shivat*). Others, however, believe *shivat* comes from

---

1. The NJPS places the verb tense in the future: "When the Lord restores the fortunes of Zion . . . we shall be filled with laughter."

a word that means "captive" or that which was "captured" (*shavah*). Thus *shibat* carries more the weight of "restore the captivity of," to reverse the consequences of captivity. It pictures not only a release of captives, but also a restoration of everything that was plundered. It is not only being released from prison, but also being granted a full restitution of everything that was unjustly taken.

One thing is certain. *Shivat* was a buzzword generated by the exilic prophets to signal God's great reversal of the exile. It was an umbrella term synonymous with salvation. A critical part of that salvation was, of course, the return of those in exile but it encompassed much more.[2]

For one, the term reminisces over a time in the past when "Jacob prospered." It is not easy to locate precisely what time in the past that was. To speak of some romanticized vision of prosperity past is to collide with the thorough going condemnation of the prophets. They struggled relentlessly and often times hopelessly against the lure of wealth that created opulence at the expense of the poor. Regardless, the bottom line was always that the people of God abandoned the covenant.

There was one time that is spoken of in terms of a kingdom of prosperity that made every attempt to have the covenant front and center—the reign of Josiah. Although short-lived, the time of Josiah did experience a time of prosperity centered on a covenant commitment from the king on down.

There are several other features associated with the "fortunes of Zion" (*shivat*) all of which relate to the great reversal of the exile. These features are spoken of frequently in the Songs of Ascents and were experienced in the reign of Josiah.

A joyous union primarily expresses Zion's fortune with God. It is the gathering and worshipping community that is Zion's fortune. But even more so, it is the One "housed" in Zion who is the true treasure.

> *The LORD is exalted, enthroned on high.*
> *he fills Zion with right and justice.*
> *That which makes her seasons lasting,*
> *the riches that save her are wisdom and knowledge;*
> *the fear of the LORD is her treasure.* (Isa 33:5–6)

The gathering of God's scattered people is salvation indeed.

---

2. The summary of "the fortunes of Zion" or "the fortunes of Jacob" provided here is derived from the following pictures of restoration where the word *shivat* is found in: Isa 19:24–25, Jer 30–31, Ez 16:59–63, 39, Deut 30, Ps 14.53, 85.

> *At that time, says the LORD,*
> *I will be the God of all the tribes of Israel,*
> *and they shall be my people* (Jer 31:1).

The gathering of God's lost sheep will be cause for tremendous rejoicing. The pilgrims of Psalm 126 are actually experiencing what Jeremiah could only wish for:

> *"Rise up, let us go to Zion,*
> *to the LORD, our God."*
> *For thus says the LORD:*
> *Shout with joy for Jacob,*
> *exult at the head of the nations;*
> *proclaim your praise and say:*
> *The LORD has delivered his people,*
> *the remnant of Israel.* (Jer 31:6–7)

The Gospel of Matthew repeatedly points to the gathering activity of Jesus as a sure sign of the coming kingdom, and we should not fail to miss that each time we gather together for worship and a shared meal, we are participating in fulfilled prophecy. The greatest "fortune of Zion" is the great reunion of God and humanity. It was, is, and will be a cause of great joy.

> *He who scattered Israel now gathers them together,*
> *he guards them as a shepherd his flock . . .*
> *Shouting, they will mount the heights of Zion,*
> *they come streaming to the LORD's blessings.* (Jer 31:10–12)

The return of God's people is also signaled by a profound repentance. The people will truly desire God's will and listen to his words. This turn around will not just be in the head, but in the heart as well. The return comes first of all in the land of captivity when one *brings to mind* the covenant with Yahweh and turns toward the Torah with *all your heart and soul* (Deut 30:6). Out of a loving response to God, the land itself will produce its fruits. Blessing will flourish (Deut 30:5, Jer 31:5, 12–14).

These pictures of restoration make clear that the prosperity for all is due to righteousness and justice flowing out from Zion. Whole-hearted adherence to the righteous and just demands of the covenant generates prosperity. *Shivat* signals a release from those who captured the people of God. The pasturing rest is not just from those who would attack the people of God with threatening armies (Isa 11:6–9, Ez 39:9–10), but even more so from those who impoverish the land through economic injustice.

Several psalms share strikingly similar sentiments as Psalm 126 in this regard.

In Psalm 14, *shivat* is synonymous with a salvation that primarily is expressed by economic equity. The "fool" who says there "is no God" is an economic atheist (Ps 14:1). He is one who says that God is not involved in business. This kind of atheist is "corrupt" "vile" and "bad." His conniving ways are contagious, sorely tempting the righteous (Ps 14:2).

The portrayal of an economic atheist in Psalm 14 leaves little doubt that the corrupt, evil, vile, and hater of good atheist is primarily one who disregards economic justice.

> *Will all these evildoers never learn,*
>   *they who eat up my people just as they eat bread?*
> *They have not called upon the LORD;*
>   *then they shall be in great fear,*
>   *for God is with the just generation.*
> *You would confound the plans of the afflicted,*
>   *but the LORD is his refuge.*
> *Oh, that out of Zion would come the salvation of Israel!*
> *When the LORD restores the well-being of his people,*
>   *then shall Jacob exult and Israel be glad. (Ps 14:4–7)*

These same words are found in Psalm 53, but that psalm adds a line in verse five specifically setting God's vehement opposition to the "evildoers."

> *For God has scattered the bones of your besiegers;*
>   *they are put to shame because God has rejected them. (Ps 53:6)*

In Psalm 85, *shibat* connects the very land to the Lord's favor and liberation. In a real sense then, *shibat* refers to captives and that which was captured. This is what makes the economic injustice so grievous. Those returning are still "captives" by economic hardship.

In another sense, the land itself was captured. The archeological evidence points to a great destruction of the land and its resources in the aftermath of both the northern Assyrian and the southern Babylonian conquest. The prophets speak of the land laying fallow, hence having a Sabbath rest.

Psalm 85 connects the captivity more directly with the sin of the people. Because of the general language of the Psalms, it is easy to read this in that kind of personalized Christian way. The sins of the people were more of a personal moral nature. But if read more from the perspective of

Psalm 14 and the prophets like Amos and Hosea, we know exactly what kind of "sins" are being addressed. It is precisely because the people of God did not take responsibility for each and every covenant member that God gave up his protecting presence and the land was captured.

This psalm makes clear that goodness—reflected in a bounty of the land—is largely dependent on qualities of the covenant people:

> *Kindness and truth shall meet;*
>   *justice and peace shall kiss.*
> *Truth shall spring out of the earth,*
>   *and justice shall look down from heaven.*
> *The LORD himself will give his benefits;*
>   *our land shall yield its increase.*
> *Justice shall walk before him,*
>   *and savation, along the way of his steps. (Ps 85:11–13)*

The fortunes of Zion are really a unified people of God entered into a celebration of the covenant. If this is truthful, authentic worship, then what will come forth from Zion is a righteousness that permeates all of life, particularly a life that produces blessing for *everyone*.

Thus, the fortune of Zion is when everyone shares in the blessing and prosperity of the land. This profound truth or vision is what so tormented the prophets of Israel. In a plethora of ways, sometimes shocking and offensive, they tried to shake Israel out of its own twisted sense of righteousness—You cannot smugly pronounce God's blessing on yourself when your neighbor stands there with nothing! One cannot advocate freedom while enslaving others.

At the beginning of Psalm 126, there is truly acknowledgement, thankfulness, and joy being expressed because the congregation has experienced a salvation from God in the very fact that God has returned his people to Zion. If we place this psalm in the time of Nehemiah, we then are reminded that this restoration has been on going for over 50 years.

And it is still occurring. But as the expedition continues to ascend to the Holy Mountain, we are reminded that the return and the restoration have only just begun. This song expresses the deep interplay of our own struggle, between what is fulfilled and what is yet to be fulfilled, between our own encounter with God and the stark reality of a violent and extremely unjust world we still live in and to which our own sin still contributes to.

We were like those who dream.

It is this tension between what is and what we know should be (especially we who are informed by God's revelation of Himself in Jesus) that leads the singer to the next line: *we were like those who dream.* The active participle gives the sense here of something ongoing. It is being caught up in a dream. It is the moment when one has dreamed of being somewhere all of one's life and then she actually finds herself there. It is that adrenaline moment when something so deeply longed for finds human expression.

The dream of course, was the restoration of Zion. It was a dream that captivated every faithful Israelite even in the darkest of times. Americans also speak of a dream. It is a picture of how society should be. These kinds of dreams drive the corporate psyche of a people or nation. Dreams like these paint an ideal, which can turn into a nightmare or a lie.

The title of a humorous book aptly describes the danger of dreams that take hold of a people—*America, Again: Rebecoming the Greatness We Never Weren't.*[3] Simply put, dreams are prone to distortion and exploitation. We dream romanticized visions of our "beginnings" or of some Camelot period. Dreams like these serve as guides for returning to "the way things were." They tend to erase complication and place things in stark contrasts, especially between the bad guys and the good guys. The Tea Party movement in America over the past few years is a shining example of how a particular version of a nation's past has much more to do with the current conflict over a nation's future. It is more a *reaction* to the current political situation than a genuine or accurate *remembrance* of the past.

Since my earliest experiences as a Christian, I have been filled with visions of how to live my life as a Christian or what church life should be like. There have been times when I have been with a group of Christians and have experienced "mouths filled with laughter" and sang songs "full of joy." I have lived and still experience on occasion Christian community where the fellowship and love is genuine and daring.

But I've experienced in those very same communities bitter breakdowns in relationship and disastrous dissolution of communal bond. I have seen people lose faith completely because of it. I would dare say that many Christians have experienced something similar. It is especially the case for those who dare to take Jesus more serious than occasionally going to a church service and putting some money in the basket. Inevitably

---

3. Colbert, *America Again.*

in the midst of communal crisis, there are some whose call for a return to some pristine simplicity around the "fundamentals" or "origins" becomes a suffocating slave master, shutting off any avenue for true renewal and a way forward. Their picture of the past is more dictated by a desire to control the present.

Dreams are dangerous if they become dictatorial ideologies, if they are really the product of our own imagination. Dreams lean more toward false images of us and drive toward self-serving ambition. Following one's dream often leads to the negation of another's hope. It often tends to think that natural and human resources ought to be at the service of the dream, leaving a trash heap of resources and ruined lives.

Dreams of restoration became a major source of contention between the prophet Jeremiah and the prophets employed by the Temple. This conflict is especially pertinent to our psalm here because that conflict had to do with competing "dreams" of Zion. The court prophets saw dreams in which God would always defend Zion regardless of how God's people were behaving toward one another. To the contrary, Jeremiah insisted that there would be no peace for Jerusalem if they did not repent. Jeremiah's call to repentance was crucial precisely because he was led by a counter-vision, a vision that is at the heart of Israel and its relationship with God. It is not a vision born of kings in palaces or corporate boardrooms, but of stormy threatening sky over the turbulent waters of the Reed Sea or the crucified Jesus. It emerged from the mud-clogged wheels of chariots mired in their own relentless pursuit of power, spinning wheels bogged down in their own impotence at the flight of terrified slaves.

The song of victory at the Reed Sea is the original song of Israel (Ex 15:1–18). All other dreams are smoke and deception if they don't align with that song. The Songs of Ascents beckon us in our time of repentance to continually ascend to the open heaven. Part of repentance is allowing God's dream for humanity to overtake our own dreams.

Then our mouths were filled with laughter, and our tongues with shouts of joy

Liturgically, there is a stair-stepping effect centered on joy throughout this song. The word *rinah*, translated "shouts of joy," is repeated three times in this psalm as a way to move the congregation upward and forward. It is like the mountaineer's step my dad taught me for negotiating the sometimes scary lack of breath one experiences climbing at high altitude. The lack of oxygen makes one feel like "I just can't take another step." Lemon drops are of no help up there. So, Dad would instruct: take two or three steps up. Stop and take one or two slow and deep breaths. Then, two or three steps up. Then . . . It requires a methodical patience with less focus on the summit or a cushy grassy spot to plop down. But it keeps one moving, and sometimes that is one of the more important actions we take as disciples of Christ—plod on, plod on, plod on; stop, rejoice, rejoice; then, plod on . . .

Joy and *gladness* describe the greatness of the Lord most often expressed at a festival or to put it in more modern terms, a party. It is most readily connected to the harvest festival, celebrating the abundance of harvest. Since the Songs of Ascents make consistent references to the land, it is likely that happiness is the experience of receiving the fruit of the land that once was lost to them. But it is equally important to stress the corporate nature of such joy. It is the joy of shared prosperity of a unified people. It is as the psalm states:

> *The lowly shall eat their fill;*
>   *they who seek the LORD shall praise him.*
> *"May your hearts be ever merry!" (Ps 22:27)*
>
> *Give thanks to the LORD for he is good,*
>   *for his kindness endures forever.*
> *Who can tell the mighty deeds of the LORD,*
>   *or proclaim all his praises?*
> *Happy are they who observe what is right,*
>   *who do always what is just.*
> *Remember me, O LORD, as you favor your people;*
>   *visit me with your saving help,*
> *That I may see the prosperity of your chosen ones,*
>   *rejoice in the joy of your people,*
>   *and glory with your inheritance. (Ps 106:1–5)*[4]

Shouts of joy (*rinah*) carry a similar meaning as the word that starts off the Songs of Ascent in Palm 120:1. It is a crying out, either in joy, distress, or complaint. Most important here is that it is a corporate and very vocal expression. It is often translated as exaltation, but this a tad too religious in its depiction. One would do better to imagine the frenzied,

---

4. Psalm 106 goes on to confess the sins of the people for "acting wickedly" by *not* acting justly toward the poorer members. The voice of the one in this psalm is one who has not enjoyed the shared prosperity of Israel.

raucous shouts at a rock concert or sporting event than the polite applause of a symphony concert. (Although, those who've been to operas know the boisterous exuberance expressed in the audience's approval: "Bravo!" "Bravo!"). This kind of outward corporate expression is of course rarely if ever experienced in a liturgy so we only make pious connections through analogy.

Then they said among the nations: "The LORD has done great things for them."

Here we have the first switch in perspective, going from "we" and "our" to "they", and in this song, it again reflects the tension of the fulfilled and the unfulfilled. The important perspective, however, is that it is from those ascending Zion in liturgical procession.

The insertion of "they" is abrupt and vague. For one, it is the only mention in the Songs of Ascents where those "outside" the procession are *not* spoken of in terms of bitter enemies who are opposing the expedition. Most of the discussion of "the nations" in the Old Testament tends toward viewing the nations as those who oppose Israel and God. Here, "they" are broadly identified as the nations, and to this extent, we probably have a mixture of truthful reporting and theological idealism. It goes back to the dream.

Surprisingly, "the nations" are spoken of very little in the Bible. In one perspective, Israel is to be a "holy nation" and a "kingdom of priests" that would be the source of blessing to all nations, and hence fulfill the blessing of Abraham (Gen 10). Another perspective envisions Israel as the model nation to which all the nations of the world would desire to emulate (Isa 2:1–5). In this psalm, the nations speak as if to offer an encouraging word. This is a rare perspective in the Old Testament.

To remind, the restoration of temples was an imperial policy of the Persians that equally applied to temples across the empire. Even the Babylonian temples were restored. This saying may simply be a kind of polite acknowledgement. Given that the more localized "nations" in Palestine around the time of Nehemiah would hardly be glad at the prospect of an emerging Jerusalem, the saying probably came from people more remote, perhaps from the Persians themselves who were promoting such policies. The Persians did have an official presence in the city.

Most certainly, the Bible reserves a rather scathing recollection of Edom who especially aided the Babylonians in their scourge of Judah. Samaria, Syria, and Egypt also gladly watched the demise of Jerusalem as a way to advance their own situation or to ward off the Babylonians. The deepest remembrance of being "scattered among the nations," however, focuses on the deep breach of covenant by God's people. The gift of land and home was forfeited, mainly because God's people no longer saw the land as gift, but of a right won by extortion and power grabbing.

In a liturgical historical rehearsal of Israel, the people are reminded that God Himself had "handed them over to the nations":

> *And the LORD grew angry with his people,*
>   *and abhorred his inheritance;*
> *He gave them over into the hands of the nations,*
>   *and their foes ruled over them.*
> *Their enemies oppressed them,*
>   *and they were humbled under their power.*
> *Many times did he rescue them,*
>   *but they embittered him with their counsels*
>   *and were brought low by their guilt.* (Ps 106:40–43)

Later in the Psalm, the decree of Darius is recalled:

> *He* [God] *won for them compassion*
>   *from all who held them captive.* (Ps 106:46)

The next line in the psalm demonstrates the tension and the progression of a mighty act of God in gathering the people of God from among the nations. Here it is a prayer that God would *continue* to gather his people from the nations, and this occurrence would be a great source of thanksgiving and praise for God's people.

> *Save us, O LORD, our God,*
> *and gather us from the nations,*
> *That we may give thanks to your holy name*
> *and glory in praising you.* (Ps 106:47)

The gathering of a scattered people in praise and thanksgiving is then a major sign that God's kingdom is being reconstituted. For many like Nehemiah and Ezra, the establishing of worship at the temple in Jerusalem becomes critical.

The last line of Psalm 106 parallels the sentiment expressed in Psalm 126. This saving act of God is cause for "all the people" to praise and give thanks.

> *Blessed be the LORD, the God of Israel,*
>   *through all eternity!*
> *Let all the people say, Amen! Alleluia.* (Ps 106:48)

It is possible that "the people" here only references Israel, but it may also extend to those mentioned above who "pitied" the captives.

In the height of the iconic vision of Zion during the days of Josiah, the dream was that Zion would be "the highest of mountains." This metaphor commonly used to express the utter dominance of an empire was applied to Zion, but the central importance and influence of Zion was rarely envisioned as a dominance of military might and economic power, but of the overwhelming presence of the Lord and His glory that would subdue humanity's aggression and oppression and compel "the nations" to succumb to a just and righteous way of living in the world.

> *Observe them carefully, for this will give evidence of your wisdom and intelligence to the nations, who will hear of all these statutes and say, "This great nation is truly a wise and intelligent people." For what great nation is there that has gods so close to it as the LORD, our God, is to us whenever we call upon him? Or what great nation has statutes and decrees that are as just as this whole law which I am setting before your today?* (Deut 4:6–8)

The LORD has done great things for us, we are glad.

The nations' acknowledgement of God's greatness is mainly used here to set up the second part of the verse by way of encouragement. The long road back for the people of God (and for us even today) was fraught with discouragement, disappointment, and tension. It is easy sometimes to give in to despair. This verse plays off the acknowledgement of "outsiders" to encourage those people. "Look, even our captors acknowledge that our God is acting on our behalf." This we affirm in our continued ascent: "Yes, that is right! The Lord has done *great* things for us and we will be glad about that."

The Eastern Christian perspective on sin places a large emphasis on dispositions that lead to actions or inaction. In this regard, one hears scattered throughout the liturgical prayers the occasional mention of the sin of despair. It is one of the primary sins mentioned in the prayer of St. Ephrem that is repeated throughout the Great Fast:

> *O Lord and Master of my life,*
> *Take from me the spirit of sloth, despair, lust of power, and idle talk.*
> *But give rather the spirit of chastity humility, patience and love to thy servant.*
> *Yea, O Lord and King,*
> *Grant me to see my own transgressions*
> *And not to judge my brother,*
> *For blessed art Thou unto the ages of ages. Amen.*

Some might take the request to remove despair as almost offensive, sounding as if it views depression as wrong or even evil. Certainly, Eastern piety does not advocate some kind of smiley-happy-face piety nor seek to deny feeling low sometimes. It does, however, seek the direct help of Jesus in warding off a true enemy of faith—hopelessness.

If confessions were told, I despair at times. American types of Christianity seem to express the opposite of the gospel of Jesus, and to this extent it is odd how "lust of power" is included in the list that seems to target laziness and depression. Believing St. Ephrem to be one who is careful with his words, I assume there is an important connection here, and there is. The use of a little force can be effective in preventing sin. We can always *make* people line up with what we think are Christian values. After all, the world would be a better place for it, even if people are not acting out of genuine conviction. The Church, to our shame, too readily gives in to the temptation to buddy up to power.[5]

The songwriter here is echoing the same sentiment. If the book of Nehemiah is read along with these psalms, a mostly negative situation is depicted, one which has already been talked about in this book. One is tempted, then and now, to be overwhelmed with the facts—this "dream" will not work, not in this world. It is not realistic. What seems to surround the believer is trouble, not the Lord.

This leads to the critical importance of thanksgiving. Having been unemployed and underemployed for the past several years, I have found

---

5. One of the more cutting parts of St. Ephrem's prayer also directs me to focus more on how all those sins I see in my fellow Christians is working in my own life: *Grant me to see my own transgressions and not to judge my brother.*

myself saying along with many others that I never thought I would be in this situation at my age. I have despaired at times. But almost like a rebuke, I've been reminded of what great things God has done for me, the primary one being that I know about Jesus and have learned to trust God through Jesus. This, I should constantly affirm and "be glad" about.

> *This is the LORD's gate*
> *the just shall enter it.*
> *I will give thanks,*
> *for you have answered me*
> *and have been my savior (Ps 118:20–21)*
>
> *You are my God, and I give you thanks;*
> *O my God, I extol you.*
> *Give thanks to the LORD, for he is good;*
> *For his kindness endures forever (Ps 118:28–29)*

Near the end of the Pre-sanctified service, the choir sings while the church participates in the Eucharist: "Taste and see. Taste and see, that the Lord is good."

The tension is felt in this line, the tension of what has truly happened and what has not happened yet. Indeed the tension exists precisely *because of* God's great saving acts. We should not allow the repetition of the word "great" to numb us. That the God of Israel *brought his people back* to their homeland is truly astounding. Ranier Albertz, a prominent Old Testament theologian, put it this way: "It is one of the great miracles of human history that the exile, the loss of Israel's national and territorial integrity, did not spell the end of Israel's history."[6] As the prophet Ezekiel describes in a vision, it is like dry parched bones reassembling themselves, taking on flesh again, and becoming living human beings (Ez 37). God' people who were once dead and non-existent have become alive again.

We should not neglect to see in this verse a foreshadow of Christ's resurrection and our own. In the crucifixion of Jesus, the Lord *has done great things* for all of us. We who were estranged from God have been "brought back." Jesus rebukes his followers for failing to see these wisps of the resurrection in the Old Testament (Lk 24). He calls them "foolish" for not seeing; even so, he is compassionate and goes on to explain that the *whole story of Israel* has been steadily marching toward his passion.

---

6. Albertz, *Israel in the Exile*, 2.

The Eastern liturgical tradition is designed in a particular way that wonderfully plays with the tension of the now and not yet aspect of salvation. Fundamentally, it sets the resurrection of Jesus as a clear demarcation and point of no return. Thus every Sunday, regardless of any seasons of repentance, is a resurrection Sunday. We always sing resurrection songs to begin our entrance into the Eucharist.

A no more telling display of this interplay is the Vespers of Forgiveness which is the service that ushers in the Great Fast in the Christian East. At the end of that liturgy, each person bows before every member of the congregation one-by-one and asks for forgiveness. This act is in direct response to Jesus' exhortation that without forgiveness toward one another, God's forgiveness does not make sense.

While the congregation goes through this process, the choir sings the resurrections songs of Pascha. Thus, even in our descent into a season of repentance, we are reminded of what "great things" have already happened in the passion of Jesus. We are compelled even when we take stock of our own parched state because of sin to carry the reality of God's salvation joyfully in our hearts. "The Lord has already done great things; we are glad."

The interplay of rejoicing and repentance is played out in a story in the book of Nehemiah. There was a great gathering of all the people to celebrate the Lord's favor and to beseech him for a successful harvest. As Ezra reads from "the Book of the Law," the people's celebration turns to mourning as they realize their waywardness from the covenant: ". . . for all the people were weeping as they heard the words of the law" (Neh 8:9). But Ezra and Nehemiah exhort the congregation: *Go, eat rich foods and drink sweet drinks, and allot portions to those who had nothing prepared; for today is holy to our LORD. Do not be saddened this day, for rejoicing in the LORD must be your strength* (Neh 8:10).

**Restore our fortunes, O LORD,
  like the water courses of the Negeb.
May those who sow in tears
  reap with shouts of joy.
He that goes forth weeping,
  bearing the seeds for sowing,
shall come home with shouts of joy
  bringing his sheaves with him.**

The second half of this psalm turns in several ways. There is an appeal to make the dream more real. Keep the restoration going even while the current situation continues its sorrowful march. But it wraps the whole song in prophetic hope.

Here, we get the kind of agricultural orientation of the Songs of Ascents that reflects the rural population's struggles and desires. It reflects the solid connection the return to exile has with the land.

Here, we have the kind of play of language that sometimes backfires on us. The precarious description of farming is not metaphor or figurative language. It is real life reporting. It reflects the harsh reality of many returning exiles. Uprooting themselves completely, they traveled at great peril across harsh and dangerous terrain and arrived with an almost dizzying expectation of a dream come true. Upon arrival, however, they were plunged into a near chaotic, disheveled, bitterly divided land where the "landed" aristocracy is exploiting the *shivat*—the returning ones—making their condition worse than if they had never ventured.

There are times when I struggle deeply with whether I would have been better off never entering the Christian scene at all. Certainly, I would have been better off financially. Although the difficulties with "getting along" is no different than with any other group of people, the struggles are deepened by the kind of *expectation* connected with following Jesus. We are, in fact, called to "love one another," "honor one another," and to "do good" even to our enemies. I can't just turn away from someone, nor can I turn him or her away. Thus, we are called to "endure with one another," and to do the seemingly impossible—forgive one another over and over again, to be merciful as our Father in heaven is merciful.

The depiction of the *apiqim,* watercourses, is a fitting image for the whole psalm. I am sure that these dry, hard waterbeds on the border of the desert are similar to the ones I've seen at Joshua Tree National State Park. Although dry as a bone most of the year, one can see the obvious signs of when the spring rains turn these empty ditches into torrential rivers. One year I visited the area after an especially wet spring. I did not see flowing water then, only the remnants of standing water, but I did see the stunning results: beautiful wild flowers against the back drop of a normally browned and parched floor carpeted in green.

There is a dual current constantly flowing in this psalm. On the one hand, there is a current of anxiety and faint heartedness. There is the desperate situation of plopping dry seed on parched soil hoping against hope that if all conditions favorably collide, one will reap a harvest and ward off not only starvation, but also enslavement, being so debt ridden that one forfeits not only one's land but also one's family. The picture is grounded in the real life high stakes drama of mere survival. The farmer's tears drop like seed. As he turns around to look at a dim trail of seed upon dry soil, his own tears become the first drops of hope for the spring showers.

Concurrently, however, there are the *rinah*, songs or shouts of joy. Exuberant applause is the mountaineer's step to keep us moving forward and upward. Joy is the breath one must focus on for the moment, not the summit. It is the proper perspective to move in the present, to reflect on the past and to orientate toward the goal.

The appeal for restoration in verse four is pivotal, not only for this psalm, but also for our own expedition into repentance. The petition is none other than this: "Thy kingdom come, Thy will be done, on earth as it is in heaven." Thanksgiving is the foundation—the Lord has done great things for us. The songs or shouts of joy (*rinah*) are the pillars as we recollect the "good times" sponsored by "the goodness of the Lord."

> *Blessed are the poor in spirit,*
>   *for theirs is the kingdom of heaven.*
> *Blessed are they who mourn,*
>   *for they will be comforted.*
> *Blessed are the meek,*
>   *for they will inherit the land.*
> *Blessed are those who hunger and thirst for righteousness,*
>   *for they will be satisfied.* (Mt 5: 3–6)

9

Psalm 127

THE EXPEDITION HAD REACHED a summit, and after catching its breath, they allowed the sober realization to sink in. The final summit still awaits them. They now must reassess their position, take inventory, and recalibrate their bearings. Trust in the Lord is their energy supply (Ps 125) and joy is their breath (Ps 126). Sounds like Lent to me.

The next two psalms comprise a sermon on the mount. The temple sermon,[1] or a reading and interpretation of the Torah, was an ancient tradition that picked up new steam in the exile and post-exilic periods. Ezra is the prime example of a "teaching priest" who was devoted to studying and teaching the Torah so everyone could understand it (Neh 8:1–3). Without a royal sponsorship, the "Israel project" stressed adherence to the Torah by *every* Israelite as critical.

A Song of Ascents of Solomon

Gauging by the title, we have another special guest speaker from Israel's past. The congregation now hearkens back to the building of the first temple.

Psalm 72 is the only other psalm "of Solomon." There it is addressed *to* Solomon. It is as an inaugural address extolling the virtues of a righteous king. Psalm 127, however, sounds more like Solomon admonishing

---

1. The teaching of the Torah was actually in one of the outer courts of the temple (Neh 8:1–3). It has probable connections to communal activity "within the gate" as discussed below.

the people. There is a preachy tone to this psalm. It is a stern warning wrapped in an encouraging word. Sermons like these could be rather scathing rebukes (Ezra 10).

I have not witnessed the kind of radical and full-scale repentance described in the last chapters of Ezra. After hearing Ezra's rebuke, the people cried, and took radical action to compensate. A similar circumstance is described in Nehemiah (Neh 8).[2] Even though Eastern Lent is more rigorous than others, I confess that I do not experience any gut-wrenching sorrow or radical changes in behaviors. In Christian Eastern spirituality, a tradition of "the gift of tears" is long standing. Crying out in sorrowful tears is often mentioned in the Orthodox prayers during the Great Fast. I don't try to falsely manufacture such tears, but I do wonder why repentance does not go that deep for me.

In our day, people are aroused to radical committed change more by anger and rivalry than by a fundamental sorrow over the ravaging effects of sin on our world.

Taking a clue from Nehemiah (Neh 13:26–27), Solomon is one who knows the up and down sides of allowing the house to be built by the Lord. The mention of Solomon conjures up a ghost of Israel's past. It is within that precarious state of half-realized dreams, that Solomon interjects an admonition, a word that is both threatening and promising, one intended to push the faint hearted. From his own experience, Solomon warns of a smug self-confidence that presumes too much of God's grace and conversely of one's own ingenuity, hard work, privilege, and giftedness. All that one might think one has accomplished for God may in fact be worthless if in the end, God's concern for justice and righteousness is ignored.

This psalm falls in line with "royal" psalms which proclaim the righteous rule of Yahweh's king (Ps 2, Ps 72). Our psalm echoes many of the same themes. Most importantly, blessing and fruitfulness of the land will come primarily through a righteous and just rule that solidly defends the poor:

> The mountains shall yield peace for the people,
>   and the hills justice.
> He shall defend the afflicted among the people,
>   save the children of the poor,
>   and crush the oppressor . . .
> He shall be like rain coming down on the meadow,

---

2. Acts also mentions a radical response to the sermon of Peter (Acts 5).

> *like showers watering the earth,*
> *Justice will flower in his days,*
> *and profound peace, till the moon be no more . . .* (Ps 72:4,6–7)

> *For he shall rescue the poor man when he cries out,*
> *and the afflicted when he has no one to help him.*
> *He shall have pity for the lowly and the poor;*
> *the lives of the poor he shall save.*
> *From fraud and violence he shall redeem them;*
> *Aad precious shall their blood be in his sight.* (Ps 72:12–14)

In the context of the Songs of Ascents, we have arrived in Jerusalem only to be confronted with a rather humble temple building, a work in progress. The host city is vulnerable and disheveled. There are economic jitters among the aristocracy over whether the Nehemiah/Ezra revival will seriously undermine the economic vitality of their ventures. As we ascend the steps in procession, how might these words be heard? Who are the recipients?

Again, we must hearken back to the dominant theme of this second group of songs—*trust in the Lord*. There are competing voices in the city. Some are not worried about the temple at all, only commerce. They worry about the impact a fully functional temple of Yahweh might have on their profits. They worry, and legitimately, that the temple will once again become a flash point to set off yet another rebellion, this time from the Persian over-lords and yet again another violent campaign against the city. There is surely a great tension here. Some sixty years prior, Darius fiercely snuffed out the energetic hope of a renewed Davidic kingship. Nationalistic talk of an idyllic independent kingdom or empire like Solomon's was sure to raise the ire of the Persians who were graciously sponsoring the rebuilding of Jerusalem and the temple—albeit for a "return" on their capital investment.

But they also worry that the temple would become the right inspiration for the poor and debt-ridden rural inhabitance to advocate for "justice and righteousness" to permeate throughout the land. They may rally to demand their rights to their inheritance which is so prevalent in the Torah of Moses and in the prophets.

Some in the assembly have lost patience and determination to put up with all the infighting, the bickering, the arguments, the contention, the incompetence, and the petty squabbles. They need reminding that however painful the process, it must be done "the right way." One cannot cut corners if it is to be done right.

The last verse of this psalm gives a clue to where this whole song is going: *to contend with the enemy in the gate*. Whoever the enemy is, they are inside the city and a part of the worshipping congregation. Those who wish to be a part of the worshipping congregation must get past them. They are "within" in the gate.

This song is about our ascending entourage passing through the gate of judgment. There is a border patrol, a check point, a sentinel that blocks the way and can bring the long ascent to an abrupt and foreboding end: Access Denied. No Trespassing. We have all seen enough movies of armies taking over cities. No matter what, the attacking army must get through a gate. The war imagery is appropriate here.

Those "in the gate" control access to the temple. They control the city. The lines between brother and accuser are blurred. Everyone involved in the "Israel project" is trying to "build a house." They are trying to build a livelihood for themselves and for their children. But to everyone involved, both accuser and accused, Solomon echoes from times past: it is all worthless effort if it is not squarely centered on the Lord.

The thrice-repeated word, *in vain*, follows on the heels of the last psalm. With all the encouragement away from despair and hopelessness encountered so far in the Songs of Ascents, it is odd how this song drives toward that very thing—worthlessness—if *the Lord does not build the house*.

Unless the LORD builds the house, those who build it labor in vain.

Im Yahweh lo . . . shave'. Im Yahweh lo . . . shave'. "Unless the Lord does not . . . worthless." "Unless the Lord does not . . . empty." Yes, in English this is a double negative of sorts, but in Hebrew, the repeated phrase serves a double emphasis. For one, the *im..lo* formula expresses an emphatic oath, an imprecation, emphasizing a stark contrast of choices. It is like saying: You have your choice. You can either choose A or B, but you better not choose B.

The phrase also places the whole "Israel project" on God alone and hearkens back to the opening line of the Second Antiphon: *In the Lord*, place your trust. No Israelite within hearing shot of this phrase would fail to connect it with the third commandment: "You shall not lift up the Lord's name for worthless purposes."

In the case of the third commandment and our verse here, it speaks of a false, empty, and ruinous dependence on human effort, especially in the face of a crisis. Psalm 60:11 states it well: *Give us aid against the enemy, for the help of man is worthless.*

Even more so, the command sternly warns against hiding evil intent behind pious God talk.

> *If only you would destroy the wicked, O God!*
> *and the men of blood would depart from me!*
> *Wickedly they invoke your name;*
> *your foes swear faithless oaths. (Ps 139:19–20)*

Both Jesus and John denounce a gross abuse of piety that strips people of a livelihood and seals the deal with a "God bless you."[3]

Unless the LORD watches over the city, the watchman stays awake in vain.

Centuries earlier, Isaiah envisioned Zion as the center of the world in which all nations would ascend to the "chief among the mountains"(Isa 2:1–5). As a result, all peoples would *descend* the mountain equipped with God's *torah* that would effectively end human conflict.

Something of that vision is expressed in this psalm. The tiers of a society built on righteousness and justice are depicted here. The house of the Lord towers above (v1). The host city "watches over" the temple (v2), and both create a hub for thriving households (v3–5).

The house of the Lord towers above, inviting all to ascend to a joyous communion with Him who is "enthroned in the heavens." We as well as the Israelites of Nehemiah's day could readily envision "the house" as the temple built upon Zion, and that is certainly part of what is referred to here. Before the exile, however, the royal house was connected to the temple, so a very strong connotation of government is also inferred. A house refers to a society or kingdom, an integrated economic, religious, legal and political bond, as in "the house of David," "the house of Judah" or "the house of Jacob."

Just as important, this is the first reference to a fundamental longing that undergirds the Songs of Ascents. The Third Antiphon calls it out explicitly (Ps 132). The people of God are back in the land. They have

---

3. Mt 7:21–27, 25:31–46; 1 John 3:11–20

repopulated the city and rebuilt the walls. They are planting crops and reaping harvests. The temple is built. The people gather for worship and learn from the Torah. But there is no king, no anointed one, a messiah, the Christ. God's eternal promise to David stands as a gaping hole in the reconstruction project like a wounded ship half-submerged.

The extended family or tribe provides the fundamental building blocks for a kingdom house. The tribes have elders who provide local governess and representation in the larger "kingdom" or nation. The elders "judge at the gate" and legislate along with the temple priests and local magistrates appointed by the Persian king.

The ancient Israelites dreamed of a nice house to create a home in just as Americans do. The opposite of having a house in the ancient world was to "live in tents," to be transient, unsettled, a wanderer or immigrant. For the returning exiles, however, more critical than *having* a house, was *being part* of a house, to be incorporated into the fabric of a thriving kingdom. It is to have an inheritance, "a portion." In Hebrew, it is called the *nahalah* (Ps 127:3).

Anytime a group of people is violently uprooted from the land, a monumental breakup of family and social fabric occurs. For the American Indians, the American slaves, the survivors of the Holocaust, or countless other contemporary examples, the effects of this obvious truth last for generations. Even when people find a place to live and houses to dwell in, something restlessly nags the heart. They are no longer *connected*.

In God's great promise to David, the picture of the kingdom as a "house" bond together. There, God promises to "build a house" for David (2 Sam 7:27). This promise means much more than some dreamy, multi-chambered castle. It means: "I will establish your *lineage.* Your name will be remembered to successive generations. Here we can easily make the connection with another key word in Psalm 127:3: the *nahalah,* inheritance. Despite our notions of inheritance that lean more towards having a right to property or wealth, the Israelite idea firmly grounds it in gift with strong overtones of codependency. An inheritance is a portion that has been divvied out.

The essential character of *nahalah* as a gift that one shares creates a strong undercurrent associated with God's righteous laws and decrees and is a source of constant torment in the Psalms where this notion is thwarted. A *nahalah* cannot be traded away, used as collateral, forfeited to debt, stolen, or extorted. The owner is the Lord, and the beneficiaries are one's children.

We may also refer back to Psalm 122 and the idyllic picture of the city "housing" the Lord. We cannot neglect, however, the critical feature of God's kingdom promised to David. Only God can be the builder. The Bible contrasts kingdoms built by men and a kingdom built by the Lord in the starkest terms. The disparity torments the prophets and is the bottom-line source of "distress" that opens the Songs of Ascents.

That disparity ought to distress us if our season of penance is genuine.

Lest we think monarchies are a thing of the past, we should think again. Empire building is as popular as ever. Whether it is business, corporations, education, health, sports, politics, or religion, we humans drive our institutions toward utopia, shiny cities on the hill, beckoning as always our docile submission more than active participation. And of course, these imperial cities are always walled, keeping out all who do not belong.

The difference between a house the Lord builds and that of the man-made variety is often magnified in the Psalms.

Psalm 118 reverberates with several similar themes as Psalm 127. A distressed supplicant cries for help (Ps 118:5). His enemies surround him, conspiring to snuff out his life (Ps 118:10–12). Trust in the Lord (118:8–9) is the antithesis to trusting in "men" or "princes" whose help is worthless because it is connected to falsehood, conniving, and conspiracy.

The northern "house" of Israel fell to the ravaging Assyrian army. They conspired with other nations in a big plan to resist Assyria (Isa 7:1–9). They threatened Ahaz if Judah did not join. At the rebuke of Isaiah, Ahaz withdrew. The house of Israel was crushed. Hezekiah, the son of Ahaz, faced the Assyrian threat head on and alone, but took Isaiah's council and "trusted in the Lord."

> *It is better to take refuge in the LORD,*
> *than to trust in man.*
> *It is better to take refuge in the LORD*
> *than to trust in princes.* (Ps 118:8–9)

Miraculously, the Assyrian army withdrew. Judah was spared. This event spurred a great revival in Judah to which we owe much of the Scriptures. It was a daring yet humble act of trust that took the "rejected stone" (house of Judah) and made it the capstone of "the Lord's house" built on trust (Ps 118:23). Trust is the building material for a house "built strong by the hand of the Lord."

Trust in the Lord is the only stage-pass for entering the gates of the righteous (Ps 118:19–21). Entrance into the Lord's house requires humility, not hubris, for the supplicant understands the Lord's response to covenant breach (118:17–18).

Hezekiah's foundational trust inspired the returning exiles struggling to survive. The siege of Jerusalem by the Assyrian army provided a compelling analogy to those whose family and property were under "siege" from threatening creditors.

As in the Songs of Ascents, those under siege "cry out" to the Lord because there is no other (Ps 69:1–3). They are surrounded by conspiring foes seeking to devour. They are accused of "robbing" their creditors because they cannot pay back the debt (Ps 69:4). They face cruel justice "within the gate" as their creditors seize their inheritance. Their children, home, land, and citizenship is repossessed, they are overtaken (69:5–19). They asked for mercy, but received bitter herbs for food and vinegar to drink (69:21). They languish while the wicked gloat over their misfortune (Ps 69:26).

The supplicant knows how wrong this is and turns to the only righteous God "who hears the cry of the poor" (Ps 69:33). His only sacrifice is praise and thanksgiving since he can afford no other (Ps 69:30–31). He longs for the day when righteousness will be the rule of the land and justice its partner.

The last verses of Psalm 69 resonate with the vision of a reconstituted Israel so prevalent in the Songs of Ascents. Zion will be redeemed, the cities and towns rebuilt, and one's inheritance recovered for *those who love his name.*

These psalms, which starkly contrast a kingdom built by God and those of men, find their inspiration with certain prophets in Israel's past. I say "certain" prophets because it is often presumed that the prophets recorded in the Bible were the only ones around. We too easily assume that "had I been there," I would have listened to the prophets. But there were competing and confusing versions of "thus says the Lord" then just as there is now. For the most part, the prophets of the Bible were mostly scoffed at and ignored in their own time. They could not compete with the more popular version of: "Thus says the Lord, there will be peace and prosperity."

Listening to God's voice is a difficult task requiring diligence and training. A season of repentance is a time to tune-up our listening devises.

Amos sternly rebukes the people of God for expanding elaborate estates at the expense of the poor.

> *Therefore, because you have trampled upon the weak*
>   *and have exacted on them levies of grain.*
> *Though you have built house of hewn stone,*
>   *you shall not live in them!*
> *Though you have planted choice vineyards,*
>   *you shall not drink their wine. (Amos 5:11)*

The abuse was compounded by smug piety that used the collateral of those in debt as the sacrificial offerings in worship (Amos 2:8). Isaiah warns that a kingdom must be built on righteousness and justice towards the poor and not on "arrogance and pride of heart" (Isa 9:8). Jeremiah complains bitterly at the expansion of real estate gained from gross economic disparity:

> *Woe to him who builds his house on wrong,*
>   *his terraces on injustice;*
> *Who works his neighbor without pay,*
>   *and gives him no wages.*
> *Who says, "I will build myself a spacious house." (Jer 22:13)*

In contrast, both Jeremiah and Isaiah envision a rebuilding of a kingdom that is firmly established in justice and righteousness. In a passage that Jesus quotes, Isaiah describes the great reconstitution of Israel where "the poor" (those returning from the exile) will have good news preached to them and they will "rebuild the ancient ruins" (Isa 61).

> *They shall live in the houses they build,*
>   *and eat the fruit of the vineyards they plant;*
> *They shall not build houses for others to live in,*
>   *or plant for others eat. (Isa 65:21)*

It is in vain that you rise up early
  and go late to rest,
eating the bread of anxious toil,
  so he gives to his beloved sleep.

The preacher turns directly to his audience and with pointed finger exhorts. The target of such stern speech is left rather vague. For sure, they are people like us, who worry tremendously about the struggles of making ends meet.

They are hard workers, working long hours, yet they are anxious, very anxious. This exhortation could be a reference to those who are afraid to stop the markets in Jerusalem on the Sabbath (Neh 13:22).

There may be a subtle reason for the cryptic reference, for it points to a malady that plagues every devout person—pointing the finger at someone else's sins. Usually, we pardon our own sins by diligently seeking out pristine examples of our sin in another. Some famous person once used the analogy of extruding a plank out of one's own eye before attempting to pluck a speck out of someone else's (Mt 7:1–5). The prayer of St. Ephrem perpetually tugs us away from our proclivity: *Yea O LORD and King, help me to see my own transgressions and not to judge my brother.*

The truth is irrefutable in this regard: the abused become the abuser, the oppressed become the oppressor, and the revolution creates the reason for the next revolution.

Whoever the "you" are here, the preacher is sure of their diet: they eat bread *of anxious toil*. The term, *ha'etzavim*, describes an emotional torment, especially grief. It is to be vexed, hurt, pained even to the point of anger due to actions or words inflicted by humans. Interestingly, the definite article in front of the noun indicates a particularly well-known kind of grief, and there is plenty of it to go around because the word is in a plural form.

Anxious toil is a good translation here, and it speaks to one of the most common experiences of most humans on the planet. Our worries can overwhelm us between unpaid bills, tensions at work, or tensions of having no work. There is the unpredictability of the markets as well as the countless ways that an accident or illness can radically alter one's life. We worry about our loved ones and over dangers of all kinds. The verse here speaks of the day in and day out worries that don't ever go away. They are always there.

Equally ambiguous is the identity of "the beloved." The word of course conjures up memories of the Lord's love of David, whose name means "loved one." Solomon, however, was also "loved by the Lord" and Nathan the prophet named him "Jedidiah" meaning "beloved of the Lord" (2 Sam 12:25).

Even if this is a possible reference to the king or a messianic hope, it still relates to the faithful covenant member. The peace that a king enjoys is supposedly what the whole kingdom enjoys. As goes the king, so goes the kingdom. But there is a strong current that also insists that God loves all who are faithful to the Torah. This is especially the case with the second commandment where the rewards for obedience are visited "down to the thousandth generation, on the children of those who love me" (Deut 5:10).

It is possible that this line brings closure to the three vanities mentioned in verse one, referring to all three. God's love extends to the temple, the royal house, the city, and to the population both in and surrounding the city. Ultimately the building of the house on all levels has to do with a faithful adherence to the Torah.

In this regard, this verse strongly resonates with a prophecy given by Jeremiah before the exile (Jer 12).

Jeremiah complains, questions really, about Yahweh's notion of justice. He brings up one of the classic complaints of the Psalms, one which resonates not just with poor Israelites, but with poor people everywhere—Why do the wicked prosper and have a life of ease? (Jer 12:1–4). We can forget about the fine distinctions we have today between CEOs of large banks and a leader of a large drug cartel. It was way too obvious how most wealth was gained in the ancient world, shear extortion and exploitation.

Jeremiah continues with his complaint using the imagery of a planted field: *You have planted them; they have taken root;/ they keep growing and bearing fruit* (Jer 12:2). As he continues, he speaks to a kind of torment of mind, that eludes the wicked rich, but not those who are aware of Yahweh's covenantal stipulations: *You, O Lord, know me, you see me,/ you have found that at heart I am with you* (Jer 12:3).

Here, I will side step just a bit. Right here is for me proof positive that the exodus story really happened. This notion of being freed from the exploitation and slavery of the power machines of the ancient empires constantly drives its way into every part of the Hebrew Bible. That Jeremiah knows of Yahweh's gracious and miraculous acts and the covenantal responsibilities that result from it torments him in a sense. He cannot just go along with "the way things are." There is no better explanation for this profound sense that things can be and indeed need to be different than a living memory of a dramatic experience of radical reversal—slaves became free and empires got stuck in the mud. This "dream" with its basis in a real radical reversal is what pushes those on expedition to continue ascending until they get to Zion.

Jeremiah reveals two critical things about these wicked. They too are Israelites who call on the name of the Lord (Jer 12:2). They believe in God, and probably like Job's friends believe God has given them wealth.

Jeremiah alludes to this himself when he complains that Yahweh has planted them, given them root, and caused them to be fruitful. Second, Jeremiah directly attributes their wickedness to the famine and draught conditions of farmers (Jer 12:4).

The source of Jeremiah's complaint is clear. Many threaten Jeremiah with death if he keeps on prophesying doom on Jerusalem. There is a great parallel here with Nehemiah. The message is the same—stop doing what you are doing or else. The threat of death is a pretty good deterrent unless one has a competing word whose voice is equally threatening. And in Jeremiah's case, he did—the Lord. God answers Jeremiah similarly to those who face the loss of livelihood "at the gate." *Do not believe them* (specifically Jeremiah's own family), *even if they are friendly to you in their words* (Jer 12:6). The bottom line issue is trust.

In the Lord's response to Jeremiah's complaint, all the themes of our psalm powerfully resonate:

> *I abandon my house,*
>   *cast off my heritage.*
> *The beloved of my soul I deliver,*
>   *into the hand of her foes.*
> *My heritage has turned on me*
>   *like a lion in the jungle.* (Jer 12:7–8)

In the prophecy that follows, the Lord makes clear that this exploitation of land and people by the "wicked" will lead to a complete decimation of the land (Jer 12:9–13). The "vanity" of hard work is mentioned:

> *They have sown wheat and reaped thorns,*
>   *they have tired themselves out to no purpose;*
> *They recoil before the harvest,*
>   *the flaming anger of the LORD.* (Jer 12:13)

This "way of the wicked" that leads to prosperity all the while working a desolation of the land is referenced here as something that the Israelites acquired from their neighbors. In essence, they mimicked their neighbors way of doing things rather than listen to the Lord's way of doing things and this to their own destruction. The end result is that the Israelites are "uprooted" from their inheritance.

The Lord continues, however, and promises to have compassion on his people (His inheritance). Interestingly, the Lord speaks of his people returning to *their own* inheritance (Jer 12:15).[4] Most critically, this inheritance is based on the rejection of a loyalty to Baal and an adherence to "learning the ways of the Lord," and this applies both to the people of God *and* Israel's neighbors (Jer 12:17).

**Lo, sons are a heritage from the LORD,
  the fruit of the womb a reward.**

Of all the talk of what is at stake in "the dream," the second half of this psalm seems to interrupt it or at least forcefully interject an admonition to look or perceive things in the right direction. It beckons the ascender to avoid defining trust and faithfulness in terms of one's current economic situation. More than likely, the ones ascending are those referred to in the last psalm, *sowing seed with tears.*

The closing verses of Psalm 127 revolve around a *man* who is *happy* because he has properly and fully equipped his *sons* to *contend with the enemy in the gate.*

That sons are the *LORD's inheritance* and *reward* may hearken to the notion of the firstborn and Levites belonging to Yahweh. It may also refer to the royal Davidic line and to tribal affiliation. There is no preposition attached to the Lord here, making the interpretation a bit nuanced. Basically it states: "Behold, inheritance Yahweh, sons reward." The verses adamantly affirm what is powerfully at stake *for God* with both Israel as a people and as a land.

Even to this day, the issue of right proprietorship of Palestine is a serious and dangerous issue. The sound track to the Exodus movie boldly proclaims: "This land is mine, God gave this land to me." That Israel's claim to the land goes back to these very verses is indisputable, and so it appears to many that the Scriptures themselves advocate apartheid, discrimination, and forced emigration. This book is not about addressing those issues, as they are complex; we must clarify, however, what is the Biblical affirmation concerning land and the Lord's inheritance.

Most importantly, as is confirmed in the Songs of Ascents, the inheritance is the Lord's to give. No human being or group of human's can make an absolute claim on the land. Land as well as every good thing comes from God. The gift of land is framed in the book of Deuteronomy

---

4. There is a strong connection between God's inheritance of people and land, and the people's inheritance of God and land.

as a covenantal token or pledge to the Israelites. As the prophets so repeatedly reminded, one can only make claim to the land within the context of a reciprocal relationship with God. This required obedient responses to the covenant stipulations. The Israelites are duly warned—if they neglect the just and righteous stipulations of the covenant, the land itself will spit them out (Deut 28–39). This truth is powerfully portrayed in Isaiah's "song of the vineyard" (Isa 5) to which Jesus reiterates in his vineyard parables (Mt 20:1–16, 21:33–40). The Israelite's occupation of the land from Abraham to this very day is a "precarious landedness," and we would do just as well to have a similar position toward our own wealth. All is gift; therefore, I can give.

The latter part of Psalm 127 affirms what is most at stake *for God*—people. After all, He is "the lover of mankind." We came across this in our previous discussion of restoration in Psalm 126. The biggest part of "the dream come true" was in the very act of a people liturgically processing through the streets of Jerusalem and up the steps of the temple. It is our very singing of these songs during the Great Fast. It is in every gathering of even two or three around Jesus. It is in "the nations" drawn by a righteous, just and merciful rule pouring out from Zion to give thanks to "the maker of heaven and earth." It is in every Eucharist celebrated in every town, village and city around the world.

The children envisioned here are those with a bent toward living according to the Torah. It is here where properly building one's household and God building His household coalesce. It is in children living in just, righteous and loving ways where God is rewarded.

The word *hinah*, "lo" or "behold," signals an announcement in which the listener should take special heed, and in this case it points us to another aspect of repentance, which is to turn one's focus away from our worries, concerns, fears, doubts and anxieties and focus instead on something else. But we cannot simple try and deny the realities of our lives without affirming something in its place.

So far in this psalm, the emphasis has been on the wasted effort if one does not go about it the right way. As many a craftsmen knows, one needs the right tool for the right job and the right way to go about building the house, protecting the city, and making a living is to go about it the Lord's way. This does not mean passivity however. As already discussed, letting the Lord build the house is a signal phrase for taking heed to the covenant stipulations.

The important thing to notice is that the "sons" are primarily the LORD's inheritance and reward, not the father's.[5] It does *not* say sons are *your* inheritance and reward. The focus, oddly, is on what the Lord gets out of all the trouble of returning the Israelites to Jerusalem and rebuilding the city and the temple.

Oddly then, the *happy man* in these verses is primarily a reference to the Lord. It still is a reference to those obedient to the covenant, but it speaks profoundly about what is at stake in following the Lord. We can all too often engage in nitpicking over details and lose sight. Our reward, happiness, and pleasure are bound up in God's reward, happiness, and pleasure. This, for some, may appear rather selfish and self-centered on God's part. "Make me happy and give me what I want or I'll make your life miserable."

Yes, it can, until we look at what it is that God wants, what makes Him happy, and it is here where we must return to the dream. The dream of Zion is that the gates are open to all nations, that they are compelled to come because righteousness, justice and love come out of Zion. It is as Paul says in the New Testament; God wants "to sum up all things in Christ, in heaven and on earth" (Eph 1:10).

What makes God happy is the happiness of humans. Lest this become a circular argument, however, the affirmation here as well as throughout the Scriptures is that "Father knows best." He knows this because he has created us in His image and likeness. We are wired like God is.

What God wants for me, he also wants for others. The challenge of covenant living is to go about things in a way that procures blessing for all, not just for the few. It is precisely here, where we Americans come up pathetically short. Every other year we have elections, and we are terribly consistent in what is a bottom line for winners and losers—what is in it for me? Will I be better off than before? Whose policies will have a bigger impact on my wallet? This is somewhat legitimate, but this pales in comparison to what God wants. Until we come to the realization that it is not acceptable that I should live in comfort and security while most humans live in abject want and dangerous vulnerability, then my happiness will continue to be elusive.

The word "happy," *esher*, connotes a strong sense of the right way, the good way. It is a favorite wisdom word. It doesn't mean doing something in some kind of formulaic procedural way, guaranteeing a positive

---

5. The NJPS translation brings this out by capitalizing "His": "the fruit of the womb, His reward."

outcome. Wise living, as so aptly brought out in a reading of Proverbs, has more to do with living in a balanced, reasoned and consistent way, but most of all living in the "fear of the Lord," another code phrase for the covenant. To live in the fear of the Lord means to live reverently *referring* to God's desires above our own and *deferring* to God's desires when we lose sight of who we are, what we are doing, what is important, and as often the case when we have conflicting desires.

This reverential *and* referential outlook, our singer assures, is our best offense when confronting our enemies both internally and externally who pose an obstacle to our ascent. In addition, it is the next step as we continue upward.

Like arrows in the hand of a warrior
  are the sons of one's youth;
Happy is the man who has
  his quiver full of them.
He shall not be put to shame
  when he speaks to his enemies in the gate.

The war metaphor is well chosen, for the happy man's children must defend themselves in court. The last line makes evident where this whole sermon (and the whole expedition) was heading: to a confrontation. The combination of "speaking" to the enemy and being "put shame" indicates a high stakes legal dispute of some kind. Certainly, the gate is a place of entrance and especially into the temple. It is an open courtyard either before or within an entrance.

We, of course, would think it quite rude and inappropriate to have bouncers at the entrance to the church checking credentials, but in ancient times the "gate" was where communal business occurred. Justice was to be administered within the gate. Those with criminal offenses or defaulting loans were called to account. The leading men of the city presided, but the whole assembly would be the jury. The gate also served as a kind of courtyard for public exchange. Prophets exhorted the people on covenant responsibility and the Lord's will. The sermon of Psalm 127–29 was heard "within the gate." But merchants set up shop there is well. As the city of Jerusalem swelled on holy days, the merchant's eye grew big with the prospect of a steady flow of customers (Neh 13:15–22).

The gate was supposed to be the place where wickedness—that is economic exploitation—was rectified. Those who took advantage of the poor were to be denied access to the temple unless they made restitution. Ideally, the assembly of the righteous would discern "the way" of each worshipper according to the righteous demands of the Torah (Ps 1:5–6).

The unfortunate reality—lest we forget that the dream is always butting up against "the way things are"—was mostly the opposite. Those with bills unpaid faced the frightening specter of bankruptcy at the gate. All that a man had, his inheritance, could be "repossessed." The poor were the ones denied access. This was especially grievous since the temple was the main place the poor could petition God for help.

Understanding this sheds light on what was at stake with Nehemiah's mission to rebuild the walls and gates of Jerusalem—a reversal of control. For rich and poor alike, for Israelite and non-Israelite alike, one's livelihood was at stake with jurisdiction of the gates. The issue was whether the courts would be a "council of wickedness" and a "seat of mockers." Would it be the place where those who could not pay down on their debts are ironically accused of "robbing the rich" (Ps 69:4), where the poor are being "trampled"? Or will it be a place where the assembly "delights in the Torah of the LORD" and the "way of the righteous prevail" (Ps 1). A later prophet tersely framed the question this way: *My house shall be a house of prayer, but you are making it a den of thieves* (Mt 21:13).[6] It all depends on the gatekeepers.

As of the writing of our song here, the gate is occupied by "the enemy," and is the place where a war of words must take place. The only weapon for battle is *trust in the Lord* that produces an unshakable understanding that God loves those who are upright in their heart. Trust in the Lord, this song proclaims, will be enough to breach the enemy's seemingly invincible lines.

To be *put to shame* is a scapegoating phrase. It is to be made a public spectacle, an object of scorn where the community's violence can be conveniently funneled away from itself. For the victim, shame means a return to exile, to be stripped and exposed. It also means that "the enemy" is from within.

It is always easy to blow off or contend with some threat from outside one's circle of acquaintances, friends, colleagues, family or neighbors. In fact, having a well-defined enemy "out there" solidifies and energizes

---

6. Jesus is merely quoting the prophets Isaiah (Isa 56:7) and Jeremiah (Jer 7:11).

a community. It is quite another thing, however, if the one being hostile toward you is within your own community, when he sits in the pew next to you. It is as the Psalmist complains:

> *If an enemy had reviled me,*
>   *I could have borne it;*
> *If he who hates me had vaunted himself against me,*
>   *I might have hidden from him.*
> *But you, my other self,*
>   *my companion and my bosom friend!*
> *You, whose comradeship I enjoyed;*
>   *at whose side I walked in procession in the house of God!*
> (Ps 55:13–15)

But the promise is profound here. Those who trust in the Lord will not be put to shame, but will continue ascending to the Presence of God.

> *Blessed are they who are persecuted for the sake of righteousness,*
>   *for theirs is the kingdom of heaven.*
> *Blessed are you when men insult you and persecute you and utter every evil against you [falsely] because of me. Rejoice and be glad, for your reward will be great in heaven. Thus they persecuted the prophets who were before me.* (Mt 5:10–12)

10

Psalm 128

THE SERMON CONTINUES IN Psalm 128, but the tone decisively shifts. The stern warnings have subsided, and the confrontation within the gate is absent. Instead, the travelers turned worshippers ascend in rapid upbeat step. For a brief moment, the present tensions spiral upward like smoke to a sure hope. "Happy are all." And one more bouncy step up, "happy are you." "You will enjoy." Spring to the next step. "You will experience the good life, the good life that comes from Zion." "The Lord will bless you." Skip up. "I said the Lord will bless you from Zion." And a leap up two steps. "You will know fruitfulness, vitality, peace, *shaloam*." It is as if the entourage has snuck under the pointing finger of the accuser and is making a b-line for the front row seats. They are on a fast track to the temple courtyard where sacrifices will be made and appeals for God's intervention will be heard.

The metaphors of a good life blend together, one hope serving as a metaphor for the other. One's family is a field and one's orchard a family. The fertility of a man's wife is like a grapevine, and his children are compared to budding olive shoots. The images speak of one of the most powerful religious impulses in the human experience—procreation. It is an idyllic picture in a similar way as the "American dream." *Everyone* wants and should have a sense of home, of place, of belonging, and of sustenance. It is what blessing is all about—to survive and thrive.

Micah expressed it as: *Every man shall sit under his own vine/ or under his own fig tree, undisturbed* (Mic 4:4). In Micah's vision of Zion, this idyllic picture proceeds from another better-known hope that all war and violence will come to an end (Mic 4:3): *They shall beat their swords into plowshares,/ and their spears into pruning hooks;/ One nation shall not raise the sword against another,/ nor shall they train for war again.*

All of this is envisioned as people from all over the world "ascend" Mt. Zion in order to "learn his ways" so that they may "walk in his paths" (Mic 4:2). When people walk in God's well-trodden path, the "*Torah* will go forth from Zion."

Blessed is everyone who fears the LORD, who walks in his ways.

Trust in the LORD (Ps 125). Let the LORD build the house (Ps 127). Fear the LORD and walk in His ways (Ps 128). These are all code phrases for whole-hearted adherence to Torah living. These go back to the dream. The wish, the dream, the hope of a peaceful and fruitful existence for all is only envisioned as all, from aristocracy to servant, live with the Lord being the primary referent.

In post-exilic Judah, the term, *fear the Lord*, took on a formal designation for citizenship in a new "democratic" experiment. With this in mind, we must exercise some caution when criticizing the ancient Jews, for we tend to think of "fearing the Lord" in strictly religious terms where as the term in the Hebrew bible mostly speaks to a political governing body, a kind of voting constituency or citizenship.

Even in our day, we have intense debates around clearly defining citizenship because there is a huge difference when it comes to rights and privileges. When it comes to issues of citizenship, language identification and marriages are just as controversial today as they were then. We can also add the extremely touchy problem between those established in a place and those entering the land.

As described in the introduction, the "law" of the land of Judah was anything but settled at the time of Nehemiah and Ezra. Nehemiah and Ezra's policy of excluding foreign influence from Jerusalem and the temple seem disturbing. After the events of the twentieth century even up to today, we are extremely sensitized to the gross inhumanity when it comes to ethnic cleansing or second-class citizenship. These issues and the implications cannot be discussed here.

I do, however, need to point to a primary issue with citizenship in the newly constituted Israel because it more directly addresses the concerns of this book. It has to do with *repentance*. Ezra and Nehemiah insist that the constituents of the reforming Israel be primarily "of the exiles" because they understood most profoundly the error of their ways. A posture of repentance in their view was the only foundation to rebuild the nation. It was Israel's gross negligence of their God's will that brought a complete end to the nation, and nobody knew that better than those who "wept on the river banks of Babylon."

Repentance was the test for citizenship and the fundamental building block for the nation. That "policy" did not change even some four hundred year later when Jesus proclaimed the good news of the kingdom. Repentance was the foundational posture for the reunion with God and was the signature slogan of Jesus' ministry: "Repent, for the kingdom of God is at hand." Those who "tremble at the words of the God of Israel because of Israel's unfaithfulness" (Ezra 9:4) are the ones who pass the citizenship exam in God's "kingdom come." Citizens of God's kingdom mourn over humanity's and the Church's stubborn refusal to exchange self-centered desire for "Thy will be done."

The *fear of the Lord* is equated with a fortitude that resists corruption, an unwillingness to "cheat the system" for personal gain (Neh 7:2). It is able to carefully discern the difference between the oft-blurred lines between bribery and justice, and so the "fear of the Lord" is also a buzzword for wisdom (Prov 1:7).

Wisdom sayings are concentrated in Job, Psalms, Proverbs, Ecclesiastes, and Song of Songs. They are also found scattered throughout the Hebrew bible, and sometimes scornfully referred to by the prophets. Wisdom sayings and literature were common among the aristocracy of all ancient Near Eastern civilizations. It is inaccurate to say that Israel "borrowed" from their neighbors with their incorporation of wisdom literature anymore that it would be to say that Israel borrowed agricultural practices. Wisdom writings were simply a part of the broader cultural "scene" of the time. Wisdom literature was cosmopolitan.

Although wisdom sayings worked themselves down to the common folk, it was preeminently an enterprise of those of wealth and influence. As the book of Proverbs demonstrates, wisdom was a way to instruct the young in the ways of leadership. Fundamentally, the wise were those who were diligent, entrepreneurial, hardworking, disciplined, prudent and focused on obtaining and maintaining one's wealth and status. Wisdom literature was the ancient version of "secrets of the successful." The antithesis to the wise is of course the fool who is characterized as lazy, impulsive, short-sighted, unethical, brutish, and most of all poor. The general understanding for the "well-to-do" of the ancient world was quite formulaic. Just follow the recipe. If you do these things, you will enjoy wealth and all the nice things that come with it: health, a beautiful wife (or wives), above average children, nice things, a big house, lovely parties, influence in the gates and front row seats in the temple.

Unfortunately, the formula was often circular. One's wealth became the proof positive that one was wise, no matter how one obtained it. Job's "friends" were prime examples of this. They never gave up on the idea that Job's disaster was surely brought on by his failure to heed to certain parts of the formula.

The prophets are ruthless in their attack on the presumptuousness of the aristocracy. They saw all too well that most wealth was gained by exploitation of the common folk and maintained by intrigue, conniving, and violence.

The wisdom literature of the Hebrew Scriptures seeks to subvert, convert, and subordinate the worldview of the rich and powerful to a higher referent than the king of Persia. As I defined the *fear of the Lord* in the last psalm, it is to live reverently *referring* to God's desires above our own and *deferring* to God's desires when we lose sight of who we are, what we are doing, what is important, and as often the case when we have conflicting desires.

Yielding to the Lord, letting Him have the right of way, referring and deferring to a higher point of view is the primary definition of orthodoxy. Orthodoxy is the right or correct or most direct (*ortho*) reference and deference toward glory (*doxa*). Orthodoxy is about *orientating* our whole existence toward and in God's being.

The idea of fearing God is very problematic for many people and for good reason. For many, it conjures up images and ghosts of one's experiences with intimidating, manipulative and abusive authority figures. As a student and teacher of the Hebrew bible, I have often been taken back with the honest responses of students to the scary images of God as a wrathful king, a merciless judge, or overbearing parent. Some of them, such as God desiring massacre and genocide, are profoundly disturbing. In my responses to students about these images, I have found it precarious to point to some positive aspect or image in this. But here, I will once again, perhaps unsuccessfully, attempt it.

Of course I don't like to think of a punishing, disciplining god when it comes to the myriad of ways *I* "knowingly or unknowingly" violate, hurt, destroy, murder, exploit, hate and victimize others. But when it comes to being a victim of those things, I sure do wish that *those* people would get a healthy dose of the fear of God!

As should be abundantly clear from our journey through these songs, those on expedition are up against some profound injustice and in their very appeal for "salvation" is the hope that God will decisively act against wickedness.

The human appeal in the Psalms and the prophets is that God would deal with wickedness and injustice decisively and ruthlessly. They should be smashed, snuffed out, and brought to ruin, like what happened to Job. The tempered appeal throughout the proverbs and Psalms, however, is that the Torah would profoundly work its way into the way of the wealthy to such a degree that the wicked would choose the Torah as the primary guide for the good life and not their wallets.

Fear of the Lord, a referential and deferential preference for the Torah, fights against a true enemy known to all of us, ancient and modern—the fear of being taken down by an enemy.

> *Have pity on me, O God, for men trample upon me;*
>   *all the day they press their attack against me.*
> *My adversaries trample upon me all the day;*
>   *Yes, many fight against me.*
> *O Most High, who I begin to fear,*
>   *in you I trust.* (Ps 56:1–4)

We all have things we fear, deep down. All mythologies have monsters, representations of our fears coming to get us and for no other reason than to get us, to destroy us.

For most of my life, I have been depth perception challenged. This comes out on a regular basis when I have wrongly presumed the correct distance of a low lying branch or open cabinet door and my head. When the utter shock and deep pain strikes me, I at that moment feel a complete assurance that that cabinet door deliberately and maliciously attacked me simply for its amusement, gleefully gloating over my anguish, pain, and rage.

Fear is one of the most profound and fundamental emotions in us. A healthy fear keeps us away from danger, but all too often our fears can overtake us, domineering and commandeering our choices and responses to situations. Those with no fear are usually considered foolish and for good reason. One of the most consistent and direct commands in the Bible is "do not fear." Essentially, "do not fear" homelessness, unemployment, terrorism, liberals, relativism, guns, the lack of guns, or the list goes on. Instead, fear the Lord. Direct all fear to God. More accurately, make fear yield to mercy, God's mercy (Ps 56:1).

There is a counter-balance to the command to deny fear, and we have already encountered this on our ascent. When we choose to enter the procession and join the expedition, we must shed the extra and non-essential weight of our fears, like climbers who must with precise calculation select only the gear that will enable and not hinder an effective ascent or like the sailors on Jonah's ship who had to choose between lightening the load or perishing.

With each step upward, we leave our fears on the side of the trail.

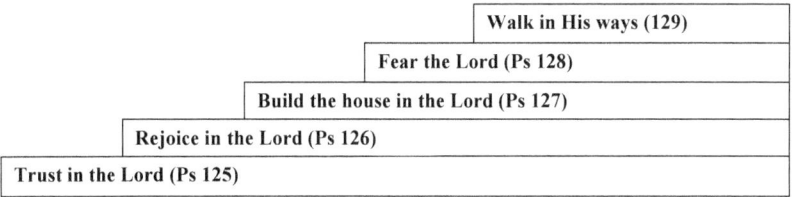

As already mentioned, "fear the Lord" is a referent to the Torah, to giving a supreme reference and deference to the Lord's desires above our own. It is also, especially in the Psalms, a referent to the worshipping community

> *You who fear the LORD, praise him!*
>   *all you descendants of Jacob, give him glory;*
> *Revere him, all you descendants of Israel . . .*
>   *so by your gift will I utter praise in the vast assembly;*
> *I will fulfill my vows before those who fear him.* (Ps 22:23, 26)

The next verse is critical because it is in "fearing the Lord" and "searching" for God in worship that: *The rich will share their wealth, the poor will eat and be satisfied, all the ends of the earth* will *turn to the LORD and worship God* (Ps 22:25–29).

"Obeying the law" is never isolated in the Hebrew Scriptures from loving God with all strength, soul, mind, and heart. Here we have a window into the importance of gathering for worship.

When I became a Byzantine Catholic, it took several years for me, coming from a Protestant orientation, to get used to a liturgical life. I was used to attending church services on a regular basis, but I wasn't used to orientating my whole calendar around the liturgical year. The Eastern tradition is very liturgically centered as it is based on the monastic ideal. One could spend a good deal of every week in liturgical services. At times, I have struggled with whether too much time is devoted to that at the expense of getting out there and "doing something for the Lord." For certain, pious diligence can lull me into an indifference to the world I live in and make me presumptuous toward what God requires of me. Jesus and the prophets frequently complain of such piety. Nonetheless, we are not called to avoid assembling together in worship. No matter what my mental condition or sinful state, it is critical that I keep orientating my life to its primary source. Sometimes we act like going to church is doing God a favor when, in fact, it is God who has lavishly poured out the favor to us.

There is one fundamental fear that permeates the scriptures: the fear of returning to the desert, that is, the loss of place, belonging, and home. It is a wandering place with no rights, no claims, vulnerable to the attack of weather, marauders, or enslavement by powerful kings or landlords.

This fear played itself out countless times in the ancient Near Eastern world. Before the Israelites began settling in the land, archeological evidence points to a significant period of immense decline in the region. Cities and villages were destroyed or mysteriously abandoned. Without the cultivation of orchards and fields, the desert creeps in and slowly chokes out vestigial remains of human activity. No doubt when the Israelites began settling, they came across "ghost towns," disheveled stone structures smothered in sand and thistles with scattered tools and shattered pots bemoaning a vibrancy vanquished. Sometimes these very mounds served as a foundation for a fresh attempt at a settled existence.

The second fear is one that we have become very familiar with in our ascent through these songs—the fear of "the enemy in the gate." It is an enemy from within the community. The enemy is always a collective, an accusing mob. It equally destroys lives, and like the desert, it slowly strangles those whose vigilance slips. Their weapons are forged more from malice, accusation, conspiracy, and manipulation than from iron. But they are frightfully accurate and deadly.

Both the desert and the mob behave like a deadly snake. Stealth is its perfected strategy. Not accidently is the fatal temptation in the garden portrayed by the wise snake.

Interestingly, the *nakedness* of the original couple and *wisdom* of the snake derive from the same Hebrew word and intentionally play off each other. The word in Hebrew means to be stripped like a barkless tree or an exposed heap of dirt.

As far as its use in the garden story (Gen 3:1), it of course means shrewd or crafty. The craftiness of the serpent holds a double sense. Its primary sense is to expose or strip away the essence of something from the non-essential, yet simultaneously, it suggests a kind of toying with what is concealed and what is exposed. It strongly implies a sense of command over the dynamics of a situation, a hubristic knowledge that confidently controls what is exposed and what remains hidden, and this especially applies to desire.

Wisdom is precariously double-sided depending on how and who wields it. It can just as easily destroy as create, kill as give life, tear down as build up. The scriptures constantly push away from the presumption that we ourselves confidently control it, like magicians who expertly control what is concealed and what is shown. Scriptural wisdom drives toward subordinating all "know how" toward "know who," that is, knowledge and awareness of God.

There is another interesting allusion to the garden here, and perhaps the image is helpful. The happiness that comes from fearing God is in *walking in his ways*. In the midst of the crisis in the garden, God is said to be on a walk-about. To "walk in his ways" imagines a God who goes before us and lives what he wants us to live. Curiously, Eve and Adam did not seem aware of this fact. They had lost their orientation toward that.

This is precisely what is at issue when Jesus encounters a rich, young ruler in the synagogue. When the young man asked Jesus, "What must I do to inherit eternal life?" (Lk 18:18–27), we cannot know to what extent it is an honest or a manipulative inquiry. Both Jesus' answer and the young man's response are Torah centered. Jesus does not negate Torah adherence, but pushes the inquiry to its heart and center. He asks the man to focus on following a living model of a God fully engaged in this world and in his life. The essence of the Torah is the same in the Old Testament as in the New. Walk as God is walking, follow as God leads, live as God lives. "Follow me," Jesus says. Walk with me. Live as I live. Remember the image of God on expedition from the last antiphon (Ps 121)? He is one who is our guardian and bodyguard (Ps 121).

**You shall eat the fruit of the labor of your hands;
you shall be happy, and it shall be well with you.**

As is typical of the psalms, they often speak in lyrical platitudes so it becomes difficult to locate a real life context behind the verse. The beauty of general poetic verse is its ability to speak into a wide variety of lives and situations. It is what makes "pop" songs go "viral." It has an amazingly broad appeal. It "strikes the chord" of how a large amount of people are feeling or sensing about the current situation. This being said, those ascending who are well off are possibly hearing this as a positive affirmation of God's favor, especially when one has made due diligence to trust in the Lord, let the Lord build the house and to fear the Lord.

I think of the rich young ruler who approached Jesus. He was honestly doing his best to walk in the ways of the Lord.

I believe, however, that the hope of "enjoying the fruit of your labors" rang more profoundly for those whose efforts at a sustainable living were precariously held in balance by environmental and economic forces. The fear that creditors would devour one's strenuous effort at yielding a crop and making a living comes out repeatedly in these psalms.

As the snake in the garden so masterfully displays, there is a double-sidedness to wisdom and it is the precarious task of a wise person to sort this out, to be aware, not gullible, presumptuous, or prideful. As the struggling farmer abandons his field in order to ascend in procession, vulnerable to human and natural predators, the words of the last three psalms are meant to give strength and faith to the faint hearted. They are words of promise and quiet assurance painted against the background of looming realities. The foundation is not the temple, nor the hill that it is built on, nor the city that houses it. It is the God who acts to rescue those in slavery and who by his word, provides a way for the people to walk in. The temptation may be to abandon the Zion project altogether.

To those who are ascending, both the poor and the wealthy, there is admonition as well as encouragement. The heart of the temptation for each is economically driven. To those on the edge of poverty and enslavement, there is the temptation to abandon the Lord, that is the God of Israel, his Torah, and his covenant. It would be either to retreat to the gods of the tribal ancestors and live a sequestered existence or to yield to the imperial gods of Egypt or Persia.

To be sure, all wealth at the time of Ezra and Nehemiah was channeled through the Persian Empire. Cooperation was essential. The essential temptation revolved around whether there was any benefit to involvement in the Zion project. Furthermore, there was considerable risk.

The book of Nehemiah indicates that exploitation of the poor by the wealthy was a huge problem:

> *But see, we today are slaves; and as for the land which you gave our fathers that they might eat its fruits and good things—see, we have become slaves upon it!* (Neh 9:36)

Your wife will be like a fruitful vine
within your house.
Your children will be like olive shoots
around your table,
Lo, thus shall the man be blest
who fears the LORD.

It should be remembered that if one did not prove to have proper citizenship, that is, had foreign wives, one could lose everything. The claim to citizenship, and thus to its rights and privileges, depended on the wife. She must prove her lineage.

The claim here is that if one "fears the Lord" one can have confidence that he and his family will enjoy the full rights of citizenship and be protected from exploitation.

Nehemiah indicates that foreigners could partake in the assembly if they "feared the Lord," if they were willing to abide by this law of the land. The assembly consisted of all who were able to understand (Neh 8:2).

May the LORD bless you from Zion.

The act of blessing implies and requires a reciprocal relationship, usually from a superior to a subordinate. Curiously, it is derived from the Hebrew word for knee, perhaps connoting the idea of bending the knee in humble request and the petition being granted at bended knee. Usually it is the greater who bestows blessing on the lesser. In this case, it denotes the granting, empowering, or bestowing of life's generative force, not just in procreation but also more broadly with the idea of "thriving."

The curious and reciprocal aspect of blessing is that the lesser can also "bless" the greater as in the well-known exhortation to "bless the

Lord." It is in a response of thanksgiving that the greater receives a generative force in return. It is a kind of giddy reciprocity, generating its own life force. "Father bless me." "Blessing be upon you child" "Bless you Father. Bless you!" "No, bless you, child. I am happy that you are happy." "No, bless you, Father. I am happy that you are happy that I am happy." Like the childhood song, "This is the song that never ends," blessing has a self-generating quality to it.

Having come to the holy city and contended with the accuser in the gate, the pilgrims have passed the final check point. They have sworn allegiance to One God, one people, and one covenant and have placed their trust *in the Lord alone*. They are ready to proceed to the temple floor, and with that, the preacher pronounces a blessing.

There is very much a trickle down theory at play here, but it is diametrically opposed to those ideologies being propagated in my day, advocating as they do that the wealthy need to maintain and increase their wealth in order for everyone else to enjoy prosperity.

The song is clear. Blessing is *from the Lord* and is to go forth and descend from Zion. It envisions abundance within the walls of Jerusalem itself that is the source of prosperity for all. But as has been mentioned several times on our ascent, the wealth of Zion is measured more in an abundance of God-centered wisdom, righteousness, and justice, than the accumulation of houses, estates, and enterprises. It is a prosperity based on a trust in the Lord and Torah understanding, rather than of money and power. The generative source of Zion's wealth is a powerful sense of belonging to and being responsible for God's people. This sense is to be an inspiration for "all nations."

The fear of God refers to a just, loving, and righteous way of life in which all are esteemed, all have a share, and all are able to survive and thrive. The archenemy of this posture is to presume way too much on one's own good fortune (and wise investments) as God's favor all the while "trampl[ing] upon the weak" (Amos 5:11).

It is here where I return to the precarious duality of the snake's craftiness. We all too easily can turn *our* hard work, *our* diligence, *our* know-how into a boastful claim of self-sufficiency and mastery. Of themselves, these attributes are valuable and necessary, but they become "wickedness" when they get cloaked in pious God talk, especially when our prosperity depends heavily on the exploitation of resources and people. Pious claims of God-given prosperity become a stench to the Almighty, when we cloak our wealth in pious platitudes and religious celebrations and are complacent to injustice, cruelty, poverty, and abuse. This is where wisdom turns to pride. And this is where the prophets angrily appeal to a just God and envision Him saying:

> *I abhor the pride of Jacob,*
>   *I hate his castles . . .*
> *Yet you have turned judgment into gall,*
>   *and the fruit of justice into wormwood. (Amos 6:8,12)*

> *I hate, I spurn your feasts,*
>   *I take no pleasure in your solemnities;*
> *Your cereal offerings I will not accept,*
>   *nor consider your stall-fed peace offerings.*
> *Away with your noisy songs!*
>   *I will not listen to the melodies of your harps.*
> *But if you would offer me holocausts,*
>   *then let justice surge like water,*
>   *and goodness like an unfailing stream. (Amos 5:21–24)*

The prosperity trickling down from Zion is not primarily of lavish feasts sponsored by God and king in which the well-to-do parade their good fortune to the struggling and destitute as God's bonus for loyalty to the company, holding out some unobtainable carrot to those who must work on the holiday to makes ends meet. "See what prosperity awaits you, when God likes you." (See Amos 5 and 6). It is not, as Paul so angrily rebukes the church at Corinth, where the rich enjoy their gourmet banquets inside the house while the servants and the poor wait outside until they are done and then clean up and perhaps get a few scraps. This is all done before the church service where they will all gather as one body and give thanks to one Lord (1 Cor 11).

Justice and righteousness are the primary commodities that Zion and the city should deal in. Justice and righteousness should *not* trickle down to every part of society, but rather pour forth like a great river. This is wisdom primarily informed by "the fear of God." It is the difference between a worldly wisdom born of one's one craftiness or a wisdom orientated around God's glory and amazing grace.

"Let justice surge like water,/ and goodness like an unfailing stream," says Amos (5:24). This is the blessing that comes from Zion and the prosperity of Jerusalem that is the basis for the prosperity of all. This is the great guarantor for those looking to Zion for salvation.

> **May you see the prosperity of Jerusalem**
> **all the days of your life.**
> **May you see your children's children.**

"Prosperity" here is translated from the Hebrew word for "good" (*tov*). *Tov* denotes wellness, pleasure, or value. In other words, *tov* means "the good life" with a primary emphasis on enjoying the basic necessities of life. Goodness is God's response to his creative activity in the first chapter of Genesis , and it is only as God "saw" it that he pronounced its quality. Goodness is connected with seeing, savoring, or tasting. Goodness is experienced, not thought. It is most closely connected to seeing as indicated by a common biblical phrase "it was good in his own eyes" or in verse six of this psalm "may you live to see." In order for it to be good, it must be visual and a part of our experience. And it is *shared*.

As already discussed, there is tension between what has been experienced and what should be experienced. The disparity can easily lead us into extreme positions. Nonetheless, the blessing pronounces a confidence, but it concludes exactly where this antiphon started (Ps 125)—with the Lord. Blessing, happiness, prosperity, and the good life not only have their source in God, they also are defined by it.

Often times in both Jewish and Christian history, the disparity between "the dream" and the reality are so severe that it pushes believers into only imagining God's kingdom being completely of another world. A profound and wrong effect of this thinking is to condemn or at least forsake God's creation and most of humanity. In more mundane terms, it often leads people to abandon the gathering together of believers. I readily admit my own temptation in this regard.

To whatever extent one wishes to have his family live a prosperous, fruitful, and blessed life, he and his wife need to turn toward the Lord and orient their lives on Him. But one must never forget that God's blessing and goodness go as the people of God go.

It is as *all* of God's people are blessed that blessing comes to me and my family.

We today, must keep our focus constantly on what is clearly the express wish of the True God. Thy will be done, *on earth* as it (already) is in heaven. We must never separate the continuity between heaven and earth, this world and a world to come, the mystical from the common. We should notice the parallel between this prayer from Zion and the prayer that Jesus taught his followers. Jesus did not invent a new prayer; rather, he encapsulates all the prayers of Zion in the Psalms and of the prophets.

Our Father who art in heaven—May the Lord from Zion.

Hollowed it be Thy Name—Trust and Fear the Lord.

Thy kingdom come, Thy will be done—refer and defer to Torah/Gospel.

On earth as it is in heaven—Let justice and righteousness gush forth. Let all share in the prosperity of Zion.

Peace be on Israel!

The word "peace" (*shaloam*) summarizes this last song combining, goodness, happiness, vitality, and enjoyment in not only one big affirmation, but also a proclamation as the assembly of Israel proceeds.

Of course peace also means the absence of hostility, and given how much the "enemy" and the "wicked" are tormenting those on expedition, this last phrase may also be a cry for help, and as much as the ascenders "trust in the Lord," "fear the Lord," and are letting "the Lord build the house" it may also be a call for hope.

> *Blessed are all those who mourn,*
> * for they will be comforted.*
> *Blessed are the clean of heart,*
> * for they will see God.*

11

Psalm 129

THE LAST SONG OF this second antiphon is pivotal. From the very start of our expedition (Ps 120) until the blessing of Psalm 128, we have been ascending to the very threshold of the temple. More properly speaking, the second antiphon (Ps 125–29) is more about reaching (almost) the destination. We arrived at the hills of Jerusalem and passed through the scoffing gates of our creditors. We ascended the temple steps in joyous procession and rising affirmation. We gathered as the *qahal*, the assembly of citizens of "Israel," those "trusting and fearing in the Lord." We have heard the sermons as if Ezra, Nehemiah, and even Solomon delivered them, exhorting us to rejoice and acknowledge God's great work of returning that which was lost. They have admonished us not to lose heart, to walk as God walks, to live in His ways, and to trust in a kingdom building project where God Himself is the builder, guardian, and investor. We have been injected with a firm affirmation that God wants us to be happy, blessed, joyous, and rewarded. All of our desires can find a home in God's desire.

At the end of the sermon, the priest pronounces the blessing (Ps 128:5–6). As he calls out, "Peace be upon Israel!" we all in one joyous accord shout out "Peace be upon Israel!" Suddenly, however, the tone turns back to the torment of the conflict. Abruptly, "they" are back on our minds, those "plowmen" who scourge the back like plowing a field. "They" hate Zion, and it is "they" whom we must once again face as we conclude this stage of our exhilarating ascent and contemplate another small descent and the conflict with "the scepter of wickedness."

Even when the faithful make the final ascent to the courtyard of the temple, "they" will be there. Some of them will not go any further than the gates of accusation. As the expedition ascends to the temple court, the pilgrims leave some of their enemies and tormentors behind. "They" fade away.

Before the final push upward, the assembly ponders the descent from the holy hill. They realized that the long sought after goal was a "false summit." They will have to descend once again in order to attempt the final pitch. They will have to pass through the enemy in the gate on that descent, which makes it even worse than the ascent up.

For those who do not climb mountains, it is reasonable to assume that going downhill is much easier that going uphill, but for many, like myself, going down is in some ways worse. Going down steep pitches puts a slow, constant stress on muscles and ligaments from hips to ankles. I don't have to deal with burning lungs, but the constant knifing pain in knees and ankles at times feels worse than anything suffered on the way up.

"Sorely have they afflicted me from my youth."
  Let Israel now say.
"Sorely have they afflicted me from my youth,"
  yet they have not prevailed against me.

The voice has abruptly changed. It is now "Israel" who sings as one voice, and it is not just the voice of those preparing to ascend the mount, it is Israel of the past and Israel of what is yet to come. It is the voice of all those who trust in the Lord alone. The line *let Israel now say* indicates that a preacher still leads the congregation in what is now a call for courage and inner strength.

The caller cries out: *Sorely have the afflicted me from my youth.*

The choir and congregation respond: *Let Israel now say.*

The caller cries out again, as if straining to hear the half-hearted and faint response. I said:

Sorely have they afflicted me from my youth.

The choir and congregation are now stirred to a more confident response: *Yet they did not prevail against me!*

The repetitiveness, so evident here, serves as it has throughout the antiphons as steps, but for a moment, they are steps downward. Having come so far, however, has changed everything. These steps are not the descent into the despair of exile, but of a resolution firmly based in God.

The word *sorely* comes from a basic Hebrew adjective to describe multiplication. It is often translated as much, numerous, great, enough or abundant. In other words it refers to "a whole heck of a lot." In the famous covenant formula known as the *shema—Hear O Israel. The LORD our God is One LORD*—the word is translated most often as *all your strength*, but it carries an accumulative sense that one should love the Lord with *everything you've got*.

And the one thing that Israel affirms they have way too much of is *tzarar*, affliction. Thus, we return to the opening line of the antiphons: in *my distress* (tzarar) *I called to the LORD* (Ps 120:1).

The affliction is compounded even more because it has been *from my youth*. This phrase is difficult to pin down with precision because there is no one event that clearly signals the constitution of Israel. Does it refer to the semi-homeless wanderings of Abraham, Isaac and Jacob? Is it the enslavement of the Hebrews in Egypt or the struggle of the loosely connected tribes against strong city-states and the invasion of the Philistines? Does it refer to the ever-threatening cloud of the great empires of Assyria and Babylon which loomed over most of Israel and Judah's history as kingdoms? Or does it perhaps refer to the internal enmity between two warring brothers, Israel to the north and Judah to the south?

The phrase probably refers to all of the above, but my guess is that the internal conflict is the most grievous and the one that best fits the historical context. As we have encountered all along in these songs, the bitterest opposition facing those ascending to Zion are themselves occupiers in the land and in Jerusalem itself. They are keenly invested in the economic development of the region and are vying for the "official policy" of the land from the Persians. For the most part, they too worship the Lord.

What they most oppose is any notion of a unified people under one God (*Yahweh*), one king (David), one place (Zion) and one government (*torah*). This opposition, as we have encountered many times already, is strongly energized by the need to hold on to wealth and power at the expense of most of the inhabitants of the land, but especially the vulnerable exiles returning to the land. They advocate a limited scope to a kingdom whose king is God.

Probably most important, this opposition was willing to "prevail" over Israel by not only refusing aid to Jerusalem when it was under siege by the Babylonians, but also assisting in its destruction.

The term "prevail," *yekol*, alludes to the story of Jacob's change of name to Israel (Gen 32:22–31). Importantly, this incident occurs as Jacob is on his way to encounter Esau where the outcome is uncertain. It could end with reconciliation or in disaster. In that story, Jacob wrestles with "a man," but he could not subdue (*yekol*) the stranger. The "man," impressed with Jacob's tenacity, changes his name to Israel because of Jacob's willingness to struggle (in Hebrew *sarah*) with God.

The prophet Hosea is the only other writer who connects Jacob's struggle (*sarah*) with prevailing. There are two significant things about Hosea's recollection of Jacob's struggle with the stranger. First, Jacob "prevailed" against the man, and yet "wept and begged for his favor" (Hos 12:4). Hosea's whole argument is that "Israel" gained his blessing by tenacity *and* humility.

Second, Hosea contrasts Israel's humble tenacity with the arrogance of those who have gained wealth by partnering with Egypt and Assyria and have sorely extorted the poor of the land, haughtily proclaiming their innocence.

Hosea speaks of a partnership that God desired for Ephraim and Judah. The two are described as a plowman (Judah) and his heifer (Ephraim). The seed to be planted was righteousness and love (Hos 10:12), but what was sown was "wickedness," "evil," and "deceit," and all because of their lack of humility and their trust in power (Hos 10:13).

As the pilgrims shout out this verse in ascent to the temple, they likely conjure up images of the prophet Jeremiah as well, for the term "overcome," *yekal* was favored by him. The term carries the sense of overrunning a boundary like armies taking a territory or stronghold. In Jeremiah as well as Hosea and Genesis, there is a strong connotation of being betrayed (Ob 7), indicating that the struggle is within the community.

For Jeremiah, the term was both a comfort and a threat. The Lord promises that Jeremiah's enemies will not prevail against him (Jer 1:9, 15:20). Ironically, when Jeremiah resists the call to be the Lord's prophet, the Lord promptly promises that He will prevail over Jeremiah's objection (Jer 20:7–12). Jeremiah becomes the field of battle over which the Lord will contend with the people of God. The Lord will overtake his rebellious people and Jeremiah's enemies who seek to silence his message. God prevailed through the struggle of his servant who willingly submitted to God's will.

The plowers plowed upon my back; they made long their furrows.

Ploughman comes from a Hebrew word that generally depicts cutting or engraving. It is also used to describe those who carve images on stone or wood. The image is clear enough here. Israel has had a long history of those who have lacerated the back (mainly of the poor) and scoured huge swaths of enmity, discord, and division, mainly opting for the game of gods, power, wealth, and exploitation instead of the dream of brothers dwelling together in unity (Ps 133:1).

The ancient Hebrews connected certain attributes or qualities to parts of the body, and this is true of the back. The curvature of the spine like those of mountain ridges brought to mind the idea of loftiness, exaltation, and dignity. To gouge deep lacerating wounds upon the back leaves the victim with protruding tattoos of shame.

The picture of cultivating a field is a stock Ancient Near Eastern image for building a kingdom. It conjures up a collage of readily understood connections between a king and his territory with a farmer doing likewise with a field. Both invest time, talent, effort, and resources in an all out gamble to reap rewards. Both plow the field as the first step in a great expectation of a harvest.

As most kingdoms went in ancient times, plowing the field simply meant violently seizing resources, often by killing the men in battle, destroying or greatly disabling a city, and taking the women, children and livestock as plunder. In other words, plowing the field meant "wiping the slate clean" like excavators leveling the ground for the foundation of a new development.

Micah thus prophesied of Zion:

> *Zion shall be plowed like a field,*
> * and Jerusalem reduced to rubble,*
> *And the mount of the temple*
> * to a forest ridge. (Micah 3:12).*

Ezekiel uses the plowing image to simply refer to a brutal destruction by an invading army (Ez 21:31).

The prophets, however, vehemently objected to this notion of "kingdom building" as related to their God. Yahweh indeed desired to plant a garden (Gen 2), a vineyard (Isa 5), or a field (Jer 12) in hopes of a great return on His investment. But the prophets insist that what the Lord prepared the ground for in his "mighty saving deeds" was that humility and faithfulness would be sown in the hopes that righteousness, truth, love, and justice would be harvested, a bounty the whole world could reap the benefits of.[1]

> "*Sow for yourselves justice,*
>   *reap the fruit of piety;*
> *Break up for yourselves a new field;*
>   *for it is time to seek the LORD,*
>   *till he come and rain justice upon you.*"
> *But you have cultivated wickedness,*
>   *reaped perversity,*
>   *and eaten the fruit of falsehood.*
> *Because you have trusted in your chariots*
>   *and in your many warriors,*
> *Turmoil shall break out among your tribes*
>   *and all your fortresses shall be ravaged.* (Hos 10:12–14)

The Israelites were constantly tempted and readily gave in to plowing the field like the other nations did and to which their gods sponsored in hopes of reaping power, wealth, and prestige at the expense of most of the lands inhabitants. The prophets bitterly complain about this gross misconception of "the mighty One of Jacob" and reserve some of the nastiest diatribes for those who sow the wickedness of the gods of nations. (See Jer 12, Isa 5).

The LORD is righteous;
he has cut the cords of the wicked.

The contrast between the god sponsored wickedness of the nations and the dream of Zion is so stark here that the lyricist does not even bother with a conventional contrasting conjunction. The abrupt assertion, *the LORD is righteous*, nearly in and of itself rudely severs the cords of the wicked. To remind, "the wicked" do not refer to moral reprobates hanging out in bars, cheating on their spouses, and getting into brawls. It refers to those engaged in and perpetuating systems of injustice, primarily of the economic kind. The chords to which Yahweh's righteousness cuts off probably refer to both the breaking up of the often impenetrable unified front the powerful and wealthy present as well as its strangling effect on the vulnerable (see Ps 120).

1. See Hosea 12 and Isaiah 5.

The Hebrew word for cut (*katzatz*) conjures up similar images to that of the wicked plowmen in the last verse. It depicts a terminal act of severing something that was once a unity, such as severing a limb from the body. The word is association with hewing boundary markers, jagged and protruding edifices split from one piece of solid rock. *Katzatz*—the word itself has a cutting sound to it—connotes a decisive and forceful break. A noun form of the word (*kits*) depicts the decisive end of a time period or era like at the end of the forty days of rain in the time of Noah (8:6).

In one psalm depicting Zion, both the noun and verb describe Yahweh's mighty acts of laying wickedness to waste:

> *He has stopped wars to the ends* (kits) *of the earth:*
> *the bow he breaks; he splinters* (katzetz) *the spears;*
> *he burns the shields with fire.* (Ps 46:10)

The verb form here emphasizes the decisive irreversibility of the act. Yahweh, by virtue of his righteousness, has already accomplished this and there is no turning back.

Once again, the general statement that *he has cut the cords of the wicked* could have countless references. It may be that it is an accumulative affirmation. In a rehearsal of the history of God's people from God clothing Adam and Eve, sparing Noah, calling Abraham, rescuing Isaac and Joseph, snatching the Hebrews from Pharaoh, delivering the Israelites from the Philistines, sparing Jerusalem from Sennacharib's siege, returning the exiles from Babylon, restoring Zion in the days of Nehemiah and Ezra, we can see the all encompassing righteous action of God.

And once again in this single terse statement, we see God's relentless campaign toward the resurrection. Jesus' statement on his resurrection has often baffled me. He rebukes his followers for not seeing how everything that was written in the Law of Moses, the Prophets, and the Psalms was moving, pushing, and driving towards God's mighty act in resurrecting Jesus from the dead (Lk 24:36–49).

Don't we get it? The righteous God can act in no other way than to "sever" wickedness. Our repentance must begin by allowing God to do that within ourselves. The image of plowing the field was also employed by the prophets to depict the rough, jagged, lacerating work of breaking up the sin hardened ground of our lives. "Break up for yourselves a new field,/ for it is time to seek the LORD," the prophet Hosea exhorts (Hos 10:12). With each strategic "resurrection" move, Israel's God repeatedly and emphatically affirms that the "kingdom of God" is not "of this world." This does not mean that God's kingdom is pie in the sky; rather, it means that God's kingdom is not based on the same principles, ideas, and images of the kingdoms that men build.

May all who hate Zion
be put to shame and turned backward.

As we have traveled, traversed and terraced our way through the antiphons, "they" have been ever present. Their presence has at times seemed more evident than the Lord's presence. As these final lyrics of our current song close off the second antiphon, however, so does the curtain close on "them." "They" are never spoken of again in the Songs of Ascents.

As is often the case in the Psalms, there are dramatic and unexplainable turnarounds. The singer goes from a litany of despair to an exaltation of praise with only an empty space between verses as explanation. Here, silently and inexplicably, some kind of resolve about one's enemies, about God's enemies, has festered inside those who made the arduous ascent, escaped condemnation at the gate, and rallied as one with those who *trust and fear the Lord*. Something has happened to those who let that crazy dream sneak by the security gates of the heart.

This verse is the reverse side of the benediction pronounced in Psalm 128. There, a blessing is pronounced for those who "fear the Lord." What is implied from this verse is that they also *love* Zion as opposed to those who hate it. We have been presented with several images of Zion throughout this second antiphon that converge into a single composite image. From the very first mention in Psalm 120, Zion has been depicted most of all by the gathering of God's people in radical trust and worshipful response to God's presence. They are those who abandoned a comfortable existence in exile, for the discomfort of a difficult ascent upward to a rule among humanity where God's desires win the day.

At first glance, these closing verses of the second antiphon appear to be one of those nasty curses sometimes found in the Bible. Cursing one's enemy was a conventional practice in the ancient world, and the ills wished upon an enemy could be vile and nasty. Mostly, however, the imprecation wishes for a flip-flop of fortunes. May my misfortune become his, and may his fortune become mine. Something of that wish is expressed here, but oddly, the wish for misfortune tones down as it proceeds. It goes from imprecation to lament for "those who hate Zion."

Jesus' words, "blessed are those who mourn for they shall be comforted," resonates in these verses as well. The focus is not on the misfortune of those tormented by their enemies, but on what the haters of Zion will lose out on. Most importantly, those who love Zion understand that Zion is the source of true blessing, the *only* true foundation. To turn away from Zion simply translates into turning toward the mean ways of living so prevalent in our world today. It is the natural result of human existence that is not whole-heartedly orientated to God and his righteous, just, and merciful ways.

Hate, *saneh*, is more the sense of being unloved, starved of attention. When this is done to children, they demonstrate clear signs of "failure to thrive" (the opposite of blessing): gaunt faces, empty stares, inappropriate social responses or an absence of it. Hate in these terms does not carry the ferocity that our word often does. Those who hate pay the object little or no heed. They do not value it. They ignore it. They do not take it seriously. Especially, they withhold love.

I am reminded of the merchants Nehemiah confronted over the Sabbath (Neh 13:15–22). They simply did not take Zion or the Sabbath command seriously. This view of hate is much more in line with the way most of us really "hate" people. We do not seek their doom, nor do we wish violence against them. We are not even mean to them but exchange polite little greetings with them. We simply avoid them. Live and let live. Thus there is a strong sense of turning one's face away from that which is not loved. Blessing, on the other hand, is asking someone to turn his face toward the supplicant.

We can be reminded, and perhaps reprimanded, by Jesus who teaches us to "love your enemies." Jesus does not allow us one bit of wiggle room here. We are to "turn toward them" in active and demonstrable ways. We are to "do good" to them.

There is a subtle double-play here. May those who "turn away" from Zion be "turned backward." In other words, may those who do not orientate their life toward Zion be disoriented. This is not so much a wish of destruction as it is an affirmation of truth. The presence of God is the only direction we can turn to have direction. Without a compass and a map, one will inevitably get lost.

The progression downward in this song began with a sweeping remembrance of Israel's difficult past and its struggle for existence, and a quick look upward to remind that the righteous Lord has cut the cords of wickedness.

Often times, a "false summit" is a raised part on a ridge. In order to proceed upward, I must descend for a little bit. On many climbs, a climbing group must consider the members who for various reasons feel like they cannot go any further. Sometimes those climbers choose to stay in the same place and wait to rejoin the group on the way down, and sometimes they choose to start back down. Those who choose to continue try to keep an eye on those left behind, but as they continue the ascent, their figures become smaller and smaller.

In these last verses of the second Antiphon, there are three steps down as the congregation reflects on the next encounter it will have with "them." They must descend a little in order to proceed upward. The real descent, however, is that "they" choose not to go further. They will not go to the Holy Mountain because they are far too entangled in the "scepter of wickedness." Those who stood in opposition since the very start of the expedition decline to proceed. As the expedition begins its final pitch, the haters of Zion begin to get smaller and smaller.

The first downward wish is that they *be put to shame and turned backward*. The wish that "they" experience shame is found several times in the Psalms, and when we compare those psalms, several other common features emerge.[2]

"They" seek the life of the petitioner. Psalm 35 directly connects the "life" in peril with the poor and needy who are robbed of a livelihood (Ps 35:10). The wish is often a response to the enemy's gloating presence and conspiring ways. In other words, the biggest torment seems to be their arrogant boasting at the demise of the petitioner, and in this regard, the supplicant hopes for a reversal where "they" feel the confusion, disgrace, humiliation, and shame that is the supplicant's experience. In other words, the supplicant wants his persecutors to fall victim to their own trap (Ps 35:7–8). The petitioner's appeal is for vindication, but not so much that they are destroyed or come to ruin, but more in the simple fact that the victim survived their assault and stands in the assembly praising God (Ps 35:26–28).

The sense here is that the exaltation of Zion is enough to shame those who oppose it. In other words, the more Zion is built up the more those who *turn away* from Zion *will continue to turn away*.

This turning away is not something "they" do as much as it is something that happens to them. May they be turned away or repulsed. It

---

2. See Ps 35:26, 40:15, 70:3, 71:24

carries strong overtones of retreating in cowardliness or betrayal, and it is here where we once again get the indication that "they" are in the midst of the congregation and not outside it. "They" should have been loyal, should have been a trusted colleague, a trusted partner. The word is used in the well-known verses of the suffering servant in Isaiah. The servant has suffered greatly because he was not rebellious. He did not *turn away* from those who struck him (Isa 50:6–7).

Turning away also carries the idea of a slip or fall, and once again we return to our analogy of mountain climbing. A slip or fall can be pretty harmless. One can simply get up and brush off a bit and carry on. But sometimes it can be dangerous or fatal. One thing is for sure, however; the mountain rarely causes the fall. The climber incites it.

There is a strong sense of reciprocation here and it centers on shame. Shame held a powerful sway in the ancient world. Shame is one of the umbrella terms to express the whole exile. It borders on the miraculous that the Scriptures from prophet to psalmist consistently witness to the *shame* of failing their God as a people rather than the *blame* of powerful enemies. One of the signature signs of those returning from exile is that they wear "faces of shame," as the prophet Daniel describes it (Dan 9:7). Those returning to Zion profoundly understood that the only foundation on which to rebuild Zion was that of humility and trust. They understood their utter failure to heed the covenant. The singer desires those who turn away from Zion experience in some way the shame that the exiles felt.

In a real sense, the exiles were the first to come to terms with the fact that they themselves had hated Zion. The promise to David (Ps 132:11) was abused by presumption, and covenant responsibility was violated by greed. If the returning exiles had any "right" to Zion, it was only be virtue of their shame. If one did not understand that, and our antiphons give ample witness that there were many who didn't, then Israel was destined to repeat once again its own calamity. Once again, this very posture reverberates right on down to John the Baptist and to Jesus, and it is a powerful reminder that we ourselves ought to soberly approach the Great Fast. "Repent," Jesus and John say, "for the kingdom of God has arrived." May our own "hatred" of Zion bring us to our own shame.

Our ascent toward the resurrection only begins with our descent into the shame of exile. Only from the loss of "our" world do we begin to enter the kingdom of God not of our worlds and our kingdoms. Experiencing the shame of exile means comprehending to some degree what it means to be an outcast, to be homeless, to be on the losing end of the way the world likes to do business. This is one reason why serving the poor in some real human-to-human way enables us to see this from our comfortable armchairs.

I am reminded of a fellow who entered our adult initiation program a few years back. As part of our program we ask the initiates to serve at the church's sandwich line. Sam welcomed this idea and enjoyed the experience so much that he volunteered on his own many more times. Upon his baptism and chrismation into the church, we reflected on the year's journey. The sandwich line experience was a highlight for Sam. It was comforting for him to know that he would be received at our church regardless of *which side of the line he was on*. I knew enough of Sam's life at that point to know that the struggle for daily sustenance was not theoretical.

There is also the sense here, which is often the case with the Biblical view of sin, that the sin is also the consequence. Turning away from Zion, from the source of blessing, simply means that one turns away from blessing. It is as the Psalmist says; their own trap has ensnared them (Ps 35:8).

Let them be like the grass on the housetops, which withers before it grows up,

The second step downward or backward wishes that "they" live a shallow empty life that fades from memory as soon as it dies.

The imprecation starts with a general word for existence or living: *let them be*. There is a subtle admonition to the congregation here about their tormentors. Perhaps it is similar to Jesus' exhortation to his followers about rooting out the wicked weeds in the field (Mt 13:24–30). The temptation, which we are reminded of almost daily now in the news, is to violently oppose our enemy. Root them out! Get rid of them! How often is the cry to "get rid" of some problem person, never even giving a second thought as to what it means for someone to be expelled? Jesus warns that to "get rid" of the weeds will also uproot the wheat. He reminds his followers that only God can properly deal with those who oppose *his* kingdom. Most often *my* enemies are the one who opposes *my* kingdom.

Again, the implication here is that a life not centered in God's presence has its own short shelf life. It will expire in due time by its very nature or design.

Grass of the open prairie lands and semi-desert can under certain conditions flourish to abundance. After a rainy spring season, the Great Plains deceptively impress as lush and green. The grass grows hip-high in strong green abundant stock. The comparison of those who prosper through unjust means to this kind of wild grass has often instigated a complaint by those who experience the flip side of someone's profits: "Why do the wicked prosper?"

It only takes, however, just a few weeks of parched, hot, and dry conditions to turn the oceans of green into brown, brittle grass. This would especially be the case as in this psalm, if the grass grows not in open fields but on housetops. Their limited growth area coupled with the lack of shade or shelter make the grass especially exposed to withering. Grass on a housetop is especially useless since no herds can pasture there. This kind of wild grass became a preferred image in reference to Israel's enemies.

Wild grass grows spontaneously and flourishes abruptly especially in semi-arid areas along river banks, near an oasis or spring, or in open fields exposed to heavy seasonal rains. It is a choice metaphor in wisdom literature and the prophets to refer to wealth and power acquired by human ingenuity and exploitation, but also readily subject to seizure (Isa 15:6). The important connection in the metaphor is its uncultivated nature. Thus man's wealth is not viewed as something designed, planned for, or manipulated. That picture certainly flies in the face of a popular notion that one's ingeniousness and hard work win wealth. The importance of the connection is its contrast with God's kingdom being compared to a cultivated orchard or vineyard. It is planned, designed, intentional, and tended to. Most of all, however, its fruits are for *all* to partake.

With which the reaper does not fill his hand,
  or the binder of sheaves his bosom.

The metaphor is extended and it subtly reminds us about enemies—there is nothing to be gained from them. Nothing they have is worth desiring. One cannot "reap" some benefit from them. The songwriter knows what is insidiously lurking behind our enemies—*envy*, some perceived treasure that he or she has and won't share (Ps 35:1–2). The desire for "it" consumes us and drives us toward investing energy and torment of mind into a harvest that will never produce anything of value, especially "it." When all is said and done, "it" cannot even produce a handful of value.

While those who pass by do not say:
The blessing of the LORD be upon you;
We bless you,
  in the name of the LORD.

The last step backward speaks of a life devoid of mutual blessedness. "It" especially won't produce reciprocal love, a one-to-anotherness.

The main thing one will not get from "them" is a kind of reciprocity that comes with having partaken of God's presence with others. As mentioned earlier, blessing is a term of exchange, most often of one greater to one lesser. But here in this verse, we glimpse a vision of blessedness that grows out of that exchange; it is an exchange of shared wealth. It is what the New Testament calls *allelous*, one-to-another.[3] Although it is expressed here as a simple greeting, there is a great deal implied.

For one, it implies a society, culture or community that is guided and orientated toward God's presence and God's word. The outcome of that is a strong sense of mutual care and common share. *All are blessed* in God's kingdom.

In this progression downwards, we have arrived at a flip-flop of fortunes. The ones "loving Zion" feel disgrace and shame and the scourge of those who plow upon the back. Those who "hate Zion" will inevitably turn away and most of all miss a kingdom whose king is the Lord. As the sermon ends on Zion's mount, all those who trust in the Lord and fear Him now exchange a greeting that is infused with not only a hope but also a pledge. God's blessing upon me is my promise to you. "We bless you by the name of the Lord."

The temple sermon, and the second Antiphon, comes to an end with a benediction, but unlike the blessing of the previous psalm where the preacher called out the blessing, here the congregants exchange blessings to one another. As "those trusting in Zion" proceed to the place of sacrifice, they bid a final farewell to the enemy. "They" are not mentioned again. This last song was dedicated to all those who have opposed God's righteous rule; in other words and ultimately, the song is an ode to humanity, to all of us who have at various times, by our actions or inactions "hated Zion."

Not all things concerning our posture towards enemies can be addressed here. Critically, our singer is not focused on the enemy. He does

---

3. "so we, though many, are one body in Christ and individually parts of one another" (Rom 12:5). See also Rom 13:8, 15:5, Eph 4:25, Gal. 6:2, Col 3:13).

not seek the all out destruction of his enemy. He is not obsessed with his enemy. He merely acknowledges that the enemy is clearly an obstacle toward his goal, an impediment. His main appeal is that their binding cords be broken. His imprecation slips to lamentation for his enemy, for "they" will miss out on a wealth and prosperity generated by justice, righteousness, generosity, and mutual care.

Often I find repentance or the act of reconciliation (confession) to be awkward and confusing. I find it hard to account for specific sins. My confessions sound about the same every time. I tend to confess to general sins and dispositions that nearly every human comes under.

Perhaps one way to inventory our lives is to do as the singer of these songs does. He gives full account of his enemy. He grapples greatly with how his own struggle, anxiety, and fears are wrapped up in his enemy. He struggles with how much his own desires and dreams are more dominated by envious repulsion of his rival than on his desire to "love God with all of your heart, soul, and strength."

The Third Antiphon—Psalms 130–134

ANOTHER LITANY IS CHANTED by the priest between the second and third Antiphons. All of the intercessory prayers between the Antiphons end with this prayer:

Help us, save us, have mercy on us, and keep us, O God, by Thy grace.

The priest then chants the prayer of the final Antiphon:

O LORD our God, remember us Thy sinful and unprofitable servants when we call upon Thy holy and venerable name, and put us not to shame in our expectation of Thy mercy, but grant us, O LORD, all our petitions which are unto salvation, and make us worthy to love and fear Thee with all our hearts, and to do Thy will in all things.

 The expedition is seemingly on the last pitch of their ascent. Having made it past "the enemy in the gate," they climbed to the very courtyard of the temple. As they continued their ascent, the powerful sway of the enemy slips backward. The higher the pilgrims get the smaller the enemy becomes until they cannot be seen at all.

 It is natural to suppose that we would encounter great jubilation in this last set of five psalms, but we do not. Instead, a great somberness engulfs each member of the expedition as sacrifices for sin are being prepared. Some will be fortunate enough to offer an animal for sacrifice. An animal, after all, makes for a better gift since it requires a great loss on the part of the sacrificial victim and the one giving it. The supplicant will himself prepare and aid the priests in the shedding of the victim's blood all the while being reminded of the cost of sin in his own life and the life of the nation. The greatest consequence was of course the shame and loss of exile.

Others, especially those who have escaped the howling accusations of their creditors, have nothing except their poverty stricken soul, a prayer of thanksgiving, and a last ditch cry for help to offer the Lord. They will depend entirely on the sacrifices offered by the priests for all of Israel as their only sacrifice. The humiliation of their bankruptcy is compounded by the empty-handiness of their offering. Even in the assembly of the righteous, some subtly wag their heads in derision.

The mood is somber. The sacrifices proceed methodically and reverentially, each quietly contemplating the gruesome necessity. A low, growl-like hum of individual prayers murmured under breathe hovers in a foggy haze as sacrificial smoke spirals to the heavens.

"The dream" itself fuels the fires of sacrifice as the expedition now turned into "all of Israel" earnestly seeks forgiveness—a cancellation of debt and a chance at a new beginning (Ps 130).

Rarely have I witnessed jubilation at the top of a mountain, especially the higher the altitude. We start before the sun is up, and for the next eight to ten hours we battle muscle strain, lung-burning gasps for air, and a mental tug-of-war between failure and victory. For the most part, climbing groups take a sigh of relief, find a quasi-level place to sit down, and quietly take in a contemplative rest. If the weather is mild, many will reverently commune with the mountains, the sky, the sun, and a few hearty creatures.

On several occasions, I have gone through old slides[1] with my kids of climbing trips my family took when I was young. Memorably, my son once commented: "Dad, if all you had to go on were these pictures, you would think that climbing mountains and skiing is all you did as a family." Of those countless sets of slides, many depict my dad in a classic mountaineering pose on top of the mountain—one knee a step higher than the other, ice axe in hand, and looking out. As a refugee

---

1. Okay, for those of you who don't know, a "slide" was made from the film of a non-digital camera. It was placed in a slide projecter and shown on a screen.

of the Holocaust, he came alone to this country as a scrawny teenager, never to see his family again. He loved climbing mountains and in those pictures of him at the top, it seems as though something of eternity was experienced there for him. Something of pains past found resolve in that outward look from the top.

In sorrowful contemplation of each one's failure to live into the great invitation of the God of "heaven and earth," the expedition comes to a gripping realization—this is not the final destination. This is another false summit, but they are so near the top that only quiet resolve and renewed hope emanate. They have done all that they could do. Now they must *wait for the LORD* (Ps 130:5–8). In that moment of quite retrospection, each member of the expedition takes deep breathes and rests in confident expectation (Ps 131).

The expedition realizes the unfinished business because "David" "your anointed one" (*messiach*), and the "ark of Thy might" are absent (Ps 135). The great "Israel project" is incomplete. The realization is deepened by the gross injustices and corruption that infect the people. Prayers go up for God to act mightily on His promise to David.

As with most of my family's climbing trips, we would try and arrive on top by early afternoon so as to enjoy our lunch. Better to go down with a full stomach than up. Cheese and dry sausage sliced from a Swiss army knife were inevitably on the menu, garnished with gratuitous handfuls of "gorp," dried fruit, lemonade, and conversation. For just a brief respite, all was good.

In a similar way, the expedition takes a break and enjoys the "all is good" moment around a sacrificial meal (Ps 133). There on that Holy mountain and in that meal of fellowship everyone can "taste the heavenly bread" and the "cup of life," and "see how good the LORD is."[2] In that moment where past, present, and future commune in God' merciful presence and faithful promise, the assembly sings; "The Lord has commanded the blessing, life forever more."

The antiphons end, not with an unhappy prospect of descending with hopes dashed, but with an exchange of blessings and inspiration to keep ascending. The assembly blesses the singers who have accompanied them the whole way with odes of encouragement, admonition, and hope. The summit is in sight now: "May the LORD, maker of heaven and earth, bless you from Zion (Ps 134).

2. The communion hymn in the Presanctified Liturgy.

12

Psalm 130

It is perhaps difficult for us moderns, especially Christians, to imagine the critical importance of a temple for the purpose and means for making appeals to God. We have confidence that anywhere, at any time, and without any mediator, we can "call out to the Lord." This notion was not foreign to ancient Israelites either. People could cry out anywhere (Gen 4:26). The Israelites prayed and had festivals in local and regional locations. In fact, the local temples became a considerable problem as they were prone to sectarian forms of worship and foreign ritual. Certainly, the exiles with their incipient forms of synagogue worship based on lamentation in far off Babylon understood that prayers could be lifted up anywhere.

There are two things, however, that local sanctuaries and private prayers could not accomplish. Places of worship unite the community. But when it is local, it cannot unite the local community to a greater unity, a greater community, a kingdom. Second, when there is internal conflict, and there always is, a local community may not be able to resolve its internal violence without an appeal to a greater community.

At the top of the mountain (almost), we don't expect contrition, yet this psalm and this last Antiphon return to the same cry for help that first jettisoned the supplicant to expedite an arduous journey. The distress of the opening psalm (Ps 120:1) gushes out in yet another cathartic appeal.

The confession of sin and the cry for mercy indicate that the penitent one is in the temple where sacrifices are being offered. Heads of households offer sacrifices for individual sins, but every morning and evening a sacrifice is offered for all of Israel. The expedition celebrates *yom kippur*, the day of atonement where a great sacrifice is offered to purify the priesthood, the temple, and the people. The debilitating effects of sin are still present, even in the temple.

A great innovation had occurred since the days when the king presided over the temple. Whereas before, sacrifice was the exclusive work of the priests, now the people participated in it. A massive altar was set up in the outer part of the temple where priest and worshiper offered sacrifice and prayers. There was less separation between priests and laity, especially Levitical priests. The second temple was much more of a "populists" temple than anything under royal supervision. Its self-administration without royal oversight made it all the more a focal point of unity for all of Israel.[1]

The congregation would arrive at the *ulam*, the outer courtyard of the temple. With the assistance of priests, any Israelite could sacrifice a "burnt offering." The word for the burnt offering, *olah*, derives from the same word as our Songs of *Ascents*. In this case, the *olah* goes up, referring to the smoke produced from the whole, sacrificial animal being burned on the altar. The people's altar in the *ulam* was considerably elevated, perhaps rising to twenty feet or so.

The *olah* was offered every morning and evening by the priests for all of Israel. In that moment, God promises: "I will meet you and speak to you" (Ex 29:39–42).

Each Israelite who offers a sacrifice performs most of the work, including killing, skinning, and cutting the victim into pieces. The priests wash the parts and place it on the fire. It is "an aroma pleasing to the Lord," not because God likes barbeque, but because of the supplicants display of commitment and devotion.

Many of the sins requiring sacrifice also required restitution. Violations towards others of extortion, swearing falsely, unwillingness to testify, or not returning stolen or lost property were to be compensated. For many suffering in the social crisis, just being present at this place of sacrifice might possibly mean that a just and equitable solution was given, and that the guilty confessed their sin (Lev 6).

---

1. Albertz, *A History of Israelite Religion*, 461.

Out of the depths I cry to You, O LORD.
O LORD, hear my voice.

It is strikingly out of place that the supplicant expresses trauma while standing near the top of the mountain he has so longed for. In general, the "deep" (*emeq*) refers to any geographic depression like a valley, cavern, cave, pit, or well, but especially one in which its vastness and depth make it impossible to get out of. In human experiences then, it connotes the lowest of the low or rock bottom. It couldn't get any worse, like Job. "I am in *deep* trouble now." There is no conceivable way out.

Although valleys are positively associated with fruitful plains, more often valleys are the place where the devastation of war plays out and where humans discard their trash, including unwanted or unclaimed human corpses. Thus, *emeq*, is connected to *sheol* or hell, the abode of the dead (Jer 31:39–40; Prov 9:18). To cry out from the depths means the supplicant is as good as dead, a dead man walking. He is doomed, tried, convicted, and condemned.

To compound the matter, the word is plural. "Out of the depths" is rarely mentioned in the Hebrew bible. It means to be completely overtaken by calamity. Other than our psalm here, the plural form is only used once in Ezekiel and in Psalm 69. We have already encountered that psalm in relationship to "the enemy in the gate" (Psalm 127), but we will need to return to it now, for the picture of this one crying from hell itself is becoming clear.[2]

Although the "enemy" who has hounded the expedition from the start is no longer visible in the text, they have not left the mind of the supplicant. There is good reason to believe that "they" are in the assembly offering sacrifice (Ps 69:19), and even now, they insidiously listen in on the supplicants prayer, hoping to use the supplicants own words as evidence against him (Ps 109:6–7).

I have spoken much about the poor land owner or merchant caught in the pit of insurmountable debt, but back in the introduction of the book, I also talked about those of the aristocracy, like Nehemiah, who were willing to put their wealth at great risk to sponsor the Israel project. As we look again at Psalm 69, we realized that this one who is now "condemned" was likely one from that class whose risky investment in

---

2. Psalm 69 is one of the psalms read aloud in the Bridegroom Matin services of Holy Week as the congregation liturgically follows the path of Jesus from exuberant entrance into Jerusalem to his crucifixion.

"the dream" was sabotaged and his life destroyed in the process. He was like Job, an esteemed leader of the community who fell into scandal and accusations of corruption. Now, he is the scoffing subject of song for drunkards (Ps 69:11–12). He above all others should now denounce "the dream" of God's counter empire where justice and righteousness rather than greed rule the day.

As I paint the picture of this supplicant, we will come to a clearer understanding of this cry for help and its importance to the Songs of Ascents, for in many ways, this moment before God in His temple has been the long sought after height that the expedition has struggle so hard to reach. For the moment, I will call this supplicant, "the ruined one."

Evidence of his ruin is obvious on the temple floor. He stands in the back of the crowd with those who are so poor they cannot even offer a bird or handful of grain. All he can offer is a song of thanksgiving (Ps 69:30–33).[3] He has lost everything and is reduced to the endless toil of slavery (Ps 69:23, Ps 109:9–13). Although he has come from the land of captivity, he has found himself excluded even in his hometown. He ought to have been welcomed by his family, but instead, he was taken advantage of (Ps 69:33). "I am a stranger to my brothers," he cries out, and "an alien to my own mother's sons" (Ps 69:8).

He came from far off Babylon empowered by the dream, but for those long settled in the land, the rules of the game were dramatically different. They knew how to prey on the dreamer's lofty hopes and play upon his ideals of a house of integrity (Ps 69:9). They deride his pathetic prayer rituals of lamentation from the exilic community (Ps 69: 10–11, Ps 109:9–11). They lured him with displays of new wealth ready for the taking if one signed on the line (Ps 69:22). "You can increase your own pockets and help the newbies settle in," they promised. Once the ruined one took the bait, however, the pit became even more slippery. They kept secret the small print (Ps 69:23). They took advantage of the ruined one's vulnerability, preying on his sensitivities to the covenant demands for equity.

---

3. The prayers of thanksgiving (Ps 69:30–33; Ps70:6, Ps 109:22), where an appeal for God to listen to the impoverished, come from the very real experience of one who does not having a sacrifice to offer for his sins. All he can offer is praise and thanksgiving. Some of the anti-sacrificial statements in the Psalms come from this experience. The rich could afford a sacrifice, but ironically, it was the very rich who robbed others of such and opportunity. (Albertz, *History of Israelite Religion*, 522)

**Let Thine ears be attentive
to the voice of my supplications.**

It may seem odd to ask God to pay attention as if He was possibly distracted or dozing off, but that is not really the picture here. The word, *qahav*, denotes an active engagement with someone else, often times in a legal case before a judge. To ask for the attention of a judge strongly connotes a decision is forthcoming that will change an outcome.

Isaiah connects this kind of focused attention as a critical feature of a kingdom where righteousness and justice prevail. In this respect, the judges will no longer be blind and deaf to corruption (Isa 32:1–8). For Jeremiah, complacency to corruption is the inevitable outcome of ignoring God's word (Jer 6:19–20).

The appeals for God to listen and to be attentive in the Psalms are nearly always related to someone who has or is suffering economic injustice. Constantly, the supplicant appeals to God because a gang of accusers who by their conniving intrigue have figured out ways to "cheat the system" surrounds him. These appeals are often associated with the sacrifices for atonement (Ps 5).

It is not easy for us to understand the seemingly fastidious attention to sacrificial purity often detailed in parts of the Bible. Here, I can only focus on one point in comment about that. The writers of those sections always connect ritual impropriety with murder, corruption, and economic disparity.[4] The lack of explanation for that connection can and does lead to a gross abuse of piety—paying zealous attention to ritual detail devoid of economic justice—a practice strongly condemned by Jesus (Mt 6–7). But I believe the intent went a different direction. The emphasis on offering a pure and unblemished sacrifice moves away from the temptation to "cheat the system." The unblemished, choice sacrifice on the altar served as a powerful model. Just as you would not cheat God, so do not cheat your neighbor. If God is not a system to toy with, neither is your neighbor a commodity to be exchanged on the market. Something of this idea was behind the statement: "Love your neighbor as yourself" (Lev 19:18, 34) *and* "be holy for I, the LORD, your God, am holy" (Lev 19:2). Don't turn gift into grift.

---

4. See Lev 19 for a prime example.

If Thou, O LORD, should mark iniquities, LORD who could stand?

Slowly the trap engulfed, more bills, more debt. Then, at the just the right time, the ruined one is taken to bankruptcy court. He is accused of extortion. Suddenly, a host of accusers line up with the same suspicious line. The ruined one realizes that his own conflicting desires got him into this mess (Ps 69:5). He knows he is not completely innocent. He is as guilty as his partners in crime. But that is why he must pray at the temple during the sacrifices. It is the optimum "favorable time" (Ps 69:13–14) to seek pardon. But even on the temple floor treachery lurks. Some have taken bribes in order to wiggle close to the ruined one even at his most vulnerable time and record his own confession as evidence against him (Ps 109:6). The guilt of the ruined one must be exaggerated and embellished, cloaking the rest from suspicion (Ps 69:20). They offer choice animals for sacrifice and offer their scraps to the poor displaying their favored status before the Lord. The ruined one has nothing but his trust in the Lord and his needy prayer as an offering to Him. All he can offer now is his own life.

The worrisome prayer that the sins of Israel are too grievous and numerous is echoed throughout the Psalms and in the prophets. It reflects a deep-seated anxiety that God's anger over Israel's past failure that led to the exile will never be abated. We could focus on God's anger here and critically wonder what kind of God this is. On the other hand, we could be amazed at the persistence of this ancient people who profoundly understood that:

> *With the Lord is kindness*
> *and with him is plenteous redemption;*
> *And he will redeem Israel*
> *from all his iniquities.*(Ps 130:7–8)

But there is forgiveness with thee, that thou mayest be feared.

The ruined one begged his accusers for a second chance, a forgiveness of debt. He hoped his confession of guilt and appeals for mercy could persuade a turn around. But instead, the accusations of betrayal intensified (Ps 69: 19–21). Even in his enslavement, his debts remain on the books. He wears them like a worn out garment (Ps 109:16–21). If, "in the time of favor," the Lord will forgive, then all will be made right. God is able to forgive where men will not. God is more merciful than man will ever be. In God's forgiveness, the ruined one is miraculously rescued. The dream, at one time marred beyond resemblance, is renewed in God's grace to even greater vigor, for:

> *For God will save Zion*
>   *and rebuild the cities of Judah.*
> *They shall dwell in the land and own it,*
>   *and the descendants of his servants shall inherit it,*
>   *and those who love his name shall inhabit it.* (Ps 69:36–37)

The term for forgiveness, *selichah,* is plural and intensive—*abundant forgiveness.* The plurality of *the deep* is matched by the abundance of God's mercy. It is only the miraculous rescue from exile where this form is used. In a lengthy story of the Jews celebration at the temple, Ezra rehearses God's amazing history with his people. The sermon of Ezra was probably given as a part of the *yom kippur* observance. Those who had returned mainly celebrated it. In other words, it was the exiles who really knew what confession, lamentation and the need for atonement was about.

Jesus teaches along similar lines. Only those who understand the depths of their own sin, not just in terms of naughty little habits or little failures of religious obligation, but more importantly in each one's contribution to the violence our current human systems inflict. They best understand the vast riches of God's forgiveness (Lk 7:36–47).

At one point in his sermon, Ezra reminds Israel of God's forgiveness when they rebelled against God and Moses at the base of Mt. Sinai:

> *But you are a God of pardons* (selichah)*, gracious and compassionate, slow to anger and rich in mercy; you did not forsake them* (Neh 9:17).

This particular phrase, repeating God's loving, forgiving and faithful response to Israel became a kind of covenant mantra in the post-exilic period.[5]

There are several other points of contact with Psalm 130 and this sermon of Ezra's. For one, the portrayal of the "ruined one" is probably an archetypal image for all involved in the Israel project. It is a characterization of the exile itself and of each individual coming out of exile. In other words, the ruined one in Psalm 130 is a composite iconic figure of the suffering

---

5. See Ex 34:6; Jonah 4:2–3

endured by returning exiles in the social crisis of the time. This explains for one, the dramatic shift in the song from a singular confession to a corporate hope. "I wait for the Lord" quickly turns to "O Israel hope in the Lord."

By following Ezra's sermon, we pick up on more insights into God's abundant forgiveness. For one, it is based on His righteousness (Neh 9:8). It was "righteousness" that compelled God to listen to the cries of his people in Egypt and to act. Here we might take note. Ultimately it was not sacrifice that "made" God act favorably. Only God, because of the kind of God He is, "made" God act favorably.

In that historical rehearsal, it was the rebellion in the wilderness where God in particular showered forgiveness, grace, compassion, long-suffering and abounding love (Neh 9:17). God did this when the people were offering the *wrong* sacrifice to the *wrong* god. Precisely in that moment, God did not abandon them in their rebellion (Neh 9:19). There is a whole lot we Christians need to get here on a profound level (Neh 9:31). Sacrifice does not *cause* God to forgive. Sacrifice is our *response* to His forgiveness. Sacrifice is a gift offered in response to love, not a payment offered in hopes of a loving response. Sacrifice is much more about obstinate, greedy, and violent humans changing course than it is about God doing so.

God did for the exiles what he did for that rebellious lot in the wilderness. He led them out of the wilderness and out of the land of their captors. The returning ones understood that the whole temple apparatus and the land they stood on was nothing other than undeserving gift. It is the one who goes *through* the Reed Sea, the wilderness, the exile, the expedition, and the passion who best understands that God is Love.

Here I am reminded of something our priest exhorts us toward every year during the Fast. The Eastern traditions around the Great Fast are rigorous. We are asked to abstain from meat, dairy, oil and alcohol for forty days. We should spend more time in prayer and giving to the poor. Presanctified Liturgies are on Wednesday and Friday evenings. Come Holy Week, we will have services every day. The congregation does what it can to take this season seriously. Nonetheless, our priest reminds that Easter or Pascha, the celebration of Christ's resurrection, does not make much sense if one only shows up Easter morning yet has circumvented the conflict, arrest, trial, execution, and burial of Jesus first. In a similar way, the Jews who had returned from exile insisted that identification with that horrific experience was the only way to understand and to live into the reconstitution of Israel. Repentance, penance, and lamentation were the only starting points to possibly grasp the "second chance" God was offering His people.

The time of repentance, of going through the exodus, the wilderness, the exile, the expedition, and the passion is what conditions us to "fear the Lord." It is only in understanding the depths of God's forgiving and guiding hand that the Lord's Torah can rightly guide a person. It is what helps them see how profound forgiveness of debt really is.

I wait for the LORD, my soul waits,
 and in his word I hope.
My soul waits for the LORD
 more than the watchman for the morning.
 more than the watchman for the morning.

This word for wait, *qawah*, is often used of waiting for a harvest. Isaiah uses it in reference to God's vineyard, Israel (Isa 5). There, God cleared the land, planted the seed, tilled the garden, and prepared for the harvest. This kind of waiting is based on reasonable expectation. Having done everything a farmer can and should do, he can expect a harvest if all goes well.

Waiting on God for favor sometimes takes on this quality. If one lives an upright life and diligently seeks to follow God's way, he can reasonably expect, wait for, a favorable response from God (Ps 25:21). This kind of righteous confidence was the unrelenting view of Job's supposed "friends" (Job 4:6).

Mostly, however, waiting on God in reasonable expectation turns resoundingly negative by the prophets. Israel forgot that God is also waiting on them. Isaiah says of God's vineyard:

> *He looked* (qawah) *for the crop of grapes,*
> *but what it yielded was wild grapes.* (Isa 5:2)

The gross disparity between the good intentions of the farmer and the kind of crop produced threw "reasonable expectation" out the window.

> *The vineyard of the LORD of Hosts is the house of Israel,*
> *and the men of Judah are his cherished plant;*
> *He looked for judgment, but see, bloodshed!*
> *for justice, but hark, the outcry!* (Isa 5:7)

The bad crop is one which we are quite familiar with by now: expanding estates and wealth at the expense of others. Israel and Judah had gone the way of all other nations. Greed, exploitation, corruption, treachery, and violence were the standard ways of going about business. Time and again, they fell into the temptation to turn the God who had rescued slaves from imperial powers into an imperial God who enslaves (Isa 5:8–30).

No other prophet was so tormented by this reversal than Jeremiah. Repeatedly Jeremiah laments: *We wait* (qawah) *for peace, to no avail;/ for a time of healing, but terror comes instead.* (Jer 14:19)

Jeremiah's and the people's hope for God to intervene in the Babylonian crisis was useless. The sins of the people were too great and grievous for God to act favorably. The result was exile.

Curiously, the prophets place a good deal of emphasis on God who is waiting for us. Constantly, and sometimes despairingly, the Lord waits and seeks to see the fruit of righteousness and justice. And in this sense, God's response is extraordinary. He does not wait until we get it right; instead, he acts, not because of our righteous deeds but because of God who is righteous, just, *and* abounding in mercy.

> *Honesty is lacking,*
>   *and the man who turns from evil is despoiled.*
> *The LORD saw this* (waited), *and was aggrieved*
>   *that right did not exist.*
> *He saw that there was no one,*
>   *and was appalled that there was none to intervene;*
> *So his own arm brought about the victory,*
>   *and his justice lent him its support . . .*
> *He shall come to Zion a redeemer*
>   *to those of Jacob who turn from sin, says the LORD.*
> (Isa 59:15–16, 20).

Ultimately, the foundation for waiting in confidence for God's intervention lies firmly in the kind of God the Israelites worship. Only in this sense can the supplicant reasonably expect God to intervene in his own life and the life of the nation. Only God can be counted on as surely as the watchman can count on the rising of the morning sun in the dreariness of the midnight watch. "The Mighty One of Jacob" is faithful, just, true, righteous, and loving. He cannot be otherwise. It is as the prophet proclaimed:

> *Such as they had not heard of from of old.*
> *No ear has ever heard, no eye ever seen,*
>   *any God but you*
>   *doing such deeds for thos who wait for him.*
> *Would that you might meet us doing right,*
>   *that we were mindful of you in our ways!* (Isa 64:3–4)

There are two things that the ruined one can do in his agonizing time of waiting. First, he must repent. He must realize the gross error of his ways and earnestly seek God in confession. Second, he must put his trust in the Lord, rely on his word, and fear the Lord. In Isaiah's famous encounter with king Ahaz, Isaiah places waiting trust as the antidote for fear.

> *And fear not, nor stand in awe of what they fear.*
> *But with the LORD of hosts make your alliance—*
> *for him be your fear and your awe . . .*
> *For I will trust in the LORD, who is hiding his face from the house*
> *of Jacob; yes, I will wait for him.* (Isa 8:12–13,17)

The "word" that the ruined one is especially anxious about is not entirely clear. Curiously, there is no pronouncement of forgiveness at a sacrifice. Repeatedly, the scriptures affirm that the act of sacrifice effects forgiveness: "the priest will make atonement for them, and they will be forgiven."[6] For the atonement sacrifice, the high priest was to confess "all the sinful faults and transgressions of the Israelites" (Lev 16:21), but there is no pronouncement of forgiveness.

My guess is that the "word" is more in line with a whole string of prophetic promises uttered over a two hundred year span, such as the ones mentioned above. They are too numerous to recount here, but the fundamental message was and is the same: No matter how bad the sin, God is greater. Israel belongs to God, and God will not abandon Israel. This is precisely what the last lines of this song boldly proclaim:

---

6. This formula is repeated throughout Leviticus (Lev 4:20). It does not suggest that there is a pronouncement of forgiveness, nor identify who is doing the forgiveness. There is the very real possibility that the act of sacrifice was aimed at getting the *community* to grant forgiveness, including financial debt. If God forgives, then who are we not to?

O Israel, hope in the LORD,
  For with the LORD there is mercy,
  and with him is plenteous redemption.
And he will redeem Israel from all his iniquities.

As we have often encountered in the Songs of Ascents, so we once again take note here. There is an abrupt and mysterious shift. Something happened to our "ruined one" in between verse six and these final two lines. God does miraculous things in blank spaces. Nothing appears to have happened outwardly, but something miraculous has happened inwardly. Perhaps, the corporate act of "all Israel" waiting and watching as the high priest performs the atonement and scapegoat sacrifices has revived *the dream*, not just for "the ruined one," but even in his enemies. Perhaps also, the business machine halted just long enough for the congregation to look at each other as brothers instead of objects of exploitation. For one, his anxious waiting was transformed into quiet confidence. Suddenly, he goes from supplication to proclamation, from penance to exhortation. For a brief moment, he turns away from addressing God to speak to his neighbor. Perhaps, the Levitical choir sings these last verses at the end of the *yom kippur* proceedings.

I am reminded of the kind of transformation that transpires during Easter vigil. In the darkness of midnight, the faithful have processed in sorrowful tones, still contemplating the grotesque and shocking end of the ruined one's death on the cross. They come to the doors of the church where the priest calls out to the closed doors to open "that the king of glory may enter." The doors burst open and the dirge suddenly transcends into a *shir*, a victory song. All shout in song and process in victory: "Christ is risen from the dead, trampling down death by death. And to those in the tombs bestowing life!"

All somber colors have changed to white and gold. Bright light overtakes flickering candlelight eking its way in darkness. Mournful songs in minor key give way to songs of boastful triumph. God has vindicated as only He can do. One of those joyous songs of Easter morn blurts in such giddy exuberance that we fail to notice the utter depth of what we are saying. In our normal world we would never dare to say such a thing, but in the brightness of the resurrection we dare not say otherwise:

> *The souls bound in the chains of hell O Christ,*
>   *seeing thy compassion without measure,*
> *pressed onward to the light with joyful steps,*

> *praising the eternal Pascha!*
> *Let us embrace each other joyously.*
> *Pascha, ransom from affliction!*

And the most ridiculously radical statement of them all:

> *Let us embrace each other!*
> *Let us call "brothers" even those that hate us*
> *and forgive all by the resurrection!*

Our psalm here, only sings in hopeful anticipation, but whiffs of that glorious day must have ascended with the smoke from those sacrificial embers. Here the confidence resides as everything in the Songs of Ascents does—*in the LORD alone*. Even in the darkest nights of exile and as refugees in a land far from home, prophets would dream of a great reversal, not because of the circumstances, but only because of the God they had known. Ironically, it was only in their death as a people that they understood even more so the kind of God they belonged to.

> *To whom can you liken me as an equal?*
> *says the Holy One.*
> *Lift up your eyes on high*
> *and see who has created these:*
> *He leads out their army and numbers them,*
> *calling them all by name.*
> *By his great might and the strength of his power*
> *not one of them is missing!*
> *Why, O Jacob, do you say,*
> *and declare, O Israel,*
> *"My way is hidden from the LORD,*
> *and my right is disregarded by my God?"*
> *Do you not know*
> *or have you not heard?*
> *The LORD is the eternal God,*
> *creator of the ends of the earth.*
> *He does not faint nor grow weary,*
> *and his knowledge is beyond scrutiny.*
> *He gives strength to the fainting;*
> *for the weak he makes vigor abound.*
> *Though young men faint and grow weary,*
> *and youths stagger and fall,*
> *They that hope in the LORD will renew their strength,*
> *they will soar as with eagles' wings;*
> *They will run and not grow weary,*
> *walk and not grow faint.* (Isa 40:25–31)

The question, first sung on the shores of the Reed Sea and revived among the exiles in Babylon, is put to the imperial powers of every age:

> *Who is like you, among the gods, O LORD?*
> *Who is like to you, magnificent in holiness?*
> *O terrible in renown, worker of wonders!* (Ex 15:11–12)

In each case, and in the case of those on the temple floor in the social crisis of post-exilic *Yehud*, the confidence comes from two things God had revealed to the Israelites. The Lord loves Israel unfailingly— *with the LORD there is steadfast love*. Always! Because of that, there is no sin great enough and no price too high for God to redeem his prized possession—*In your mercy you led the people you redeemed* (Ex 15:13).

> *Blessed are the poor in spirit,*
>   *for theirs is the kingdom of heaven.*
> *Blessed are those who mourn,*
>   *for those will be comforted.*
> *Blessed are the meek,*
>   *for they will inherit the earth.*
> *Blessed are they who hunger and thirst for righteousness,*
>   *for they will be satisfied.* (Mt 5:3–7)

13

Psalm 131

From the title, we recognize that David is back on the scene. Unlike the first mention of David in Psalm 122 where the reminiscence had more to do with a kind of nostalgic look back, this time David's presence is more somber and serious. Even more so, David becomes the primary focus of the rest of the Songs of Ascents for two reasons. The more obvious reason is the mention of him in the text. Psalm 132, which is exclusively *about* David, is sandwiched in by two songs *of* David. More importantly, however, David's presence in the text accents all the more his *absence* at the temple and in Jerusalem. The absence of a Davidic king reminds the worshipping community on the temple floor that they are still on expedition. They have climbed to significant heights, but they have not summited yet. The absence of the anointed one, *messiach*, is present throughout the worshipping community, especially for those who long for a rule of righteousness and justice to overtake the imperial rule of "the normalcy of civilization's violence."[1]

The formula for a kingdom whose king is God was set by the time of Nehemiah and Ezra. One needed: a land, a people, a covenant, a city, a royal house, and a Holy Mountain. All was in place save one—the royal house. This critical piece, however, was a dicey proposition. The Hebrew bible is rife with criticism of kings, and although all of Israel took responsibility for its failure, it readily understood how problematic the very concept of a king was.

---

1. A phrase by John Dominic Crosson, *God and Empire*, 46–47.

The problem of kings in Israel and Judah only served, however, to increase the stature of David to iconic proportions. Long ago, this most unique fellow conquered this ancient city. His name was "Beloved." He was loved both by God and his fellow Israelites. He was an unusual mix of lowly shepherd, musician, renegade, mighty warrior, cunning politician, diplomat, king, and priest. David managed all of that in a most humble way, never forgetting his origins as a shepherd boy or as a member of a unique nation whose psyche was deeply etched with the memory of being miraculously delivered from slavery. Other than a couple of serious mistakes, his rise to kingship had so captured the imagination of Israel, it seemed that no one since his time could really fit the part. None of his children could quite match his unique stature.

As the kingdom of Israel divided, declined, and degenerated, the longing for another king like David increased and magnified. The harder the times were, the bigger the legend of David became.

Within the Songs of Ascents, David is revived mainly because he founded Jerusalem and envisioned it as a "city of God," a focal point that could unify the people of God. Most of what has been said so far about Zion and all the dreams associated with it find some grounding in this mysterious intriguing figure. Probably most important for the Songs of Ascents is that David was a dreamer whose dreams ran ahead of logistics most of the time. In Psalm 122, David is conjured up as one who dreamed of uniting the tribes of Israel under one God, one city, one temple, one banner (the Ark), one covenant, one temple, and one king. As will be mentioned in the next song (Psalm 132), David is the one beloved by God in which God made a covenant of love with him, promising him an eternal kingship. In other words, God really liked this guy because David was so in tune with God's desires, what God dreams of.

David has several points of contact with the Songs of Ascents. Every Levitical scribe, lyricist, singer, and liturgist has been schooled through Davidic Songwriting 101. David is the father and master of Israelite liturgical song. Second, David was an outlaw. He lived the absolute opposite of what was promised. Even though he was capable of seizing what was promised, he waited patiently for his Lord to act without seeking revenge or retaliation.

But mostly here, he is called to mind as the model of repentance and humility. David went the way of just about anybody, then and now, who because of their giftedness rise to the top. Doused in accolades, he thought he was above the rules of ordinary humans, and he took a step toward "god-like" status. Unfortunately, his constituency had a deep suspicion of divinity status from their days as Pharaoh's slaves. He did not do one of those public apologies which boils down to "I am sorry I got caught." No, he repented. He returned to his humble origins. Just as a lone, half naked shepherd or a renegade hiding in caves, David returned to a true part of himself. Even in his sin and guilt, David surrendered to the mercy of God. He came back to the quiet resolve that it is better to fall into the hands of God than of men.

As I mentioned in the introduction, the "ground up" prayers dominate the Psalter, and this above all else finds its origins in David. David schooled Israel on how to love God, pray to God, worship Him, and trust him. Maybe nothing saved Israel more during the exile than that Israel had learned to pray.

A prayer of the priest after the reading of the well-known penance psalm of Psalm 51 in Daily Matins puts it this way:

> O LORD our God, You have given us forgiveness through repentance and as a model of knowledge and confession of sins. You have revealed to us the repentance of the prophet David that led to pardon.

We like to think of prophets as men who revealed something about the future, so it is significant that this Orthodox prayer that starts out every morning considers that David prophetically modeled repentance for the people of God for all generations to come.

Again, we need not concern ourselves too much with actual authorship because for certain, David is the virtual author. It resonates in Davidesque tones in several ways.

More importantly, we need to ask: who is praying this prayer, and singing this song? There is a royal flavor to this prayer. There are hints of exhortation to it, as if most within earshot are having trouble cooperating with it. We should imagine David singing a song like this, perhaps around a smoky, flickering campfire in the recesses of some rocky cleft, hiding from Saul. We should equally imagine David's "son" praying this as he returns to the throne sometime in the future.

Of course, our *ruined one* of the previous psalm prays this prayer. It is he, even from *sheol* itself, who miraculously grasped forgiveness and steadfast love arising from the sacrificial smoke. In that moment, a quiet resolve took over, a strength renewed, a vision resurfaced. His invigorated hope turned contagious. The *ruined one*, now in concert with David, call out to the Levitical choir: "Sing to all of Israel—wait for the Lord. For with the Lord is steadfast love and great power to redeem."

All of Israel—true Israel, faithful Israel, ruined Israel, rebuked and punished Israel, penitent Israel, exiled Israel, returning Israel, poverty stricken Israel, longing Israel—pray this prayer, each and every one yet altogether.

O LORD, my heart is not lifted up,
mine eyes are not raised too high.

Lust, lust, lust. Not, not, nyet. Desire is the fundamental problem of kings, the wealthy, the poor, and well, everyone. This song begins with three emphatic negations of it. Desire is the primal proposition: which of the lusty[2] trees will you partake of (Gen 2–3)? For Adam, he could have it all save one. For kings of old and those empire-builders even today, the question remains: must I acquire everything that someone else has acquired? Or is there satisfaction that requires no more? Does "profit" have a limit? As insignificant as that last piece of fruit is, it is what drives empires to insatiable limits.

For us, the heart metaphorically refers to emotions, passion, or impulse. The Hebrew concept encompasses some of that, but moves more toward the seat of will, deliberation, choice, determination, and even reason. In a sense, the heart super charges human drives by summoning all the human faculties to action. The phrase "lift the heart" has an occasional positive sense. King Jehosaphat "was encouraged [lifted his heart] to follow the LORD's ways" (2 Chron 17:6). In other words, he was encouraged and inspired toward devotion to the Lord.

In most every other case, however, it refers to a ruler or wealthy person who is overtaken with confidence that they are indestructible, that they are beyond reproach. Most Bibles translate the Hebrew idiom "lift the heart" as haughty or proud, a condition that precedes and causes their downfall. In nearly every case where "lift the heart" is used, it is associated with expanding wealth, corruption, injustice, and violence while simultaneously reducing trust in Yahweh:

---

2. The Hebrew word describing the trees in the garden could be translated "lusty," but usually it is not due to our prudish sensitivities. Regardless, we certainly understand that the primary focus of the story is not fruit trees in an orchard, but rather the direction desire will go.

> *The rich man's wealth is his strong city;*
>   *he fancies it a high wall.*
> *Before his downfall a man's heart is haughty,*
>   *but humility comes before honor.* (Prov 18:11–12)

The phrase is especially applied in the Bible to the problem of kings. The rich and powerful king Uzziah, presuming upon his greatness, entered the temple and acted as a priest, offering sacrifices (2 Chron 26:16). He suffered leprosy as a consequence, but more disastrous was the contagion that spread to his descendants and gave rise to the whole prophetic tradition in the Hebrew Bible. Uzziah's son Ahaz jettisoned the quiet Isaiah into a bold and relentless prophet. Prophets such as Amos, Micah, and Isaiah were the first to see the spread of this contagion beyond the royal house. It seethed its way into the rulers of the people, causing them to "loot" the poor, "crushing my people" and "grinding down the poor" (Isa 3:15).

God healed Uzziah's grandson, Hezekiah, of a life threatening illness, yet Hezekiah "did not then discharge his debt of gratitude" (2 Chron 32:25). Although vague, the statement probably refers to his refusal to make a sacrificial offering. God's "wrath" was on him, but Hezekiah, Jerusalem and the city repented.

No other scripture depicts the pride of empirical power as the poetic diatribe against the King of Tyre in Ezekiel (Ez 28). Certainly, the prophecy takes on iconic proportions as a scathing rebuke to lustful kings everywhere, especially because of the shockingly thorough destruction the city experienced by the Babylonians. The passage deserves a full reading, but here I can only summarize.

Ezekiel begins straight away with the heart of the issue, an arrogance that makes one think he has transcended the mere human realm into the divine (Ez 38:2). The source of pride is wealth, power, and prominence, but surprisingly not military might. Most of all, the primary source of such ascendency was the king's great wisdom and cunning in the market place, a wisdom, however, that turns on the one who presumes to have mastered it (Ez 38:17). The lust for boundless treasure and endless glory turned wisdom into greed and violence (Ez 38:16). Most of all, however, a great presumption overtook. "I am a god," the king convinced himself (Ez 38:2, 6, 9). Most of all, he lost sight of his humanness.

Zephaniah, like his contemporary Jeremiah, prophesied the inevitable destruction of Jerusalem because of the people's unwillingness to repent. But he also envisioned that the exile would cause repentance to overtake pride. Jerusalem would again be inhabited, but this time by humble worshippers like the one's singing Psalm 131 who would no longer "exalt yourself" (Zeph 3:11). Rather:

> *But I will leave as a remnant in your midst*
>   *a people humble and lowly,*
> *Who shall take refuge in the name of the LORD:*
>   *the remnant of Israel.*
> *They shall do no wrong*
>   *and speak no lies;*
> *Nor shall there be found in their mouths*
>   *a deceitful tongue;*
> *They shall pasture and couch their flocks*
>   *with none to disturb them.* (Zeph 3:12–13)

The next denial in our psalm comes in the phrase: *I have not raised my eyes to high*. Most of us know that downward look from a dog exposed to some mischievous mishap, but we also know the reverse, that certain upward glance that says: "I am above you." Raising the eyes is synonymous with lifting up the heart, but is even more associated with unmitigated desire.

At the top of the list of things God hates are "haughty eyes" (Prov 6:17). The list goes on to mention all the things associated with "the wicked" in the Songs of Ascents: lying tongue, violence, scheming after gain, testifying falsely, and stirring up discord. Another proverb plainly connects raised eyes with a disdain for the poor that "devouring the needy from the earth,/ and the poor from among men" (Prov 30:13–14).

The funny thing about desire is that the more it is fed, the hungrier it gets. The question of the garden bears repeating: is there satisfaction that requires no more? Torah advocates were keenly aware of the question and understood a devastating effect of over consumption—forgetfulness. The more people enjoyed wealth and prosperity the more their "eyes were raised" and the more they forgot from whence they came.

> *When . . . you have increased your herds and flocks, your silver and gold, and all your property, you then become haughty* (be raised) *of heart and unmindful of the LORD, your God, who brought you out of Egypt, that place of slavery.* (Deut 8:12–14)

This Torah awareness has important connections to our psalm here. It is in the gathering at the temple where sacrifices of thanksgiving are made that the Torah is read and renewed. Forgetfulness of who one is and where one is going was only magnified in David's sons. Too few kings after David were able, let alone willing to reverse the contagion of desire. During the reigns of Hezekiah and Josiah attempts at reforming the notion of "king" were made. The "ideal" king was articulated. He was not to be haughty and does not lust for power and wealth. He was not to "become enstranged from his countrymen through pride, nor turn aside to the right or to the left from these commandments" (Deut 17:20).

In one sense, the *ruined one* prays not only his own prayer, but the prayer of all Israel and of David's future son yet to come. He is to be one "among his brothers" whose denial of imperial lust enables him to remember the Torah, faithfully keep it, and lead the people of God towards. It.

I do not occupy myself with things too great and marvelous for me.

In essence, this third and final "not" statement combating desire reiterates the idyllic king hoped for in the Torah. We could assume based on the previous verse that the great and marvelous things are wealth, wisdom, and power alluded to in the previous verse, but this is not likely since the Hebrew word for marvelous, *pele*, only refers to the mysteries of God, both in marvelous, saving deeds or of God's judgments and wisdom: that is the Torah. In keeping with the previous psalm, the greatness of God's mercy in the return of the exile, the building of the temple, the reestablishment of worship should be included.

First, we can puzzle. Why would a worshipper *not* want to "occupy" himself with the mighty deeds and ways of God. The word here, *halak*, is the same as in the well-known phrase to *walk* in the ways of the Lord or the Torah. It has a wide array of meanings, but here it carries the sense of "to busy oneself" or to apply a considerable amount of time and effort into it. It is to go about the business of "great and marvelous things." When put this way, it comes closer to understanding it as a temptation rather than some kind of pious meditation to the Lord. To do so would, could lead to the temptation of Davidic kings of old: seize for oneself a share of praise that belongs to God alone, to confuse one's own saving acts with the Lords.

The temptation to confuse God's glory with one's own accomplishments, even of the most spiritual or religious kind, is singled out by the monks of the Christian East as the most ruthless and precarious. As odd as the compulsion of the desert monks to avoid human contact to extreme measures, it reflects a profound understanding of how deadly praise and adoration of one's spiritual prowess can be. "Vainglory and pride bring about every spiritual calamity and downfall . . . The Desert Fathers used to say that if we praise our brother untimely, it is like delivering him to the demons," says Archimandrite Zacharias.[3]

Can praise of God's great deeds turn into a praise of my wonderful deeds, or our wonderful deeds? Can God's triumph over Pharaoh, over Sennacherib, over Nebuchadnezzar, or over the haughty, wayward kings of Israel and Judah turn into a triumphalism on our part? Look at what mighty things I have done. Look at my choice sacrifice upon the altar, at the many blessings God has bestowed on me. Does God build his kingdom or his church or do we do it for him? Do the mighty works of God turn into boastful claims of "I built it"?

Truly from the very ancient of times even until today, devotees of God tend to confuse who "builds the house." Spiritual dangers abound the moment I presume that my faithfulness, my hard work, my money, my investment of emotion and time in the church, my diligence in prayer and attending Mass, or my dedication to the Lord's work entitles me to a return on that investment. Time and time again, from kings of old to parishioners now, we are gloriously adept at forgetting whose house we are in.

But I have calmed and quieted my soul,

According to St. Theodoros the Great Ascetic, there are three principle negative passions to which all other passions that keep us from God derive: love of pleasure, riches, and praise.[4] In the second verse of this psalm, these passions mentioned in the first verse find an antidote.

The contrasting conjunction here is derived from a Hebrew *im lo* (if not) formula which brings out a sense of emphatic resolve in the opposite direction. The emphatic denial reminds the worshipper of a border that should not be crossed. It is that boundary set in the garden: *of this tree you shall not eat*. Even though the people where able to draw nearer to the sacrifices in the post-exilic temple, they were to go no further. We may remember the boundary that God laid out for the

---

3. Zacharias, *The Enlargement of the Heart.* 14

4. St. Theodoros the Great Ascetic II, A Century of Spiritual Texts, Sec.10, from *Philokalia: The Eastern Christian Spiritual Texts.*

people of Israel at the base of Mount Sinai which the people had some problems with (Deut 5:5).

Here once again is a parallel with the *ruined one* and the future David praying at the temple floor and those of Eastern monks. For at the heart of the remedy for our illness is stillness. "Stillness," says Nikitas Stithatos,

> *is an undisturbed state of the intellect, the calm of a free and joyful soul, the tranquil unwavering stability of the heart in God . . . an unsleeping watchfulness, spiritual prayer, untroubled repose in the midst of great hardship, and finally, solidarity and union with God.*"[5]

The penitent one has resolved to calm and quiet his soul. To remind, the soul, *nephesh*, is that part of a human designed to take in Life. The soul is an "open throated" human. The goal is never to deny or destroy our desires, for we are made to consume life. Rather, the goal is to redirect our desires to the One we are most designed to be with. For this moment where the ruined one stands before the sacrifices too impoverished to offer anything other than his soul, he can only respond in quiet resolve. He has conditioned his soul to first be calm. The term connotes being settled, situated rightly. It is to put oneself in the right situation to receive grace. He has caused his competing desires to level out. Additionally, his soul is made quiet, to be made still in speech and motion, but also in resignation and resolve.

Like a child quieted at its mother's breast.

Most of us have seen the near intoxicated countenance of a baby after getting some "home brew." That image alone is enough to draw us into the contentment of the moment. Certainly most who have attended meaningful prayer or worship services have known something of the kind of peaceful quiet resolve of a congregation as they depart.

For me, St. Ted is another image that also evokes this amazing quiet resolve. I will have to change his name because Ted would not approve of me saying anything about him. Ted is one of the daily visitors at our church's sandwich line. He is always the first in line and he rarely misses. Ted greets every volunteer with a hearty good morning and an offer to help. Ted is your quintessential homeless looking man. He

---

5. Nikitas Stithatos, IV, on the Inner Nature of Things and on the Purification of the Intellect, Sec. 64, from *Philokalia: The Eastern Christian Spiritual Texts*.183

has bushy unkempt hair and beard. He wears the same grease lathered winter jacket all year round. Probably most significant about Ted are his pants, or lack thereof. Ted's pants had steadily deteriorated over the past several years. First there where holes and rips around the knees, then all the way down to the ankles. Soon the rips were moving up towards his hip. At one point, his paints looked more like a hula skirt than anything else. Of course, we offered him a new pair, but he would steadfastly refuse, and he would get offended if you said anything about his pants. What most of us who knew Ted realized is that the pants were a symbol of his repentance, for what sins none of us knew.

I lost my job during the recession and needed work. I accepted a job as the part-time janitor at our church being unable to find much else. Sometimes, I would get very discouraged. I felt like I was not supposed to be a part-time janitor at my age. I should have been somebody important or respected or at least making a decent living for my family. One very frigid winter morning, I was particularly depressed (in the depths) about my situation when I greeted Ted with his blackened knees looking especially painful in the cold. I asked Ted if he was doing okay with the cold. His reply is a word I often need to say to myself. "God takes care of me," he said with utter knowledge of the truth of it. Sorry to exegete the sayings of homeless men, but we need notice that Ted's statement is in the perfect present, not the future tense. God takes care of Ted right now and on into the future.

Like David of old, the ruined one, the expedition, or the monk in his cell realizing that the top has not been reached, St. Ted knows what it means to calm and quiet his soul in the hopeful resolve of penance.

**Oh Israel, hope in the LORD
from this time forth and forever more.**

14

Psalm 132

A PRAYER FOR A "messiah" to "sprout" from David dominates this song (Ps 132:17). From this song, it is easy to see why the early Fathers picked the Songs of Ascents as the premier Hebrew text to embed in the liturgy of penance leading up to Pascha. The term "messiah" is well-known by most Christians as a reference to Jesus. Indeed, the word "Christ" (*christos*) derives from the Greek translation of the Hebrew word, *messiach* meaning anointed.

In many ways, the Songs of Ascents has been climbing to this song, only to realize that this last pitch to the summit must be put on hold. Israel must wait in a trust-driven suspension between a *foundational past and the ideal future*,[1] a dominant theme of the expedition through these songs. For sure, there were many both in Judah and Babylon who were glad to see the end of kings in Israel and who strongly advocated for marching into the future without any reference to it. So, it bears exploring here, why this prayer? Why is it here? What drives this prayer and has it been this prayer that has driven the expedition from the start and most of all?

From the Bible's perspective, Josiah was the last real hope for the "house of David" to rule over the people of Judah and possibly restore a kingdom of Israel to a Solomonic ideal. His untimely death in 609 B.C.E. signaled the beginning of the end. Some twenty-three years later, no one of the Davidic line ruled in Judah. What I said in the historical introduction, I'll repeat here. History ends when the last king of Judah is exiled.

---

1. Zvi, "What is New in Yehud?" in *Yahism After the Exile*, 40.

There is little written evidence in the Scriptures about the Davidic line in exile. Ten years after the edict of Cyrus and nearly fifty years since the royal line was exiled, Zerubbabel, a nephew of the exiled king Jehoiachin, emerges. Zerubbabel came to Jerusalem with a wave of returning exiles to rebuild the temple around 522 B.C.E. This indicates that the somewhat privileged status that exiled royalty enjoyed in Babylon continued to some degree throughout the exile. The appointment of Zerubbabel could not have happened without the authorizing stamp of Persia.

The return of exiles and the rebuilding of the temple occurred at a time when the Persian Empire was under considerable stress from rebellious regions.[2] For a brief historical moment, the future of the Persian Empire was in serious doubt, and this lent itself to rising hopes of a worldwide shake up and a revival of a Davidic kingdom. The prophets Haggai and Zechariah provided prophetic support to such hopes (Zech 4:1–14).

By 519 B.C.E., however, this brief window was shut forever. Darius' control of the empire was firmly in hand, and he immediately took measures to shore up quivers of rebellion in *Yehud*. He replaced Zerabbabel with a Persian governor (Ezra 5). Zerubbabel and the prophets Haggai and Zechariah disappear from the historical record. The remigration of *Yehud* would proceed under solid Persian oversight. Any hopes of a reconstituted Israel would out of necessity be centered on the temple in cooperation with the needs and demands of the Persian Empire, a precarious proposition at best.

One thing is certain. When it comes to a messiahnic hope, there was no straight line from the destruction of Jerusalem and the exile of the Davidic king to the time of the second temple. There was no straight line from the time of Zerubbabel to Ezra, and there was no straight line from Ezra to the time of Jesus. Like so many other traditions, the exile changed everything. The exile seriously crippled all traditions. It was innovate or die. This held true for the Davidic/Zion tradition (and maybe more so) as for any other. To say that the Jews expected this or that kind of messiah after the exile and up to the time of Jesus is a misnomer. There were different and often conflicting visions of a future king and a future kingdom.

At issue, however, was an extremely problematic proposition: *The LORD swore to David a firm oath that he will not renounce, "One of you own issue I will set upon your throne . . . to the end of time."* (Ps 132:11–12).

---

2. Ranier Albertz, 'The Thwarted Restoration' in *Yahwism after the Exile*. 8

Pertinent to our psalm, several things should be said to clarify the prayer for a revival of David.

As mentioned in the previous psalm, Israel struggled all along with the problem of kings. There were those who were happy to be done with a king. Kings became a convenient scapegoat for all of the social ills of postexilic *Yehud*. For them, the post-exilic situation held out promise for a true nation of priests and a potential for all Israelites to faithfully follow the covenant.

The post-exilic situation only exacerbated the problem with kings since one of the main reasons for a king—temple sponsorship—was being fulfilled by a foreign king. In this case, Persia now monopolized the kingship problem. The problem of cooperation with imperial kings at the expense of adhering to the righteous requirements of the Torah was still ongoing, but the tension was felt most deeply with the occupying powers. The more apocalyptic book of Daniel exemplifies this tension. The problem of empires was now global.

The emerging prominence of the temple as the focal point of unity and identity for Israel pushed the view of the Davidic promise in different directions. The priests assimilated some of what was once under royal administration. They found a new independence in instituting reforms in line with their perspective. In another direction, God's promise to David was assimilated into the reestablishment of Zion and the holy city. After all, David established both, and the prophetic visions of old about Zion being the focal point of the nations could still be realized. From this perspective, God himself and alone would be king:

> *Who is he, this King of glory?*
>   *The LORD of hosts.*
> *He is the King of glory.(Ps 24:10)*

There was one major problem that still existed with the second temple era. In fact, the problem became increasing worse. It is the problem not so much with kings as with temples. Temples serve kingdoms. They take their marching orders from power and wealth. Temples are just as capable as kings of consolidating and yielding power and wealth at the expense of the poor. Lest we forget, Persia insisted on the rebuilding of the temple as a means to stabilize its empire. From the Persian perspective, one of the main functions of the temple in Jerusalem was to pray for and serve the empire. It may have been "the people's temple" to the Jews, but to Persia, it was an imperial temple. As I mentioned at the beginning of the book, there were those in *Yehud* who had no problem supporting the temple as a rather convenient structure to stabilize the markets, increase profits, and exploit others with little repercussions. One need only pay out dividends to the shareholders.

There were two basic groups who most longed for a Davidic king to arise that could somehow take on the mighty empires and establish a powerful independent kingdom. These groups had one piece in common. They both knew of and had heard of the "glory of the LORD" imagery so prominent in past royal theology (Ps 2) and reinterpreted by the prophets (Ez 1). But the two groups interpreted that imagery in radically different directions.

Those who had lost great wealth, prestige and power wanted to see it restored. The desire to be like the great nations, to imitate them, was the bane of the prophets. It is the main push behind the strong anti-idol sentiment in the Bible. The kings of Judah and Israel constantly gave in to the temptation to "swear to Baal" and take on the appearance of power exemplified by their powerful neighbors.[3]

There was a group of mainly military elites who retreated to Egypt in the days of Jeremiah and were determined to hold out until a great Israelite kingdom came about (Jer 32). They lasted for a while in Egypt as mercenaries in a place called Elephantine, but disappear completely from history.

There was another grouping of people who also disappear completely from history. Their families disintegrated, their land confiscated, their share in the covenant reneged due to the insatiable appetites of the economic engine. They are the ones who have appeared in the Songs of Ascents over and over again. They are the one's crying to the Lord out of great distress. They are the ones on expedition. As no other part of the post-exilic Israelite community, the poor, the marginalized, the disenfranchised, the enslaved, and the ruined were longing for a mighty and miraculous intervention to reverse the abysmal and powerless situation they found themselves in. Unlike the Elephantine community, however, they are everywhere heard of and remembered thanks in large part to the Holy Scriptures.

(Here, we may pause for just a moment to marvel at the amazing gift of the Bible that we hold in our hands. The astounding witness that there is a god "who hears the cry of the poor" pervades the Scriptures against the millenniums of the gods of power and wealth.)

---

3. See Jeremiah 12

Albertz summarizes the situation that generated the prayer for God's *messiach* to be resurrected from the dead:

> Thus the price for the liberty which the Persians granted the upper-class was a chronic impoverishment of the poor, a deep split of Judaean society, and a partial loss of solidarity. So, the prevention of restoration [of the Davidic rule] was dearly paid for.[4]

Equally certain, however, is that there were many priests, scribes, and community leaders who were not willing to give up on the "Israel project." The very inclusion of this psalm in the scriptures demonstrates this. This psalm points to a real and living embodiment of the Lord's mighty saving deeds. God did return the exiles. The temple did get rebuilt. The Torah became prominent. God really did raise his people from the dead.

The Persians had all too willingly demonstrated their ability and willingness to take care of any kingdom talk. This kind of prayer that almost sneaks itself into this series of songs was precarious at best and quite possibly fatal. Most importantly, however, it speaks of those within the temple apparatus, anonymous song writers singing little pop tunes, who cleverly and cunningly infused the troubled temple worship with "the dream" of a kingdom yet to come.

There is a curious mixture of key themes in this psalm. David is mentioned or alluded to several times with terms like "servant," "*messiach*," "throne," "sons," "horn," and "lamp." These terms are mainly in connection with another repetitive theme, that of a "place," "resting place," or "dwelling place" for the Lord. Curiously, terms of victory over an enemy also pervade the text: "Mighty One of Jacob," "footstool," "mighty Ark," "triumph," "shouts of joy," and "enemies in disgrace." These terms are tied closely to the priests and "the saints."

Often times, a climb begins in the cold, darkness of early morning. Sometimes, one will ascend for a couple of hours before the light of day illumines the mountain. We always hope for one of those glorious Colorado days of dazzling sunlight where one can view the summit from the very start. This is not always the case, however. Many a climb starts out on a gloomy overcast day where the peak is shrouded in misty fog. Sometimes, the clouds indicate a bad weather day ahead, but other times, the clouds will slowly dissipate with the warmth of the sun and

---

4. Ranier Albertz, "The Thwarted Restoration," in *Yahwism after Exile*, 17.

unveil the treasured destination. One is always energized afresh when the goal is in sight.

Beyond doubt, this psalm has caught a glimpse of the summit peaking through clouds. It envisions a perfect situation. The temple is full of the "loyal ones" and led out by priests clothed in righteousness. The king triumphantly enters the city with "the Ark of Thy might" heralding victory over a threatening enemy. Most importantly, this triumph will signal a great turn around. It is not the wealthy who rejoice that the victory has protected their assets, but the poor. It is the poor who will be satisfied and filled.

Remember, O LORD, in David's favor,

In the New Testament, we are presented with a pretty consistent image of God as Father. In the Hebrew Bible, however, the depictions of the Lord are quite varied, and many times, they can carry an undesirable or unintentional affect. The appeal for God to remember something, in this case to remember the covenant with David, implies that God is forgetful. Perhaps a little dementia has set in.

When it comes to a covenant, however, forgetfulness carries a different connotation. Covenants varied in the ancient world, but they all convey a critical social, political bond. To "remember the covenant" does not mean so much to think about something, but rather to energize oneself toward action. Remembering a covenant means to activate it.

I am reminded of a phrase my son used all the time when he was very little. He would ask his mother or me if we could do something for him. "Mom, could I have another glass of juice?" he would politely ask. Mom would say yes, and then he would reply matter of fact, "Then do it." It is a bold statement, but it is based on the belief that someone's affirmative word is good. In a sense then, asking God to remember his word to David is like saying, "Do it."

Remembering a covenant is often referred to in the Hebrew bible. Most of the time, the problem was in reverse. The Israelites chronically suffered from memory loss. Ultimately, it led to a total breakdown between God and his people. The bond unfurled. Israel and exiled Judah. It is again one of the marvels of the Bible how God is said to respond to such a breach. Although it repeatedly reminds of how any normal party would respond, by tearing up the contract and seeking retribution, God does something drastic. He implements the covenant even more, *despite* the response of his covenant partners!

> *He took note of their affliction*
>   *when he heard their cry;*
> *And for their sake he was mindful of his covenant*
>   *and relented, in his abundant kindness.* (Ps 106:44–45)

A similar response is depicted in the father who receives his wayward son in Jesus' parable of the lost son (Lk 15:11–32).

To this day, we make covenants and contracts based on mutual benefit. You do this for me, and I will do this for you. Here are the consequences if you renege. But the major difference with human covenants and God's is this—love. What motivates God to make and keep covenants with us humans is "his great love." It is in the appeal to God's great love where the exiles took great boldness to ask God to both remember the covenant *and* forget their sins, their own sinful forgetfulness (Ps 25:7).

The appeal to God's love is an appeal from above. In other words, the basis of the appeal is placed solely on the supplicants understanding of God, on who God is. In this regard, God's love is not the only basis, especially for those being "oppressed by the wicked." No, they must also appeal to God's righteousness. In several of the psalms where God is asked to remember his people, both God's love and his righteousness are appealed to.[5]

Another common appeal for God to remember his covenant is from below. It is based, not in God's nature, but in the desperate condition of the supplicant.

> *The Israelites groaned and cried out because of their slavery. As their cry for release went up to God, he heard their groaning and was mindful of his covenant with Abraham, Isaac and Jacob.* (Ex 2:23–24)

The cry for help always prompts God to remember his covenants, and it is in this vein that the appeal to remember David is made. Most of the time, the appeal to remember the covenant is based on the believing response of Abraham. The supplicant understands that his own sinfulness is a huge impediment for God to respond, so he appeals to the whole-hearted devotion of the one to whom the covenant was originally given.

---

5. Ps 9, 25, 130,

In our psalm here, the appeal is based not so much on the actual promise given to David, but on "all the hardships he endured."

All the hardships he endured;

> *The LORD is my shepherd, I shall not want.*
> *   In verdant pastures he makes me repose;*
> *Besides restful waters he leads me;*
> *   he refreshes my soul.*
> *Even though I walk the dark valley,*
> *   I fear no evil, for you are at my side.*
> *With your rod and your staff,*
> *   that give me courage.* (Ps 23:1–4)

There is probably no more a famous prayer than Psalm 23. It resonates with every human soul in a time of darkness and death. It also resonates with what is most certainly the heart of David and why tradition places all of the prayers of ancient Israel within the sphere of David. As no other in the Bible, David taught the faithful how to pray. Not the prayers of convenience or for success or for blessing, but most importantly when one "walks through the valley of the shadow of death." No one knew that prayer more than David, exemplified that prayer, and helped others to pray it. Furthermore, he showed how to make every prayer a song and every song a prayer.

It is David who taught Israel how to pray. He taught Solomon how to pray. He taught kings and prophets how to pray. He teaches the Church how to pray. It was David who gave the words to Jesus on the cross.

As I mentioned in the introduction, the Psalms are primarily "ground up" prayers. They reverberate with the same basic theme, the same fundamental struggle we have encountered in the Songs of Ascents—the tension between what is promised and what is. It is as the writer of Hebrews states: *They did not receive what had been promised but saw it and greeted it from afar (Heb 11:13)*.

David was among the first to be a *messiach* for Israel. So in a very real sense, the Psalms are the prayers *of* the *messiach*. In the Psalms, we pray *with* the messiah. Mainly, we do not pray with the king at the temple in celebration of a great military victory. We pray with the promised king who is more outlaw than authority, more renegade than royalty, more scapegoat than scepter-holder. The stories of his man-on-the-run days must have leeched onto the exiles who were aligned with the royal house. Perhaps the best witness to the royal line during the exile was the many prayers that speak of one who has suffered great shame and affliction. David becomes the primary composite icon for all those suffering affliction in exile and even up until the days of Nehemiah and Ezra. In David, all Israel finds an empathetic partner in their continual struggle. It was his royal house that was "harshly treated" (Isa 53:7) and taken away "oppressed and condemned" (Isa 53:8). It was the royal house that suffered loss to such a degree that there were "many amazed at him—/ so marred was his look beyond that of man,/ and his appearance beyond that of mortals—" (Isa 52:14).

We have encountered several words and images of distress on this perilous ascent, and now we can add one more, David's *'ana*, hardships. This term refers to someone in a lowly, humiliated, and indentured position, usually brought on by the shear oppressive force of another. In other words, one was *made* low, poor, or a slave. It is like the ruined one of Psalm 130. And of course, who would volunteer for such a position? On some occasions, however, it speaks of someone who *voluntarily* accepts hardships and slavery for the sake of turning around a dire situation suffered by others.

How he swore to the LORD,
  and vowed to the Mighty One of Jacob:
I will not enter my house
  or get into my bed;
I will not give sleep to mine eyes
  or slumber to mine eyelids
Until I find a place for the LORD,
  a dwelling for the Mighty One of Jacob.

In the case of this psalm and in relationship to David in this psalm, the "hardships" speak of self-discipline and self-denial. As the story goes, David refused to build for himself a lavish mansion while the Ark, considered the abode of God, was wandering around the countryside. He denied himself residency because of God's transiency. There is no other account of such an oath taken on the part of David. When David expressed a desire to build a house for the Lord, he was already living in a mansion built by the King of Tyre as a gift. This time of denial refers to the time immediately after the taking of Jerusalem by David. The historical accounts delegate an urgency on the part of David to bring the Ark into Jerusalem immediately. Nothing is said of an oath or of self-denial, but giving a permanent "resting place" to the Ark was David's top priority.

The biblical account makes clear that the physical house was of little importance to God. A tent suited God just fine. But the account does bring out what is most important about the Ark being moved to Jerusalem—it was where God could be with His people. The covenant formula, "I will be their God, and they will be my people" could find a home. In fact, God refers to being with David through all of his wanderings and hardships as well as with the people of Israel as the most critical feature. The Lord further makes explicit that finding a "home" for his people where wicked people will no longer oppress them is what will ultimately please Him (1 Chron 17:1–15).

David's self-imposed affliction speaks directly to our time of fasting. If we are to be like David, and Moses, and Abraham for that matter, then we too must be willing to exercise self-denial in order to see a greater good come about.

The repetition of the reference to the Lord as *la'abir ya'akov*, "the Mighty One of Jacob," bears exploration. It is a term rarely used and only in poetic verse. It is definitely a militaristic term with a connection to Ephraim, the largest tribe in Israel and hence known for producing a good army. The phrase is put into the mouth of Jacob while blessing the tribe of Joseph. In that verse, it speaks more to "the Mighty One of Jacob" who was with Joseph even in his darkest hours of slavery in Egypt (Gen 49:22–26).

Isaiah seems to pick up on the term as a way to speak of the God who rescues his people from "their oppressors" and returns them to a place of leadership (Isa 49:26). In Isaiah 1:24, "the Mighty One of Israel" is invoked as one who defends the fatherless and widows against those who take bribes and work injustice—the victory tune is one of avenging the poor.

Having a permanent home for the Mighty One of Jacob, it appears, was to be like placing a sign in front of the church that says something like: "To all those who have designs to gain wealth at the expense of the poor, be fore-warned. Don't mess with God." *All mankind shall know/ that I, the LORD, am your savior,/ your redeemer, the mighty one of Jacob* (Isa 49:26).

> Lo, we heard of it in Ephrathah,
> we found it in the fields of Jaar.
> Let us go to his dwelling place;
> let us worship at His footstool.
> Arise, O LORD, and go to Thy resting place,
> Thou and the ark of Thy might.

The Ark, in Hebrew *aron* meaning box or chest, is certainly an intriguing and near magical object. It fundamentally served as a military banner, a critical piece of motivational apparatus. The Ark not only symbolized, but embodied an ancient notion of God's mighty Presence called "the Glory of the Lord." It was the central icon of the "Lord Almighty" especially in rescuing the Hebrews from Egypt and settling them in a land of their own. For a longtime, the Ark resided at Shiloh where the Israelites would assemble to remember the mighty acts of the Lord in birthing the people of Israel. There, the early Israelites would renew their covenant commitment to the Lord (Jos 18:1). Above all else, the Ark emanated the triumph of *Adonai ish milchamah*—the Lord, a mighty warrior—who hurled Pharaoh's chariots into the sea (Ex 15:4).

The Israelites, however, painfully discovered that victory over one's enemies was not guaranteed simply because of the Ark's presence, especially if covenant obedience was neglected. In a humiliating military campaign, the Ark was captured by the Philistines. When it was returned, the Ark was handed over to a group of non-Israelite lumberjacks at Kiriath Jearim[6] for safekeeping (1 Sam 7:1, Josh 9:27). This wooded area (*Jaar*) strategically located in between the warring tribes of Judah (David) and Benjamin (Saul) was known as "Ephrathah" to which the town of Bethlehem was situated. For over twenty years, the Ark remained "in the woods" while Israel fought the Philistines from without and themselves from within. Access to God would be "unavailable" and kept under guard by reverential "heathens" until all warring ceased.

Curiously, the songwriter of our psalm here throws the whole congregation into a "way back" machine, and we are all transported back to that time when a great culmination of conflicts found resolve because of David. He defeated the daunting Philistines who perpetually threatened any kind of settled existence for the Israelites. This defeat is highly significant to our song and to those like the ruined one in

---

6. An interesting story, but one that cannot detain us here. Josh 9.

a similar situation. They too cannot "find" God due to the perpetual threat of their enemies. In a sense, the Lord could not come out in the open until all enemies had been defeated.

Curiously in verse six and seven, the cessation of conflict enables "us" to find God even in the woods! We are taken on a rapid-fire scavenger hunt: we heard, we found, we entered, and we worshipped, not in some towering monument to imperial power, but at the Lord's woodsy hideaway! Verse seven bears repeating: the community entered "his dwelling place" and "worshipped at his footstool" in the "fields of the woods (Jaar)."

Perhaps we might reflect in our time of penance just how much our preoccupation with those we are in conflict with, both internally and externally, obscures our own ability to "find" God's home. We may also reflect how our conflicts impede the large majority of people in our world today that live in abject poverty from finding God's resting-place. It bears repeating: the cure for our illness is stillness.

The singer abruptly shifts from storyteller to commander in verse eight: *Arise, O LORD, to your dwelling place*. We often think in terms of God commanding us, but it is quite something to think of the *chutzbah* it takes to shout out orders to God. The command is as my son would say: "do it." We are likely called to imagine one such dashing and daring confident person barking out these orders for the Lord to advance in conquering step—David. Indeed, this was the case. As soon as David had defeated all of Israel's dangerous enemies and united all of Israel, he first and foremost vowed to give God a permanent residence.

Two terms are being interchanged in these verses, and they clarify how it is that the congregation can find the Lord in his *dwelling place* even in the forest, and the urgency for the Lord to establish a *resting place*. The term for dwell, *mishkan*, connotes one's living quarters, where one lives, his home as opposed to his house. When we visit someone for the first time, we go over to their *house*. We drive up and see a structure. But once we are greeted at the door, welcomed in, and view how the house is furnished and decorated, we are now in someone's *home*. We see how our friends live and for a while, we share their life. A derivation of *mishkan* means neighbor, as in this proverb: *Better is a neighbor near at hand/ than a brother far away* (Prov 27:10). Wherever God lives, even in the woods, God is home.

It is my sense that the ruined one who dominates the prayers of this last antiphon really feels like he is worshipping God "in the woods" even as he stands in the courtyard of the rebuilt temple. He pauses in the Lord's tent, knowing that the *resting place* still awaits.

For many believers today, however, they would be more than happy to have God all to themselves in a secret wooded retreat center. This seems cozy and comforting, but of course it excludes most others. If we enjoy God's *dwelling-place*, but do not sense the urgency of David and this psalm to push toward God's *resting-place*, then truly we have something to repent of.

The second term, *minuach*, connotes settling down undisturbed, to pasture. We encountered its derivative earlier in connection with the bold proclamation that God will "unsettle" the scepter of wickedness (Ps 125:3). The critical concern of *minuach* is not that God will stop camping in the woods, for He certainly does not mind that. Rather, it is so *we*—Israel, the worshipping community, all people—can more readily *find* him. No more scavenger hunts. It is so anyone and everyone can say with David and the expedition: "I rejoiced when I heard them say, let us go to the house of the LORD!" (Ps 122:1). This concern is expressed later in the psalm as coming from the Lord himself: *This is my resting-place for all time; here I will dwell, for I have desired it* (Ps 132:14).

A second aspect of the Lord's resting place is critical, however, for we must notice the verse that precedes it: *For the LORD has chosen Zion; he has desired it for his habitation* (Ps 132:13). Unfortunately, the word "habitation" does not bring out the best force of the word *moshav*, which more precisely depicts a high ranking official taking an honored seat at a communal gathering (1 Kings 10:5) or a territory where a ruler has jurisdiction. The critical feature of the Lord having his "seat" reserved in Zion is so that the right and just rule of the Lord's kingdom will be permanently in force.

The singer imagines the force of such a reign of the Lord as King. When that day comes, the Lord *will abundantly bless her provisions* and *satisfy her poor with bread* (v15). The enemies of the Lord, *will be clothed with shame* (v18) and all God-lovers (*chesedim*) will be clothed in victory and bellowing out songs of victory (v16).[7]

---

7. See "Psalms, Songs, and Antiphons" in introduction for discussion of victory song.

> Let Thy priests be clothed with righteousness,
>   and let Thy saints shout for joy.
> For Thy servant David's sake,
>   do not turn away the face of Thine anointed one.
> The LORD swore to David a sure oath
>   from which he will not turn back:
> One of the sons of your body,
>   I will set on your throne.
> If your sons keep my covenant
>   and my testimonies which I shall teach them,
> their sons also forever,
> shall sit upon your throne.

The singer envisions the expedition (and us) mobilizing before "the Ark of your might" in the forest to make that victorious final push to the summit with David and all the tribes of Israel (2 Sam 6). In verse ten, however, we are pulled back into the current situation that the ruined one is in, for the Lord's co-regent, his *messiach*, died in history past. There is no son of David and no throne for him to make right judgments. There is no *ark of Thy might* either!

As we have felt all along in our expedition through these psalms, the appeal is quite desperate, but here the desperation takes on the language of vows and oaths. We can understand now the earlier reference to David's oath to the Lord (Ps 132:2–5). It illustrates urgency. The supplicant now makes an appeal to his Lord to be urgent about his promise to David.

There is much to suggest from the prophets and the Psalms that oath-taking at sacred sites and under the auspices of sacrifice was an integral aspect of festal gathering.[8] Ratifying a business deal is likely to be performed under the auspices of sacrifice (Gen 31:51–54, Mt 23:16).

In God's promise to David (2 Sam 7), David's concern for a house and home for the Lord is reciprocated. Essentially God responds by saying: "don't worry about me, I'm fine. But Israel needs a dwelling place and a resting place" and for one reason in particular: the wicked are oppressing the people and making them transients even in the own land (2 Sam 7:10–11). God's intent for David's name and lineage was precisely to alleviate such a problem. Interestingly, the condition of adherence to the Torah by Davidic kings is not mentioned in the account in Second

---

8 Wenham, *The Psalms as Torah*, 57–76.

Samuel. Instead, the psalm here refers to Solomon's recollection at the dedication of the temple (1 Kings 8:22–53). Solomon's vision of the temple as the place *par excellence* to pray and repent matches that of our last series of psalms here. In both cases, David's son leads as a prime model of repentance. The king leads in repentance and faithful adherence to God's righteous and just ways. Zion is the place where the great reversal will occur. Certainly, the supplicant understands the miracle of the reconstructed temple and the return of the exiles as signature acts of salvation in keeping with that great event at the Reed Sea. The fact that the expedition is standing in the temple courtyard is miracle and sign that God will advance, He and his mighty Ark!

There I will make a horn to sprout for David.
I have prepared a lamp for mine anointed.

All is ready now. The need is urgent. The Lord has made an oath that cannot be revoked. The temple awaits the return of the Lord's coregent, *the messiach*, from the ash heap of history.

    A look at the book of Zechariah as he prophesied around the time of the building of the second temple is critical to understand the messiahnic expectation in this psalm as well as the time of Jesus and even in our time of penitent waiting for Christ's coming.

    Reading the whole book of Zechariah would be the best approach since I will only highlight certain features here. The lyricist in this psalm intentionally conjures up evocative images of that time with words like "horn," "sprout," and "lamp."

    The dire situation that many returning exile found themselves in and depicted in the Songs of Ascents had been going on for over 70 years since the time of Zechariah. We may want to contemplate that time span when we begrudge our paltry 40 days of fasting: seventy years, a healthy person's lifetime, languishing with the same gross hypocrisy and disparity *within* the people of God.

    In Zechariah's day, it was the time of "small things." The startup project of the temple was meager at best. Many who returned found the situation deplorable and were greatly discouraged (Zech 4:10). This is, no doubt, a major reason for Zechariah's preaching.

    It should be remembered that there were remnants of people left in the land of *Yehud* during the tumultuous years of the Babylonian and

Persian empires. It was basically reduced to a wild West condition, nearly lawless. Tribal communities scrambled to get and control meager resources and small territories just like drug or mafia gangs do today. These communities certainly begrudged a large influx of "foreigners" coming into the land especially since they claimed rights to the land and had official backing from the Persian Empire.

Needless to say, the returning exiles faced a kind of vicious passive resistance. The major plan of attack was to ruin them economically since overt military action was not viable.

Many of the communities that remained in *Yehud* during the exile were Jewish and held out bitter resentments of suffering in the exilic period with little to no help from their brothers in exile. They adapted to a way of life devoid of temple or royal administration and likely saw the new temple project as a threat to their way of life. They had little choice but to go along with the temple project, and decided to manipulate it to their advantage rather than hold up overt violent resistance. They became adept at putting on piety all the while working their ruinous agendas behind the scenes. Corruption, double-standards, treachery, and hypocrisy worked deep roots into the rebuilding project. Thus Zechariah proclaims that a curse of thievery and injustice has pervaded the land (Zech 5:1–4). Religious observance devoid of justice and righteousness was a *huge* problem (Zech 7). The "shepherds of the people" expand their wealth and solidify secret alliances by divvying up the poor. In their treacherous displays of piety, they praise God about it, smugly announcing: "Blessed be the LORD, I have become rich!" (Zech 11:5). Strong, honest, and bold leadership was needed to aggressively defend the oppressed (Zech 11:7).

Although those believing in "the dream" had some official backing, they had little political, economic, or military weight to turn things around. They could only appeal to the rightness of their cause, but even more so to the right, just, and loving God. Zechariah envisions a time when "your king" will enter the holy city in triumph like David of old. But in that time, the king will enter in humility and righteousness, riding on a donkey (Zech 9:9). He will cause all warring and violence to cease (Zech 9:1–13).

Fueled by the righteous demands of the Torah, the remigrants believed that the temple would set in motion a great turn around. There would be a national and deep-seated repentance and forgiveness of sin that would fuel a new society, kingdom, and community of mutual respect and sharing:

> *I will take away the guilt of the land in one day. On that day, says the LORD of hosts, you will invite one another under your vines and fig trees.* (Zech 3:9–10)

The Lord will dwell in Zion and it will be called "the faithful city" and "the holy mountain" (Zech 8:1–3). Just and righteous judgments will be rendered in the gates, the festivals will be truly joyous occasions based on "love, truth, and peace" and the nations will be welcomed as they flock to Zion to "entreat the Lord" (Zech 8:16–23). God will conquer all nations: *Not by an army nor by might, but by my spirit, says the LORD of hosts* (Zech 4:6).

> *The LORD shall become king over the whole earth; on that day the LORD shall be the only one, and his name the only one.* (Zech 14:9).

In Zechariah's prophecies, he sees two leaders who counter the shepherds who are devouring the flock. They are Joshua the high priest and Zerubbabel a descendant of the royal line. They are called the two lampstands, the two olive branches, and the two anointed (*messiach*) ones "who stand by the LORD of the whole earth" (Zech 4:13), especially in founding the temple.

Their role was to build up the temple as a way to prepare for a future "servant" called "the branch" (*tzimach*). Joshua and Zerubbabel are not that future royal figure, but they will prepare for him and in limited ways act in his stead. In anticipation of the royal figure yet to come, Zechariah orchestrates a crown ritual, in which the royal crown is kept in the temple until that figure "shall sit as a ruler upon his throne" (Zech 6:13).[9] They are to be lamps and servants until the future David, "the Shoot," will sprout (Zech 6:12).

Zechariah's "branch" prophecy and the allusion to it in our psalm here likely find its correlation with a pre-exilic prophecy of Jeremiah (Jer 23:5). Critically, Jeremiah's prophecy arises out of the same problem of economic violence by ruthless "shepherds."

> *Behold, the days are coming, says the LORD,*
>   *when I will raise a righteous shoot* (tzimach) *to David;*
> *As king he shall reign and govern wisely,*
>   *he shall do what is just and right in the land.*
> *In his days Judah shall be saved,*

---

9. Scholars do not agree on who the "branch" refers to. My reading here is dependent on the view of Rose, "Messianic Expectations in the Early Postexilic Period" in. *Yahwism After*, 2003. 176–81.

> *Israel shall dwell in security.*
> *This is the name they give him:*
> *"The LORD our justice."* (Jer 23:5–6)

The word "branch" is probably not the best choice because it implies a growth coming forth from an already existing tree, but *tzimach* better denotes a completely new growth sprouting from the ground. In Jeremiah's prophecy, the righteous growth happens *to* David, not from David.[10] This strongly suggests that both Jeremiah and Zechariah considered the old David line dead and gone. *The line was dead, but not the promise.* A new growth would necessarily sprout forth that would rescue David and the promise given him from its fatal blow. In essence, the expectation is that this "anointed one" would not only rescue Israel, but rescue the Davidic line from its perpetual trap of greed, corruption, and power. The future king would resolve the problem of kings and of empires by fundamentally transforming it into something else. It would be a "kingdom of God." This kingdom would not be "of this world," not meaning of some celestial ethereal place, but rather not in any way like the empires that we are still building today. This anointed one to come would depict in word, action, and life what it would look like "if'n God ran the place."

I have prepared a lamp for mine anointed.
His enemies I will cloth with shame,
  but upon himself his crown will shed its luster.

The supplicant understands what equipment the Lord has provided for the final pitch to the summit. The temple, but more importantly the God-lovers (*chesedim*) who trust in the Lord, fear him, and walk in his ways, has prepared a lamp for the Lord's messiah. Now the expedition waits in quite resolve and prepares in loving adherence to "the Lord the Righteous One." The crown preserved in the temple awaits the time to shed its luster upon the head of him who will clothe all who oppose him with shame.

---

10. Rose, "Messianic Expectations" in *Yahwism After Exile*, 179

15

Psalm 133

THE EXPEDITION BEGAN IN a foreign land far from home. It marched through perilous and hostile territory. It took every obstacle and false summit in stride and struggled with doubt, fear, and despair. In some miraculous or mysterious way, however, new strength and renewed vision was somehow mustered. The ascent gathered breathe, packed up its gear and continued upward.

With each plateau came a renewed sense of the goal, a foretaste of a new Israel, a reconstituted kingdom, and revitalized covenant with the Lord. The expedition reached its coveted destination, almost. It had reached staggering heights and accomplished unimagined feats, yet even in the very courtyard of the temple, the realization settles in. This is not the summit. That persistent faith-filled unfulfillment needles the soul incessantly.

On the temple floor, however, the windows of heaven were opened. Even when the congregation has an uneasy mix of wicked and righteous, those trusting in wealth and those trusting in the Lord, those conniving the next foreclosure and those dreaming of a head to place that sparkling crown upon, fissures widen of a kingdom coming. The solemn convocation of *Yom Kippur*, the day of atonement, makes bold a proposition: if we confess our sins, the Lord will forgive. There is forgiveness with Thee. With the Lord, things can change, people can change, systems can convert. A revolution of the heart will come.

Listen, I know as well as anyone what a preposterous statement that is. Most of the time we know, we feel, that people don't change, not just things especially cruel, unjust, and violent, but also our own dysfunction and annoying idiosyncrasies that presumptuously attack, disregard, offend, grumble, seize, step on and step over, all due to our own fear refusing the dominion of the King. At times, God's kingdom only seems to be experienced from the bottom of a well (ask Joseph and Jeremiah) or affixed a Roman cross.

Once again, the title of Psalm 133 reminds that the song belongs to the David collection because it resonates with the fellowship of the heart between David and God—the desire for the unity of God's people. It goes way beyond that, it is the unity of all people. Again, this is why God likes this fellow so much. The one so longed for in these last songs, David's son yet to come, also joined the fellowship of the heart, and he expressed it this way:

> Holy Father, keep them in your name that you have given me, so that they may be one just as we are one . . . I pray not only for them, but also for those who will believe in me through their word, so that they may all be one, as you, Father, are in me and I in you, that they also may be in us, that the world may believe that you sent me. (Jn 17:11, 20–21)

It is nearly impossible to find this kind of heart among us believers. On the contrary, we spend inordinate amounts of energy finding ways to distinguish and separate ourselves from others. Some contemplation and confession along these lines might be a part of our time of penance. May we join the Lord, David, and Jesus in the fellowship of the heart.

Behold, how good and how pleasant it is when brothers dwell in unity.

Hineh ma tov! Behold how good. We have encountered already the word "behold," *hinah*, meant to accent certainty. Unity is *without a doubt* and *surely* a good thing. The singer inserts the adverb *ma*, "how," to add an exclamation and to exaggerate or accent the value or number.

Goodness, we may remember from Psalm 125, must be something visible and tangible. Goodness is something experienced, not explained, and it cannot come about divorced of justice and righteousness. One does not call a frosted cinnamon roll "good" in the midst of oppression. The singer witnesses and participates in the very thing he sings of.

This is reinforced by the second part of this exclamation—"how pleasant." The Hebrew term is *nayim*. It refers to sensual things of the eyes, taste, sight, and sound that incite joy, contentment, or happiness. *Nayim* is a favored term in the Psalms connected with the goodness of temple worship. It is thus associated with the singing of the choir in praise. *Nayim* also speaks of a contentment based on a stillness of desires—especially of not being driven toward other gods. It speaks of contentment with limits and boundaries

> O Lord, my allotted portion and my cup,
>   you it is who hold fast my lot.
> For me, the measuring lines have fallen on pleasant sites;
>   fair (nayim) *to me indeed is my inheritance.* (Ps 16:5–6)

Goodness cannot be divorced from justice and righteousness and pleasantness cannot be separated from rightly ordered worship.

In this last set of psalms, we have sensed the unease of the expedition even as they have come so far in their ascent. Oddly, as they found themselves even at their supposed destination, distress still accompanies them. Once they realized that the final destination is yet to come, the entourage takes inventory of the mighty acts of the Lord in the here and now (another part of a season of penance).

The expedition, the singer and songwriter of this psalm, the ruined one, David of old and the David yet to come stand on the temple steps and truly behold, if but for just a moment, the fellowship of the heart. They see *brothers dwelling in unity*.

(I apologize to my sisters here for your apparent exclusion from the phase. If it is any consolation, you may want to notice the statement repeated many times in Nehemiah and Ezra that the women and children were included in the great assembly and in the hearing of the Torah. Certainly, you are included in this phrase.)

We encountered already the expedition's vision of unity in Psalm 122. There, the city itself provides a postcard image of a vibrant city with its own personality, its characteristic architecture testifying to *yachad*—unity or oneness. It is a city bound firmly together. Even the name, *Yerushalaim*, sings of a perfect union of God, city, and *shalom*. To recall, *yachad* speaks of a unique, priceless relationship with a beloved person or thing that cannot be replaced.

From the book of Nehemiah, we can determine several aspects of "brothers dwelling in unity" that our singer is experiencing. It is possible that this song was written for this event or in remembrance of it.

After Nehemiah and the Jews completed the wall, they began preparations for a series of four fall festivals: the feast of trumpets, *yom kippur* (the day of atonement, which I placed as the context of most of the third Antiphon), the feast of booths, and the sacred assembly (Neh 8–12). More than likely, the Jews had celebrated these feasts to some extent from the time of the second temple's dedication and even before, but the book of Nehemiah clarifies why this particular year would be *hineh ma tov*—extra special good.

Now that the walls were built and secure, permanent temple personnel—priests, Levites, governing leaders and administrators could move into the city. They could dwell there, be established and settle in. They could take up seats of responsibility and administration. Jerusalem could flower as the hub for those "trusting in the Lord" no matter where they were. The book of Nehemiah and the Songs of Ascents indicate that for the Israelites, the land of *Yehud* had been a very unsettling place for the returning ones. In a great Levitical sermon on the day of atonement, it is put this way: *we today are slaves; and as for the land which you gave our fathers that they might eat its fruits and good things—see, we have become slaves upon it!* (Neh 9:36)

It was not until Nehemiah took on the impossible mission of rebuilding the walls that returning Israelites could *settle securely* in Jerusalem and in the surrounding region. Until the walls of Jerusalem were secure, no Israelite was settled. They were outnumbered by those who did not take seriously the Torah as a viable rule of life against the backdrop of imperial power and theology.

The term "dwell" is derived from the Hebrew word *y'shev*, to dwell or sit. In this case, it carries a similar sense as the words "dwelling-place" and "resting-place" discussed in the last psalm. *Y'shev* emphasizes being settled and established. In one instance, it refers to that place where a plant takes root and grows. For the first time since the days of Josiah nearly 150 years prior, the Israelites could operate a "full-service" 24-hour a day temple.

The book of Nehemiah also makes clear a second critical feature to "settling in" due to the rebuilt walls. With the temple fully in operation and fulltime personnel in the city, the people of God could now participate in the appointed feasts free from interference and confusion. They could mark clear distinctions between Israelite practice and non-Israelite. The biggest distinction was the practice of Sabbath.

This may seem like petty squabbles over differing views of religious piety, but it is more in line with the persistent "distress" encountered by those on ascent—economic injustice and gross disparity. Once the gates where secure, Nehemiah was able to halt the "markets-never-close" mentality that drove hard economic exploitation (Neh 13:15-22). It created a stark contrast between a God-inspired piety or a God-damned piety.

This is demonstrated further when Nehemiah shuts down banqueting "skyboxes" in the temple precinct (Neh 13:4-9). This practice of setting up private suites for banquets violated the "brotherhood ethic" of the Torah on multiple fronts. First and in a similar way as the problem of the Corinthian church (1 Cor 11), those with wealth presume all to easily that temples are built especially for them, and it is only natural that the best accommodations and conveniences be reserved for them. Both Nehemiah and Paul get really nasty about this as well they should. "If you want to display your opulence," they would say, "then do it at home." "No one has the right to humiliate the poor in the house of God." This problem was exacerbated in the temple because these lavishly furnished banqueting facilities were designated storehouses for the Levities serving in the temple. Once again, mouthing piety while "crushing the poor."

This brings us to another "brothers dwelling in unity" experience the singer conveys—the fellowship meal. This meal is provided by a sacrifice where most of it is spared and shared. This kind of sacrificial offering is variously called the fellowship, peace, or thanksgiving offering. We recall from Psalm 130 that the thanksgiving offering was especially the delight of the poorest who had no means of offering a sacrifice themselves.

The keeping of the Sabbath and the fellowship meal come together as prime models of God's kingdom of righteousness, justice, and love. The reason God wants a resting-place is so His people can have a resting-place. The Sabbath is so everyone, especially those weighed down in conscription could experience rest and get a meal. When Nehemiah commands that the people rejoice and have a party, he makes absolutely sure the poor are included (Neh 8:10-12).

The ancient Israelites suffered from the same tension inherent in ritual observance as we do today. Ritual can go a good way or a bad way. I did not say "religious" ritual because rituals, especially social rituals, function similarly. The prophets incessantly attack the festal assemblies as opportunities for the wealthy to intoxicate themselves in their own opulence while their neighbors serve the feast with hungry bellies (Amos 4). Not only was their wealth gained by "crushing the poor for a pair of shoes," the situation is further exacerbated by the exclusion of the poor at solemn assemblies.

Ritual can numb and inoculate us from the suffering of others all the while deceiving ourselves that ritual *alone* is all that God wants of us. In the "dream" of a reconstituted Israel, many in the postexilic period, especially within the priesthood, sought to fundamentally reverse the debilitating effects of ritual. The book of Leviticus submits all sacrifice and solemn assembly to the righteous, just, and loving demands of the Torah to *care for each other*.

All "solemn assemblies" are to model righteous living. They are to profoundly *affect* the pilgrims living habits. It is from their dwellings that they come before the Lord, and it is to their dwellings that the effects of the assembly should play out. In other words, the "dwelling together" should and must be shaped by these holy convocations.

The reforming priests of Leviticus tried to radically address a problem with religious observation—we divorce it from our life, our politics, or our economics. Our rituals should inform, direct, and shape our lives. Thus in Leviticus 23 and 24, we should notice the reasons for the peculiar Israelite rituals. The ritual of bringing the sacrifices of first fruits is to remind that the Lord gave the land as gift (Lev 23:9). By making offerings to the Lord *first*, one can be reminded that resources are not ours to exploit. In all solemn assemblies, the Israelites are to "do no work—you and your servants." They are to leave the edges of their fields for the poor and alien because, "I am the Lord your God and the one who brought you out of Egypt." Worship of the Lord was to effect every aspect of the Israelites "settled" life and in this way, they could avoid the disaster of another exile.

In this regard, we should not neglect the "brother" aspect as well. The term brothers, *ehim*, is often translated *one to another* and it carries the same sense of responsibility to others as in numerous "one another" verses in the New Testament. *Love another, do good to one another, honor one another even above yourself.* Zechariah says: 7:10:

> Do not oppress the widow or the orphan, the alien or the poor; do not plot evil against one another in your hearts. (Zech 7:10)

Brother is synonymous with neighbor, especially in conjunction with canceling debts.

> . . . you shall have a relaxation of debts, which shall be observed as follows. Every creditor shall relax his claim on what he has

> *loaned his neighbor; he must not press his neighbor, his kinsman, because a relaxation in honor of the LORD has been proclaimed.*
> (Deut 15:1–2)

"Brother," of course, refers to relatives, even extended relatives. Since most ancient peoples lived in tribal-like communities these lines between family and community would be more blurred than today. But verses like these equate brother with neighbor especially when it comes to the responsibility to act justly toward them. In this sense, brother expresses a common bond in a similar way as people use brother today. A brother is one whom one has a racial, club, gang, or military affiliation with.

In the psalm here, the common bond is the covenant with Yahweh, one repeatedly called the covenant of love and consistently alluded to in the Songs of the Ascents. It is a fellowship of the heart. Here, perhaps, the lyrics sing more of potential than actual experience. Nonetheless and as I said above, when and if the poor sit down in rest with others around a meal of thanksgiving, "the good life" is pushing itself up from this world's stubborn soil. If "brothers" faithfully respond to Torah life and "trust the Lord," then "there should be no poor among you." This alone will transfer into rich blessing, "since the LORD, your God, will bless you abundantly in the land he will give you to occupy as your heritage, there should be no one of you in need" (Deut 15:4).

A brother could just mean fellow countrymen or kinsmen, but informed by Torah, brother especially means one whom an Israelite must *not* exploit or enslave. Jeremiah relates an incident which became the decisive moment for the Lord to abandon Jerusalem to the Babylonians. Zedekiah, a king put in charge of Jerusalem by the Babylonians after the deportation of the Davidic king, proclaims emancipation for all Hebrews enslaved by other Israelites in conformity to the Torah. But then (could you imagine Lincoln doing this) Zedekiah reneges on the proclamation. The nobles grab their slaves back. Jeremiah angrily prophecies:

> *Therefore thus says the LORD: You did not obey me by proclaiming your neighbors and kinsmen free. I now proclaim you free, says the LORD, for the sword, famine, and pestilence.* (Jer 34:17)

Nehemiah faced a similar problem when he first returned to Jerusalem—brothers enslaving brothers, the very ones whom they should especially treat justly!

In terms reminiscent of Deuteronomy and Jeremiah, the term "brother" is the prime word choice when combating economic disparity, exploitation, and enslavement. Notice the brotherhood language used by Nehemiah:

> *Then there arose a great outcry of the common people and their wives against certain of their fellow Jews (Neh 5:1)*

> *And though these are our own kinsmen and our children are as good as theirs, we have had to reduce our sons and daughters to slavery, and violence has been done to some of our daughters!* (Neh 5:5)

This next verse perhaps is of critical interest to our psalm, for Nehemiah takes up a class action suit against the nobles based on the Torah stipulations: *You are exacting interest from your kinsmen!* Nehemiah calls the *qahal gadolah*, "the whole assembly" in order to present his case (Neh 5:13*)*:

> "*As far as we are able, we bought back our fellow Jews who had been sold to Gentiles* [We should take notice of the wealthy who put their own wealth at risk for the "Israel project."]; *you, however, are selling your own brothers, to have them bought back by us!" They remained silent, for they could find no answer. I continued, "What you are doing is not good. Should you not walk in the fear of our God and put and end to the derision of our Gentile enemies? I myself, my kinsmen, and my attendants have lent the people money and grain without charge. Let us put and end to this usury!"* (Neh 5:8–10)

Nehemiah is able to persuade the nobles to give back everything they took in interest and emancipate those whom they had enslaved. What happens next may also be related to our psalm. He requires the nobles to take an oath before the priests. *And the whole assembly answered, "Amen," and praised the LORD. Then the people did as they had promised.* (Neh 5:13)

This last verse speaks to one other aspect of this picture of brothers dwelling in unity—corruption of justice at the gates. The word for dwell, *shebet*, is rarely used and adds a sense of being seated on a throne or in a place of honor at a great banquet or assembly. In this case, it implies having a place of undisputed honor or authority to rule, govern, and make decisions. The word "dwell" or "settle" may not only refer to the Israelites settling down in Jerusalem and in the towns, but also of having the rulers of the people seated in the assembly who trust in the Lord and who make just and equitable judgments guided by prophets, not profits.

Truly, it is good and pleasant when *brothers*—those "trusting in the Lord" and "fearing the Lord"—*dwell*—establish their temple , courts, towns, villages, and ways of treating one another—*in unity*—bind themselves to a unique and empire-busting relationship with the Lord who made heaven and earth and who is the one who has "ordained blessing, life forever more."

It is like the precious oil upon the head
  running down upon the beard,
the beard of Aaron,
  running down on the collar of his robes.
It is like the dew of Hermon,
  which falls on the mountains of Zion.

I suppose a metaphor looses all force if it has to be explained. A sampling of popular commentary on this verse demonstrates, however, metaphor run amuck. Unfortunately, we are so distanced from the picture, both geographically and chronologically, that some explanation is needed.

Critically central is to focus on what is being compared to what. In a liturgical celebration, our singer is experiencing "brothers" settled in unity. This binding together is acted out liturgically in a fellowship meal, but also in the restitution of inequitable and unjust economic situations. In the latter case, that of restitution, this was more than likely a hopeful ideal than a regular part of post-exilic life.

The focus remains centrally clear—*brothers dwelling in unity* is the *reality* to compare to. In other words, when and if covenant partners are unified, it produces "life everlasting" a long, enduring, and abundant life *for all*. The depictions of the anointing of Aaron and dew on the hills of Zion point to three intersecting "qualities of life everlasting." First, it descends and covers everything as shear gift. Second, it is ridiculously and indiscriminately opulent and lavish. Finally, it produces, even resurrects life.

Both the anointing oil and dew flow downward. This is repeated three times in this single verse. They have a pouring-down affect. Contrary to trickle-down imagery of today, the source of life for all does not first flow upwards and then come down in controlled and calculated measures from a few. In fact, the source is not measured in accounting terms at all. Again, the source is a profound sense of being bound to one another in a covenant with the Lord "who made heaven and earth."

This downward flow is not harsh, over-bearing, or forceful. The downward flow of oil is gentle, slow and even. Dew or gentle rain does not come down in life threatening down pours. The rain patterns on the Front Range of Colorado do not bear the characteristics accented by the metaphors in this psalm. Distinct, dense, and billowing clouds begin forming by early afternoon. By mid-afternoon, they darken and amass, thunder roils the atmosphere. A few large drops begin slapping the pavement, and then, the clouds pound pavement, cars, and people mercilessly. Flashes of lightening crush the spirit even of the brave. Not so the distribution of "life everlasting."

The singer emphasizes dew or gentle light rain. Dew is a classic metaphor of choice in the Hebrew bible to depict the gentle, quiet, non-threatening and unassuming gift of life's main ingredient, water. When moisture thick clouds envelop the landscape, the soul is also engulfed in its magisterial silence, beckoning submission to the misty generative force. As the prophet Isaiah contemplated: Isa 18:4:

> *For thus says the LORD to me:/ I will quietly look on from where I dwell,/Like the glowing heat of sunshine,/ like a cloud of dew at harvest time. (Isa 18:4)*

Dew brought manna in the desert and effortlessly extracts earth's riches:

> *May God give to you*
>   *of the dew of the heavens*
> *And of the fertility of the earth*
>   *abundance of grain and wine. (Gen 27:28)*

Dew, then, is Isaiah's choice metaphor for a resurrected life from exile's tomb.

> *But your dead shall live, their corpses shall rise;*
>   *awake and sing, you who lie in the dust.*
> *For your dew is a dew of light,*
>   *and the land of shades gives birth. (Isa 26:19)*

The word for oil, *shemen*, comes from the verb to make fat. *Shemen* is "fat" either from an animal or a plant. We all understand that fat is excess, and for those of us who eat meat, we, of course, know that fat is what makes meat succulent and moist, mainly because of its sugar content. Olive oil symbolizes luxury, excess, and abundance.

When the olive oil is mixed with "fragrant" spices for the anointing of holy things and persons, it becomes *shemen mishchat qodesh*, a holy anointing oil (Ex 30:22, 25).

Often oil is mixed with the "grain offering" or first fruits offering. Sometimes, the mixture of flour, oil, and spices is thrown onto the fire for added aroma. Barbeque fans know what we are talking about here.

Often time, the oil is applied by smearing and this is where we get our word *messiach*, it literally means to smear, requiring copious amounts of the lavish substance. The act of pouring and smearing oil symbolized a setting apart of someone or thing for a special, singular purpose. To anoint a sword, was to consecrate it for military use only. A soldier was not to cut salami with his consecrated sword.

The singer stretches the metaphor of Aaron's anointing for added effect, in case we miss the point. Having been a beard wearer most of my life, I know that our society does not esteem the hairy face as in the ancient days, especially when it gets long. Many a time, my children have rebuked me in disgust, when food or drink particles remain in my beard, so a good measure of "pleasant" is lost to us in this image. But the lyricist is not deterred. It was "precious" oil "running down" the head and beard, so much so that its flow continues onto his collar.

Prophets, kings, and priests were anointed, but here Aaron is particularly singled out. In the Bible, the anointing of Aaron as high priest is swiftly mentioned in a broader narrative of his consecration that centers more on the clothing and the sacrifices needed to put the priesthood into effect. Jewish tradition maintains that the anointing oil was lost in exile, so post-exilic priests were not anointed.[1] Our songwriter here highly esteems the priesthood of Aaron as indicated in the last psalm, so he views the reestablishment of the priesthood as a critical feature in the maintenance of "life forever more." Significantly, the Bible only mentions the eternal nature of Aaron's priesthood—similar to God's promise to David—only at the anointing of the high priest (Ex 29:7–9). Thus, the reestablishment of the high priesthood serves as a resurrection sign that the Lord will resurrect David somehow. Only the high priest is able to perform the atonement for all of Israel. He is the one, after all, who ritually ushers in the possibility of resurrection through forgiveness of sins.

But we cannot miss that the metaphor of oil and dew point to the reality of a unified people described above. It is the beauty of "brothers

---

1. Goulder, *The Psalms of the Return*, 107–50, 104.

dwelling in unity" that lavishly anoints Aaron and copiously waters Zion. The Levitical account of Aaron's consecration places great emphasis on its performance before the gathered assembly (Lev 8:1–4). It is rightly ordered, just, righteous, and loving interactions of the "God-lovers" that truly consecrates and makes holy worship at Zion. In a sly choice of metaphor, the songwriter subversively injects a reversal of priorities. As if in partnership with a psalm of Asaph (Ps 50), the lyricist pushes true piety to the foreground. Asaph chants:

> *From Zion, perfect in beauty,*
>   *God shines forth . . .*
> *"Gather my faithful ones before me,*
>   *those who have made a covenant with me by sacrifice."*
> *And the heavens proclaim his justice;*
>   *for God himself is the judge (Ps 50:2,5–6)*

The psalm goes on to pronounce that God does not need sacrifice at all. God does not denounce displays of sacrificial devotion, but they become worthless *especially* when thievery, evil, deceit, slander, and disregard for Torah are cloaked behind them. God reminds the "wicked" in the very temple that using piety as a mask will not go unanswered by the Lord.

The Lord places a clear priority on the "fellowship offering." If you are going to offer sacrifices, God says (Ps 50:14), offer the thank offering. Why? Because it is *spared and shared*, especially with the poor. The thanksgiving offering better models the "dream" of the Lord's kingdom coming. It demonstrates "pour-down" economics.

> *He that offers praise* [fellowship sacrifice] *as a sacrifice glorifies me; and to him that goes the right way I will show the salvation of God.* (Ps 50:23)

The fastidious attention to holy things performed by the priests likely serves as a model for the congregation. Just as the priests were to pay close attention to the observance, so too the congregation must take great heed to implement what the Lord requires. The priests are to "keep my charge and not do wrong in this matter; else they will die for their profanation. I am the LORD who have consecrated them" (Lev 22:9).

As said earlier, the prohibition against offering second-rate sacrifices may be a critical object lesson for disregarding other matters of the Torah, like enslaving others through manipulation of money systems.

We might notice in the nineteenth chapter of Levitcus, for instance, that right on the heels of a command to serve the fellowship meal (offering) with one's household and the poor and the sojourner, there is the command to leave portions of a harvest for the poor and sojourner, followed by clear, simple, and forceful injunctions against injustice. These commands address the same concerns brought up incessantly by the supplicant of the Songs of Ascents, the problems that cause "distress" and people to fall into the "deep."

> *"You shall not steal. You shall not lie or speak falsely to one another. You shall not swear falsely by my name, thus profaning the name of your God. I am the LORD.*
>
> *"You shall not defraud or rob your neighbor. You shall not withhold overnight the wages of your day laborer. You shall not curse the deaf, or put a stumbling block in front of the blind, but you shall fear your God. I am the LORD.*
>
> *"You shall not act dishonestly in rendering judgment. Show neither partiality to the weak nor deference to the mighty, but judge your fellow men justly."* (Lev 19:11–16)

The list goes on, but ends with a well-known summary statement: "Love your neighbor as yourself" (Lev 19:18). We might also notice the constant interjections reminding the congregants of the kind of God commanding such things: "Be holy, for I, the LORD, your God am holy" (Lev 19:2); "I, the LORD, am your God" (Lev 19:3); "I am the LORD" (Lev 19:18); "I, the LORD, am your God, who brought you out of the land of Egypt" (Lev 19:36).

> [But] *take care not to perform righteous deeds in order that people may see them; otherwise, you will have no recompense from your heavenly Father.* (Mt 6:1)
>
> *If you forgive others their transgressions, your heavenly Father will forgive you. But if you do not forgive others, neither will your Father forgive your transgressions.* (Mt 6:14–15)
>
> *But the hour is coming, and now is here, when true worshippers will worship the father in Spirit and truth; and indeed the Father seeks such people to worship him.* (Jn 4:23–24)

16

Psalm 134

THE EXPEDITION HAS JOURNEYED from a distant and foreign land, encountered internal struggle and external opposition and obstacles. It has picked up strength in numbers as it ascended and courage with sight of the holy hill. It ascended in procession, propelled by songs of restoration, and it has been exhorted to diligence and focus in reconstituting "Israel." They have come a long way only to realize that the destination is yet to come. For now, they will have to descend before they can ascend.

I am reminded of the countless times I have descended a peak. I have always given in to the compulsion to look back up to where I had just struggled to ascend. One thing that strikes me is how different the mountain appears from when I was climbing up. It still appears majestic and worthy of respect, but not quite so foreboding. One knows the mountain now. There is also a quite lament. For a good part of a day, most of the usual concerns of life have been discarded as the sole focus of the moment consumes all. One begins to know the mountain and the mountain knows of your presence.

This closing song of "the expedition" signals a departure. Unlike the countless departures from the temple in festivals past, this one does not signal descent of the mountain only to attempt another ascent next year. This time marked a decisive break. The walls have been rebuilt. Priests, Levites, nobles, and administrators now *settle in* as permanent tenants of the holy city. Worship of the Lord will now correspond to the just, righteous, and loving responsibilities of the Lord's covenant of love with His people. God's righteous commands will supersede the market's insatiable demands. The Lord's dwelling place will be a resting place for all people.

Yes, "the dream" will still butt heads with "the way things are." There will still be plenty who will begin their ascent with woeful lament: "In my distress, I cry to you." Brothers will still bankrupt brothers. Neighbors will still enslave neighbors. Imperial gods along with their market partners will still compete for supremacy. There is still a deep cavern that one must descend into before he can ascend. David's son will find himself crucified on a Roman cross.

This time and this ascent have transformed earlier attempts. It has reached new heights, ones only imagined in the pits of exile. Now, more than ever, the summit is in reach. The top is within sight. The expedition took a respite atop the last apparent summit. They set up yet another "base camp" to shuttle operations upward. They took inventory, renewed their strength, and assembled their gear yet another time. They begin their downward climb as the necessary start toward the next pitch. They have "tasted the heavenly bread" and "the cup of Life." The mountain is familiar to them now and has received them into the fellowship of the heart. They begin with the motivational mantra: *on Zion, the LORD has ordained blessing, life forever more.*

Come, bless the LORD, you servants of the LORD, who stand by night in the house of the LORD!

On extended mountain expeditions such as Everest, the mountain must be ascended in stages. It cannot be climbed in one day. It becomes necessary, then, to establish several "base camps" along the upward route. The camps allow for food and gear to be shuttled upward. Each new, higher camp provides the base for the next upward assault. Usually, one or two climbers must stay at the camp in order to assure a refuge for those ascending and descending along the route.

In a way, the Levites were base-campers. They maintained the refuge along the route. Psalm 134 is new in that for the first time (at least in a very, very long time) there will be 24-hour "service" at the temple. No more will they have to shutter the doors and return to their villages, hoping no vandals break in. No more are they rental tenants on Zion. They can move in their own furniture, decorate, landscape, and manage the facility as they see fit. No more will the Levites by migrant workers, wondering how or whether their service will be compensated.

In this closing song of the Songs of Ascents, that reciprocal, giddy exchange of blessing brings closure to this part of the ascent. In the exchange here, the vision of a reconstituted temple, now more a "people's temple," plays out. In times past, the high priest would pronounce a blessing on the king and then on the congregation at the closing of the festival (Num 6:22–27). "May the LORD bless you and keep you," the priests would pray.

Here, however, several innovations are revealed. For one, it is now the people who invoke the priests and Levites to bless, not them, but the Lord. We can be reminded also that it has been the Levitical choir whose music has marched us forward and upward the whole way. I cannot help but feel that the choir turns to each other at this point and sings hearty congratulations and encouragement to keep on keep'n on.

When we ask God to bless us, or in the case of the patriarchs who blessed their sons, it suggests some kind of empowerment of life. When someone great blesses a subordinate, he is transferring a generative force to them. The blessing confers a vital energy, enabling a person to flourish, flower, and fill out life. The invocation to "bless the Lord," then, seems a bit odd. Are we bestowing some generative force back on the Lord? In a sense, yes, and it is by way of thanksgiving. In the last psalm, we came to realize that the "thank offering" was in many ways the kind of sacrifice preferred by God. First off, it was offered freely and in acknowledgement of the Lord's saving grace. It was offered not because of someone's sin, but because of the Lord's mercy. Second, the fellowship offering best demonstrates blessing. It is the gift that keeps on giving because it is spared and shared. It keeps the blessing loop going. "Bless you" "No, bless you." "I bless you because you blessed me." "Well, I bless you because you blessed me when I blessed you."

It is as the story of the ten lepers who were healed by Jesus. Jesus expresses disappointment and surprise that only one returned to simply thank Jesus (Lk 17:11–19). In a world where every exchange is a calculation of cost, much of the appreciation for the countless things that people do for each other without reciprocal payment is lost. To live in a world where there is mutual exchange of blessing is to change over from a market based economy to a Sabbath based economy. And this is what is centrally important to the Levites attending to the blessing even in the graveyard shift.

The reference to "all servants of the Lord who stand by night in the house of the Lord" finds its origins in the Lord's command to Moses that lamps should be kept "before the LORD" not just through the night, but as a lasting ordinance for generations to come (Lev 24:1–4). As mentioned earlier, the Lord's concern for a "resting-place" is mainly driven by God's desire for all people to have access to him. The lights are to be kept on all night, so anyone even from far off lands could find him.

There have been times when darkness sets in before we could get back to camp after an especially long or difficult climb. Already exhausted, out of food, and sometimes battered by weather, the darkness presses the urgency of finding camp. The eyes intensely scan the night for but a flicker of light from a campfire or house light of some kind. Worries of being lost and devoured by night seep into one's thoughts. I have read accounts of climbs atop Everest where the search for base camp becomes a life or death matter. One strains both eyes and ears for the slightest hint of a flashlight or the faintest call through howling wind. The moment a light is spotted, however, all fear dissipates. All is good. All is good.

Lift up your hands to the holy place, and bless the LORD.

The Levitical choir now responds back to the congregation: "Now, you bless the LORD." The gesture of lifting the hands has several connotations, and I think in a way they come together here. A king or an army can lift the hands against an enemy. In this sense it is a display of power or resistance as opposed to helplessness or weakness. On the contrary, lifting the hand was also associated with taking a solemn oath in the same way that a witness does in a courtroom today. In this sense, God is said to raise his hand in order to enact the covenant with His people (Neh 9:15).

In this sense then, lifting the hands evokes a sense that one is bound to the Lord, similarly to the way a soldier salutes a superior.

In the psalms, lifting the hands is a gesture accompanying a cry for help. We are quite familiar with the cry for help by now. In this regard, the cry for help needing the extra expression of lifted hands is associated with prayers in the darkness of night (Ps 63:4–6).

> *Rise up, shrill in the night,*
>   *at the beginning of every watch;*
> *Pour out your heart like water*
>   *in the presence of the Lord;*
> *Lift up your hands to him*
>   *for the lives of your little ones*
> *[Who faint from hunger*
>   *at the corner of every street].* (Lam 2:19)

Since the call to "lift up your hands to the holy place" is a reciprocal exchange with the congregation, it makes sense that the Levites would invoke the congregation to a similar diligence and continued devotion to the Lord as those attending the lamps on the midnight watch. It is as if to say: "Just as we are attending to the lamps at all times, so you keep the lamp of your heart burning towards this holy place no matter where you are or what you situation is." Having a posture such as this, will invigorate God. It will bless him.

May the LORD bless you from Zion,
  he who made heaven and earth.

Only after this mutual exchange of blessing between congregation and the Levites does the high priest interject the final blessing. He reminds one last time that the Lord is in no need of temples or resting-places for himself, for he *made heaven and earth*. Nonetheless, He has established Zion as the place for all to find him and orientate their lives toward the one and true source of blessing. The Lord has also established Zion as the strategic beachhead in which his glory will go out unto the ends of the earth.

17

Conclusion

ASCENDING A GREAT HEIGHT or embarking on a long journey is a dominant theme of the Songs of Ascents and this book. It is no wonder that the early church Fathers found in this group of songs the appropriate "entrance" hymns into the season of repentance.

As many an author can probably attest, writing a book is in many ways like climbing a mountain or committing to a season of repentance. An author can chart a course, prepare a strategy, and embark on the project, but once it is in progress he has committed to an unknown adventure, a journey, an ascent. It is certainly that way for me.

For one, I did not anticipate my own struggles over employment and personal identity, nor the changes within the community I participate in. Even more so, I had not grasped the kind of internal crisis this country is engaged in. In this respect, the crisis of hope in today's world is strikingly similar to that of the ancient Jews in postexilic *Yehud* and under Roman occupation in the time of Jesus.

As I often do when starting a project, I went in far too casually. Search and rescue crews in Colorado know well the sometimes tragic consequences of hikers who take on such a posture. Perhaps in a similar way is our approach to the season of repentance.

As the Jews of the exile learned, lamentation is God's gift in the face of hopelessness. It calls us to a radical and profound action. Hopelessness causes two destructive responses. I can stew in cycles of despair, encircling into tighter and tighter circles of "giving up." We find ourselves "being done" with politics, church, family, work, "those people" and finally ourselves. I can equally grind in anger, raging against an ever-encroaching foe who seems to threaten my very way of life. I cut off all associations with perceived enemies and limit my alliances to the few who share my views. Over the course of writing this book, I wavered between both of these tendencies.

It sometimes feels futile to write a book of any kind, let alone one of a spiritual or theological bent. Realistically, my audience is limited. So few of us now have time to quietly read through a book of this nature. It is equally difficult, perhaps more so, to find the kind of dedicated time to write. For one, it requires the shuttering of lots of influences, distractions, concerns, and desires—like repentance. It was in the closing weeks of the 2012 presidential elections that I simply had to turn off the television, the emails, the mail, and even casual discussions. I could not bear the intensity of the conflict without either despairing or raging (usually a combination of both.)

It was at that time that I found a renewed focus on this book, but even more importantly "the dream." As a lifelong student of the Bible, I realize how much of it presents a challenging, alternative view of humanity. The Bible's idealism often butts heads with the ever present and ever-pressing demands of the way things really are. This conflict is deeply engrained in the Hebrew bible over issues of idolatry and Sabbath. In the gospels, the conflict is revealed to include seemingly irresistible and invisible powers that continue to posses human societies and human wills.

Yet, Jesus exhorts his followers to keep on *trusting in the Lord, alone*. So every week and within human societies racked in violence, greed, exploitation, and gross inequities, Christians all over the world appeal to their Father and dreamingly beseech: *Thy kingdom come, thy will be done, on earth as it is in heaven.*

Just as the *ruined one* of Psalm 130 and 131 sent up his appeals to God with the smoke of the *olah* sacrifice and as Jesus does even nailed to the cross, so we continue the prayer taught by our Lord. Radically, we ask that God's way on the earth begin in our own transformation away from the kingdoms of men and toward God's kingdom. We ask that God empower us to live into His rule. We ask God to reverse the destruction of this world in us:

Give us this day our daily bread. Enable us to live with enough and give enough so that this world's inequities are eliminated.

Forgive us our trespasses as we forgive those who trespass against us. Give us the courage to cancel debts and have mercy on those who are enslaved by insurmountable debt.

Lead us not into temptation, but deliver us from evil. Help us to direct our desires toward You and teach us the ways of self-giving love so that we can reverse our scandalized relationships, violent rivalries and destructive envy.

In the writing of this book, especially when I shut out many of the world's distractions and focused on the words of the Holy Scriptures, I discovered a renewed hope and invigorated faith. And as I reviewed the book many times in preparation for publication, I found myself surprised by my very words. "Did I really say that?" "Do I believe those words?" The surprise is not in the artistry of my writing skills. Rather, I am astounded sometimes at how positive God is about us humans. I am equally astounded at how those who wrote the ancient scriptures discovered and rediscovered this amazing posture of their God usually in *the least* of positive times.

A time of repentance, like writing (or reading) a book or embarking on an expedition, requires the shutting down of business as usual in order to yield to a different and greater priority. But this is only half of the formula. It also requires an openness to adventure and discovery. That kind of openness requires the willingness to leave our worlds and kingdoms behind and for good. Even though most of us will resume our "normal" way of life after Lent, we will be changed. We become antsy and resistant to *the normalcy of our violence*.[1] We become uncomfortable and less tolerant of violence, greed, and inequity, and view God's kingdom of justice, righteousness, truth, and love as the new norm.[2]

My priest reminds us every year that a season of repentance is the Church's gift to us.[3] It can and should be, but every year, we must decide once again to embark on the expedition from Babylon to Zion and the shores of Galilee to the cross and the empty tomb. On every step along the way, it requires a willingness and discipline to abstain and focus, but even more so, it demands an openness to the fullness of life that can only be found in "the Might One of Jacob."

> *Open to me, the doors of repentance, Oh Lifegiver;*
> *According to Thy great mercy.*[4]

---

1. Crossan, *God and Empire*, 46.

2. This pair of pairs—justice/righteous and truth/mercy—is repeated throughout the Hebrew scriptures (Amos 5:7, 24, Isa 5:7, Mic 3:1, Hos 2:19,20). It is a stock formula to concisely communicate the covenant demands for the common good of all. Albertz, *A History of Israelite Religion: Volume I*, 166.

3. The whole liturgical calendar is a gift to joyously participate in rather than an obligation to drudge through.

4. From the hymn of repentance sung during the priest's communion of the Liturgy of the Presanctified Gifts.

Bibliography

Albertz, Rainer. *Israel in the Exile: The History and Literature of the Sixth Century B.C.E.* Atlanta: Society of Biblical Literature, 2003.

Albertz, Rainer. *A History of Israelite Religion in the Old Testament Period Volume II: From the Exile to the Maccabees.* Trans. By John Bowden. Louisville: Westminster John Knox Press, 1994.

Albertz, Rainer and Becking, Bob. *Yahwism After Exile: Perspectives on Israelite Religion in the Persian Era.* Assen: Royal Van Gorcum, 2003.

Brueggemann, Walter, *Israel's Praise: Doxology Against Idolatry and Ideology.* Philadelphia: Fortress Press, 1988.

Brueggemann, Walter. *The Land.* Philadelphia: Fortress Press, 1977.

Colbert, Stephen. *America Again: Re-becoming the Greatness We Never Weren't.* New York: Grand Central Publications, 2012

Crossan, John D. *God and Empire.* New York: HarperCollins Publishers, 2007.

Crow, Loren D. *The Songs of Ascents (120–34): There place in Israelite History.* SBLDS, 148. Atlanta: Scholar Press, 1996.

Eagleton, Terry. "Conversation with Terry Eagleton and Arnold Eisen" Templeton Foundation. http://www.youtube.com/watch?v=BgMB_jSx3lk&list=PL78452 ADD88B14B2B 2011.

Eagleton, Terry. *Faith, Reason, and Revolution: Reflections on the God Debate.* New Haven and London: Yale University Press, 2009.

Finkelstein, Israel and Silberman, Neil A. *The Bible Unearthed: Archaeology's New Vision of Ancient Israel and the Origin of its Sacred Text*s. New York: Touchstone, 2002.

Goulder, Michael D. *The Psalms of the Return (Book V, Psalms 107 – 150); Studies in the Psalter, IV.* Sheffield: Sheffield Academic Press, 1998.

Light of Life: Part 2 The Mystery Celebrated. Pittsburg: God with Us Publications, 1996.

Ollenburger, Ben C. *Zion the City of the Great King: A Theological Symbol of the Jerusalem Cult.* Sheffield: Sheffield Academic Press, 1987.

Rose, W.H. "Messianic Expectations in the Early Postexilic Period" in Albertz, Rainer and Becking, Bob. *Yahwism After Exile: Perspectives on Israelite Religion in the Persian Era.* Assen: Royal Van Gorcum, 2003

Philokalia, The Eastern Christian Spritual Texts: Selections Annotated and Explained. Annotation by Allyne Smith. Trans. By G.E.H Palmer, Philip Sherrard and Bishop Kallistos Ware. Woodstock: Skylight Paths Publishing, 2006.

Wenham, Gordon J. *Psalms as Torah: Reading Biblical Song Ethically*. Gran Rapids; Baker Academic Press, 2012.

Zarcharias, Archimandrite. *The Enlargement of the Heart: "Be ye also enlarged" (2 Corinthians 6:13) in the Theology of Saint Silouan the Athonite and Elder Sophrony of Essex*. Edited by Christopher Viniamin. South Canaan: Mount Thabor Publishing, 2006.

Zvi, Ehud Ben. "What is New in Yehud? Some Considerations," *In Yahwish After Exile; Perspectives on Israelite Religion in the Persian Period,* ed. Ranier Albertz and Bob Becking Asem: Royal Van Gorcum, 2003).